Medicine Man to the Inuit

A Young Doctor's Adventures Among the Eskimos

Medicine Man to the Inuit

A Young Doctor's Adventures Among the Eskimos

by
Joseph P. Moody, M.D.

Arctic Memories Press
200 Union Blvd., Suite 425
Denver, CO 80228

ISBN 0-9646753-4-X

LCCN 95-78073

First printing 1995

Although the author and publisher have made every effort to ensure the accuracy and completeness of information contained in this book, we assume no responsibility for errors, inaccuracies, omissions, or any inconsistency herein. Any slights of people, places, or organizations are unintentional.

Attention: Organizations and Educational Institutions: Quantity discounts are available on bulk purchases of this book for educational purposes, gifts, or fund raising. Special books or book excerpts can also be created to fit specific needs. For information, please contact our Special Sales Department, 200 Union Blvd., Suite 425, Denver, CO 80228. 705-848-2541.

DEDICATION

Dedicated to the memory of the Inuit guides—Hakoluk, Sheeniktook, Ayranni.

Pilot—Gunnar Ingebrigtson. Co-author—W. de Groot van Embden.

ACKNOWLEDGMENTS

Special acknowledgment is due W. de Groot van Embden, whose aid and persistence helped to bring this book into existence. Thanks are also owed in large measure to Viola Moody for her advice and assistance. In addition, appreciation is expressed for the rewards derived from my many years of close and pleasurable association with that great northern family of East Arctic Eskimos and whites. Some details and verifications were also drawn from the excellent material published by the various departments of the federal government concerned with the administration of arctic zones.

Valuable assistance has been obtained from the many publications of the Government of the Northwest Territories, including *Arctic Wildlife, Heritage* and *Data Sheets*. Specific credits when indicated, are also noted in the book.

Much material was drawn from my personal diaries, archival Arctic Library and personal communications. Special thanks are due to many arctic friends and my wife, Inge Moody.

FOREWORD

This is the story of Dr. Joseph Moody, physician, explorer and photographer. It contains some of his most colorful experiences among the Eskimos while a medical health officer for the Canadian Department of National Health and Welfare, and while carrying on exploration. More specifically, it is the story of his three and a half years in the Canadian East Arctic. Dr. Moody went into the arctic in 1946, completed his tour of duty and came out in 1949. He returned in 1950 and 1954 on his own expeditions for many months.

Not all the events are arranged in strict chronological order, but taken together they present an unforgettable picture of life in those little known regions.

Joseph P. Moody, M.D., was born in Canada. He lost his parents very young, and after a stormy youth full of hardships managed to work his way through college. Originally, he wanted to study engineering but could not attend a university where a full engineering course was given.

His second choice was medicine. Here his brilliance was soon noticed and after a year he received the Leonard scholarship. In 1946 he was graduated from the University of Western Ontario, in London, Ontario, and immediately applied for government medical service in the arctic. This, again, was a second choice, for he had been encouraged by his professors to continue his study of surgery. A first rate position had even been promised the young doctor who showed such exceptional ability as a diagnostician and surgeon.

But more years of study would have piled up more debts. In 1942 he had married and although his wife, Viola, had continued working to help finance his studies, he could not support a family on the income of a student physician.

The comparatively substantial salary offered by the government made him decide to start right in on his career rather than keep to his studies in search of still further honors.

With headquarters at Chesterfield Inlet, on the west coast of Hudson Bay, he quickly acquired a reputation as a versatile and brilliant physician. He performed with success the roles of general practitioner, surgeon and medical administrator. During the great polio epidemic of 1949 he gained world fame.

As an extracurricular activity, Dr. Moody devoted time to geology and photography. He shot the full color film, "Arctic Wonderland," since shown throughout Canada. After completing his tour of duty at Chesterfield Inlet, he organized his own exploratory expedition and soon returned to the region that he had come to love.

The arctic still holds Dr. Moody's top interest. In 1954 he went back and organized a number of expeditions for tourist-explorers and scientists, taking them to many of the places described in *Medicine Man to the Inuit.*

The merits of a book like this depend not only on the writer's gift for making his experiences stand out as vividly on the printed page as they do in his own mind, but also for brilliant portrayal of the very *atmosphere* in which these experiences occur.

Dr. Moody has this gift.

Medicine Man to the Inuit is factual. Only where reputations might suffer embarrassment have the names of persons and locations been changed, then never so as to distort the real significance of the event.

It is hoped that the book will carry a message to further a wise, realistic and enlightened policy wherever our white race has infiltrated the underdeveloped areas of the world.

W. de Groot van Embden

CONTENTS

Introduction 1

Part I Arctic Doctor

1 Two Thousand Patients 4
2 Rolling North 10
3 On into the Ice Age 17
4 Diagnosis by Radio 26
5 The Excitable Trapper 33
6 Breath of Winter 38
7 Sheeniktook 44
8 The Grip of Night 51
9 Warmth Beneath the Snow 57
10 Eskimo Close-Up 62
11 Turning Point 68
12 Neophyte Patrol 73
13 Sheeniktook Redeems Himself 78
14 "Fogbound" 83
15 Dancing Airplane 89
16 "Mercy Flight" 93
17 Four Feet from Eternity 98
18 Arctic Fever 103
19 Odyssey of Death 107
20 Running an Epidemic 113
21 Strong Measures 117
22 The Reckoning 123

23   "Pokatelli Him Say Three" 130
24   Threats and Misunderstandings 136
25   Throb of a Drum 142
26   His Majesty, Tuctu 149
27   River of Fur 154
28   Tough Problem, Tough Solution 162
29   Sheeniktook Instructs the Brass 167
30   The Rough Road to Learning 172
31   Notebook Ammunition 178
32   Magistrate's Diary 183
33   Medical Patrol Report 190
34   Outpost Patrol 194
35   Father Henry's Flock 200
36   Igloolik—"Place of the Little Houses" 208
37   Calculated Risk 214
38   Escape 220
39   Camera Hunt 228
40   Private Life of a Seal 232
41   Quiet Interlude 238
42   Into the Ice Fields 244
43   Night with No End 249
44   Miracle? 256

Part II   The Eskimo of Yesterday and Today

45   A Living History Panorama 260
46   A '90s Overview 266
47   The Doctor's Prescription 271

Bibliography 280

ILLUSTRATIONS

Hudson's Bay company schooner "Severn" departs Churchill,
Manitoba, for Chesterfield Inlet, East Arctic. 13

Churchill, Manitoba, gateway to the East Arctic. A part of the
town is seen here with the Churchill River in the back-
ground. 15

End of trail. A bleak Eskimo cemetery is in the background
with a "mudded" sled runner in the foreground. 19

The Kazan Kayak has a creeping willow frame covered with
caribou skin and is an ageless and versatile craft. 21

Chesterfield Inlet community 1946—center of photo is St.
Theresea Hospital, haven for the ill with its lighted cross,
a saviour to many mariners. 24

Facial tattooing is seen only in the oldest Inuit women. 25

The Norwegian artist Giesen, has captured on canvas the
combination of radio communication and air transport to
fight epidemics. 37

Aksarnerk (Billy Brass), famous guide to many whaling expeditions, is seen here with his Cooke telescope. 45

Faithful huskies get a well deserved meal. 47

Eulalie, an Arctic beauty, spring cleaning her igloo. 52

An Eskimo puts finishing touches on his "home," an Igloo. His
whip is left on the dome, out of the reach of dogs, who
take great pleasure in eating it. 53

Baby Angote, although naked, is comfortable, and secure in her
igloo home. 55

Mother is happy knowing that the drying Arctic char will
provide many meals. 69

Wager Bay Inuit uses willow and heather for fuel to prepare a
delightful meal of seal flipper stew and tea. 71

Dr. Moody in blizzard gear, unloads komatik in preparation for
night's rest. 80

Moody and Ingebrigtson refueling their aircraft before a flight
    into the Kazan River area for patients. 85
Gunnar Ingebrigtson walks forward alongside his powerful and
    reliable Norseman. 87
The doctor equipped in full caribou clothing, suitable for dog
    team or air travel during difficult missions. 100
Quarantine diagram 119
Attwa and Sheeniktook at Chesterfield during the epidemic of
    1949. The 'Dakota' has a special ski-wheel arrangement
    for difficult Arctic landings. 125
Loading the critically ill aboard the aircraft requires all avail-
    able assistance, including the nursing Sisters from the
    hospital. 127
R.C.A.F. Canso # 11057, loading polio and T.B. patients at
    Chesterfield Inlet, August 21, 1949. 144
On board Canso is flight crew under command of First Lieuten-
    ant Rush. In mid-canoe position is Constance Beattie,
    physical-therapist. Six hours later this mercy flight crashed
    in N. Manitoba. All 21 on board perished. 147
An antler marks the carefully cached caribou meat which may
    not be retrieved for months. 156
Ayranni carefully smooths out caribou back sinew to dry. This
    is the thread Eskimo use to sew boots and garments. . . 160
Viola and Joe Moody, on ice pan at mouth of Wager Bay,
    August 1950. 222
Isolated grave at Cape Fullerton, near Wager Bay, of a Royal
    Canadian North West Mounted Police Physician, 1904. 226
Nanook, the polar bear, king of the Arctic jungle of sea ice. . 234
Oojuk—a friendly sea mammal. It is the biggest seal weighing
    up to 700 pounds. 235
Atlantic walrus—an aggressive and dangerous animal in Arctic
    water. 236
Walrus herd—although some sun and sleep, there is always at
    least one on alert for enemies. 237
Huskies in canoe. Faithful friends ready to serve by aircraft or
    canoe, in harness or as pack animals. 253
North Rankin Nickel Mines—a major force in the destiny of
    many Inuit families. 268

INTRODUCTION

Often while traveling through the arctic jungle of glistening sea ice or standing before my igloo with my Eskimo guides, watching the awesome northern lights, I found it hard to believe I was in a part of North American or even of our terrestrial globe. The Canadian East Arctic is a bizarre and intensely interesting world of its own with seal, walrus, polar bear, whale and narwhal roaming about amid the ice floes; with caribou and musk ox wandering over the multicolored, treeless tundra; with howling huskies and screaming blizzards that blanket life for days on end; with dark skinned Eskimos chattering in their strange tongue while "komatiking" from igloo to igloo over the diamond studded snow sparkling with the fluorescent midnight sun. For centuries these people did not know other human beings or land existed on earth.

The white man has found the East Arctic intriguing ever since that day 900 years ago when the first explorer, supposedly a Norwegian who was undoubtedly lost, entered the Hudson Straits. During the ensuing centuries, many men have invaded this forbidding area on various missions, principally for exploration, whale hunting and fur trading. It is difficult for us to envisage the terrible ordeals these early expeditions, like the ones of Franklin and Rae, went through while awaiting death from disease and cold during the acutely depressing, endless nights of arctic winter.

Medicine Man to the Inuit is the story of how life was in the Canadian East Arctic in the late forties. The term Inuit is the correct name for these indigenous people of this Arctic. However, Eskimo was used in the past, and I have continued to use the name interchangeably in this book. Eskimo is actually an Indian term meaning "Raw Meat Eater."

1

Part I is a fascinating history of a remarkable people and the man who ministered to them. Up to that time not much had changed over the prior centuries. The integrity and color of their lives remain intact. Photographs and sketches help readers feel closer to the subject.

During the period from 1950 to 1995, this vast land, and its people, experienced far reaching sweeping changes—some of them very traumatic. The speed and scope of this upheaval has rarely been seen in the world up to this time.

Part II acknowledges these changes. The overview that appears at the end of this book, addresses these changes and effects, and presents a comparison of the eras. These people had to literally make the transition from the stone age to that of nuclear electronics in just a few short decades.

Today, existence in the East Arctic is still dangerous at times. But in many ways it is much easier than it was in the days of the first explorers and whale hunters. Considerable progress is being made in arctic sciences and there is a good deal of mining and military activity. Some day transportation into the far north will be common-place and we may all see the Arctic wonderland. Meanwhile, if this book acts as a reminder of the sacrifices of past explorers and brings you a little closer to that vast and immensely important area of the East and Northern Arctic, and the people who live there, then it will have served its purpose.

Part I
Arctic Doctor

◆ 1 ◆

TWO THOUSAND PATIENTS!

"That's all I can tell you, Doctor."

Across the desk from where I sat in his office at Ottawa, Ontario, the director stood up with a look of smiling finality. I got up, too. My glance fell again on the huge map of Canada that dominated one wall, and it seemed there weren't so many colored thumbtacks in it as I had thought. Now that I was one of those tacks, it was hard to adjust to the fact that the Canadian Eastern Arctic, nearly one-fifth of that vast area, had suddenly become my territory, acquired merely by scribbling "Joseph P. Moody" at the bottom of the government contract.

But if the Director of Indian Health Services, Canadian Department of National Health and Welfare, was as busy as his title implied, I couldn't take up more time with questions. We had had quite a talk already. Its culmination had been my signing up as a medical health officer of the Canadian government.

Now he stood there waiting politely, as if half expecting me to say something more. Instead, I found myself gripped by a daydream of the past.

Early loss of parents—working, saving, planning for college—the University of Western Ontario—my switch from engineering to medicine—Viola—our marriage in 1942—her insistence on working so that I might keep on studying medicine—recent completion in 1946 of my hospital internship.

4

Finally, my decision, right or wrong, to forego specializing in surgery, with a sure, safe job as a reward, and jump immediately into a career by applying to the government for arctic medical service.

What brought matters to a head in our London, Ontario, home was an advertisement in the Sunday paper. The government, it seemed, wanted medical health officers. The pay sounded good. A chance for adventure in the wide-open spaces was another inducement. The job might even lead into one of my favorite "extracurricular" activities—geology. Who could tell?

Viola and I looked up what statistics we could before I took the first fateful step by calling Ottawa long distance for an appointment. We discovered, for example, that the arctic region of Canada took in 1,000,000 square miles and was divided into western, eastern and northern arctic, occupied by about 9,000 Eskimos and some thousand whites. The Canadian East Arctic, to which I would be assigned, was comprised of the districts of Keewatin and Franklin, Northern Quebec, a strip of Labrador and the Arctic Islands, including Baffin, north of the previously mentioned zones.

We learned, too, that this enormous space, consisting of some 600,000 square miles of frozen, windswept immensity, was inhabited by about 7,000 Eskimos and two or three hundred whites.

Viola wrinkled her forehead. "Six hundred thousand square miles," she mused. "Do you realize that that figures out to scarcely one person in 100 square miles?"

"H'm. But look at it this way," I said, not wholly facetious, "I'd have no competition and could be sure of at least 2,000 possible patients. The only other doctor for the zone is at Pangnirtung, Baffin Land, with the same number of possible patients."

She nodded. "Not bad for a young doctor who hasn't yet practiced officially."

We laughed a little.

When I telephoned Ottawa to sound them out, they seemed quite anxious to talk with me further. So I made an appointment, traveled to the capital and in time sat with the director. Whenever I expressed the slightest doubt of my abilities to handle the job, he quickly reassured me. He probably had encountered the same doubts before and knew the right answers.

Now the formalities were over and I stood there holding a very official looking document and staring at its shiny red seals in a sort of trance.

A hand was proffered me across the desk. I heard the director's voice repeating, "So that's about all I can tell you. Now," it went on, "I'll send you in to the North West Territories Administration. There you'll find Mr. Wright who is in charge of Eastern Arctic Expeditions." He clasped my hand. "Bon voyage, Doctor—and good luck!"

I followed an usher down the hall and into the North West Territories Administration. Behind an inner door marked Eastern Arctic Expeditions sat Mr. Wright.

He put me at ease with the prompt statement that he'd visited my area himself and could give me all the pointers I'd need. I sank into the proffered chair, accepted a cigarette and for the first time relaxed.

Mr. Wright had the paradoxical knack of bringing out all the dangers and difficulties without adding his own very evident love of the whole region. That's what I liked about the man.

"You can depend on one thing, Doctor," he began, sizing me up, "you've chosen one of the coldest spots in the western hemisphere. Sixty to seventy degrees below in winter—and winter lasts about ten months of the year. It's partly due," he explained, "to the winds that sweep across the icy plains for weeks at a time. Not all of them are eighty-mile-an-hour gales, but a lot are."

"How can you travel?"

"You can't. Nothing to do then but make for shelter. House, hut, igloo—anything will do. And you've got to stay there until the gale moderates."

Now that I had signed up, I didn't hesitate to pump Mr. Wright to the limit.

Vegetation? None of the type to which I was used, he informed me, but a great deal of the far northern type foot high creeping willows and the arctic moss heather conglomeration called muskeg. This was a swampy, tangled growth that seemed to float on the frozen subsoil.

"What about game?" I inquired, during a pause. His eyes lit up.

"You a hunter?"

"I might be," I answered, with a guarded smile.

"Fine, Doctor, fine. You'll run into caribou, snow hare and fox. These are the principal food-providing animals inland. Along the Hudson Bay coast, of course, are fish, seal, walrus and polar bear. Let me warn you about walrus if you don't know already. When you tackle a walrus," he shook his finger impressively, *"take care."*

Afterward, I had cause to remember his warning. But the lively experience that recalled it was a far cry from our long leisurely talk that afternoon in Ottawa.

I also learned from Mr. Wright that today, in order to preserve the rapidly diminishing wild life of the arctic, Eskimos are judiciously restricted in hunting, and whites are not allowed to hunt at all except under very special circumstances.

I gathered from him that the tales of fear and danger that had been built up around the Canadian Eastern Arctic were by no means legendary. Travel in those regions, he admitted frankly, was perilous, residence hazardous and subsistence often precarious in the extreme.

Uncharted waters confronted the venturesome sea captain. Even in charted sections the danger was acute because of the proximity of the North Magnetic Pole. Its pull on a compass needle threw the reading off so that in certain places the compass was wholly useless.

Ice fields, too, were treacherous. Their sudden, unexpected movements in early winter had trapped many a whaler, he said. Stories of lost expeditions, ferocious bears, charging walrus, hostile Eskimos, frozen limbs and creeping insanity—reports of all these adjuncts of the Eastern Arctic, he made clear, were enough to discourage any but the hardiest explorers.

Was I tough enough for my job? Not that he asked in so many words. It was a question that I wove into his kindly interest.

"But expeditions use planes nowadays, don't they?" I inquired.

"They do to a certain extent. But a good many fliers shun the whole region. I can't blame them." Landing with skis on moving, undulating ice fields was bad enough, he pointed out, but that wasn't all. The deep crevasses under the snow, the half frozen seas, the incalculable fuel consuming distances of the arctic had taken too great a toll of pioneering pilots and navigators to give the area a popular flying appeal.

"But surely," I put in, prompted by my own enthusiasm for geology, "a good many prospectors must have gone in there for gold and minerals."

"Some have, Doctor, but without much success. Trouble is, in order to cover up their own failures they've deliberately discouraged others from going in. Human nature, I suppose."

Further questions brought the talk around to my own professional work. The situation proved to be much as Viola had said, only it wasn't so funny now. I would be the only doctor to 2,000 Eskimos. For the smaller number of whites, I'd be the sole person capable of giving medical assistance beyond the first aid practiced by the missions and the mounted police.

Hospitals? There were only two in the whole area. One, under the authority of the Roman Catholic Mission, was at my own post in Chesterfield Inlet. This was on the west coast of Hudson Bay, some 300 miles north of Churchill.

Another hospital, which resorted under the Anglican Church, was located on Baffin Island at a place called Pangnirtung, nearly 1,000 miles farther northeast. According to Mr. Wright's records, the Chesterfield Inlet Hospital was equipped with sixteen beds and two or three nurses. The one at Pangnirtung had three nurses and a capacity for twenty-five patients.

Such were the area's facilities for taking care of its sick. One hospital for 300,000 square miles!

Except for one thing, these hospital statistics appeared to complete the information available to me at the moment.

"What sort of place would Chesterfield Inlet be," I said, as casually as I could, "for a woman?"

He looked up sharply. "You're married, Doctor?"

"A two-year-old daughter besides."

The silence seemed longer than probably it was. He came out at last with a clipped, "It's been done." Then he added, with a sudden show of unconcern, "Oh, yes, many times."

Mr. Wright was not the kind of man whose word you doubted. Nevertheless, his awkward attempt to reassure me had just the opposite effect from that intended. It started me thinking hard. Had I done right in signing that contract?

All the way back home, I kept turning this over. I was trying hard to justify the lure of high adventure at good pay, against the financial scraping of the barrel that would have been necessary were I to continue the study of surgery, as some of my professors had strongly urged.

Was it fair to Viola and our daughter for me to become a colored thumbtack on the map of the Canadian East Arctic? That stretch of frozen desolation would come to have a personal meaning to the three of us, while in Ottawa it formed only an impersonal wall covering in the director's office.

By the time I reached home to face Viola and little Gloria-May, I felt more like a culprit than a medical health officer of the Canadian government.

♦ 2 ♦

ROLLING NORTH

I can see now that my perspective had become badly distorted by the events of the day. Otherwise, I'd never have doubted Viola's attitude. She had stuck by me through difficult times before, she reminded me with spirit. If I thought my "womenfolk" too weak for the rigors of the arctic, then I didn't know women the way a doctor should.

It left me feeling that I'd be a heel if I didn't give in to the very thing I hoped for most.

"If you had refused to come," I said, when everything was settled, "I don't know what I'd have done."

She gave me a funny laugh.

Presently we were discussing, jokingly, the advisability of taking her evening dresses, handbags, umbrellas, sporting equipment, hats and other adjuncts of civilization. What we ought to take was one of the questions I'd forgotten to ask Mr. Wright.

Our friends thought us crazy to go at all. They painted doleful pictures of living in igloos, of frostbite and hunger, of shipwreck and isolation. Even cannibalism featured prominently in the morbid predictions of those happy to stay behind.

Most of them, including Viola's parents, confessed to a feeling that they were seeing us for the last time. After a while it became a point we weren't too sure about ourselves. Fortunately, the excitement of packing kept such ideas from sinking in too deep.

The day arrived in July for saying goodbye and boarding a train for the first leg of our journey. We had been brought up in southern Ontario, hence on reaching Winnipeg—that important rail center—we felt quite far north already. A look at the map, however, changed that. From Winnipeg, a thin barbed line, indicating a railway, wound north toward Churchill. This was the famed Muskeg Express, the only train connecting civilization with our new habitat out there in the arctic.

The Muskeg Express was our introduction to the atmosphere of the north. The train itself was far from luxurious. If all went well, it would make the 800-mile trip to Churchill in about three days. If not, the date of arrival was anybody's guess. Every car was jampacked with colorful characters— prospectors, officers, missionaries, trappers, adventurers, writers, photographers, explorers, research men; a few tourists who would "do" Churchill, then scamper back south to brag of their hardihood.

Many Indians moved back and forth among the passengers. In a sense, the Muskeg Express is their train because all winter they have it largely to themselves. The trainmen know many by name and, in the general informality of a winter trip, will make unscheduled stops for them or leave packages for people who appear suddenly out of the woods and disappear as mysteriously.

Viola and I could hear plenty of talk above the general confusion but, like good tenderfeet, we just sat and listened. All conversation centered in some phase of the arctic. However secretive a passenger might be as to his destination and work, he fairly gushed stories of adventure. We heard of hunts and caribou herds and upset canoes; of stranded planes, rescue parties, hard winters, northern lights, disappearing people— everything that spelled out the tale of the arctic.

Prospectors had a particular gleam in their eye to make you believe they were heading for the richest of gold fields. Scientists spoke mysteriously of ancient races and remnants of fabulous civilizations. Hudson's Bay Company people talked of foxes, the price of hides, the first boat in and the last out. We learned of Jim who didn't return, and the captain who showed up every summer with a different wife. Many times we heard about "when Mr. Brown was attacked by those Eskimos" and the flight "when Fogbound or some pilot lost a pontoon and spent three days making a new one out of tin cans"; also about "the polar bear that crushed a walrus' skull with a block of ice."

One of the saddest tragedies of the East Arctic occurred in the late twenties when Margaret Clay, wife of Sergeant Clay, R.C.M.P., was mauled by dogs and died twenty-four hours later. At the time of the incident Sergeant Clay was away on patrol. On returning, he found that Mrs. Clay had died and been buried. Her grave at Chesterfield Inlet is looked after by each Mountie stationed there, and is a grim reminder of the vicious streak that lies just beneath the surface of most husky dogs.

At every repetition Viola and I glanced at each other, wondering how true all this was. If these were facts, why hadn't we been told them before? It might perhaps have altered our decision.

Later we were to find out for ourselves that while such stories were true, and many more like them, they did not make people decide to exchange the north for a more normal life. In fact, we ourselves came to take these matters in stride; even to tell about them with the same abandon, the same degree of understatement that we observed first on the Muskeg Express.

Having left the wooded heights of northern Manitoba and proceeded into the muskeg region, we were rattling along when suddenly flames broke out in the car ahead. This caused a few moments of amused confusion. Then we stopped with a terrific jerk and men with axes chopped away the car roof. As soon as we started again, the passengers in the damaged car resumed their card games under the open sky.

A look out of our window revealed low, greenish-brown muskeg stretching from horizon to horizon. At times you could feel the rails actually move on the soggy ground. At one of our infrequent stops a lady tourist got off to pick a flower not far from the track. That was a mistake. She sank knee-deep in the peaty substance and had to be dragged out with considerable loss of dignity. Except for a larger amount of bare rock, the scenery was the same, we learned, all through the arctic. Snow and ice would come later.

Finally, amid the chattering hubbub of the train, there was pointed out to us the Hudson's Bay Company administrator for Churchill. "Now," I said with relief, "we'll find out something about our new home. Let's talk with him, Viola." The administrator, taking us for tourists, nodded a curt hello.

"We're going to Chesterfield," we told him.

"Oh, no, you're not!" he shot back, suddenly officious. "I don't let anybody go in there."

"But—"

"Can't take the responsibility, see?"

Hudson's Bay company schooner "Severn" departs Churchill, Manitoba, for Chesterfield Inlet, East Arctic.

The Post Manager's concern was genuine. It was essential to almost any person who was to live and travel in the Arctic to establish a liaison with the Hudson Bay Company. Over hundreds of years the company had developed vast knowledge of the people and the territory. They had networks of supply posts and transportation routes. To make barren land patrols, the Bay's help was indispensable for supplies, transportation assistance and advice. Many of us who did Arctic patrols will never forget the immense pleasure of a bath, hot table meals and a warm bed in the Hudson Bay Post Manager's home.

We were angry and astonished. Had no arrangements been made? Did no one know about us—not even the Hudson's Bay Company people? We were supposed to travel from Churchill to Chesterfield on one of their boats.

"We're going, anyhow," I insisted, firmly. "They're expecting us. One of your boats is supposed to take us out from Churchill. Don't you know about it?"

The man stared from my face to Viola's and back. His eyes lighted up slowly.

"Sa—ay," he exclaimed, "you're not Dr. Moody, are you?"

Assured of our identity, he became affable at once. "I've made all arrangements, folks. You're to go up on our *Severn*. She'll leave soon as you're ready."

From his manner we could only conclude that the royal yacht had been polished up, its crew inspected, and everything prepared for the doctor and his family.

As we sat in our compartment nearing Churchill at the end of the third day, an eerie feeling of foreboding crept over us. Perhaps the utter barrenness of the landscape we were passing through was responsible for it. Or it might have been the stark mental vision of wide-open spaces of nothingness ahead. More likely, though, it was because we felt helpless and inexperienced among these rough, hardy strangers who seemed so at home in a country that had obsessed them with arctic fever. To break the spell we talked about Churchill, the vast "metropolis" which the Muskeg Express was nearing at last.

Churchill was not only the most important port on Hudson Bay but was the real gateway to the arctic. It was also one of Canada's largest grain ports. In summer big freighters moved in and out and the town fairly vibrated with activity. But after September the excitement of the last boat out subsided. Everybody sat back to await the beginning of the long winter when the town functioned mainly as an air base and supply center.

To people already in the far north, Churchill seemed the place from which all good things came. During the two months of navigation the small supply boats bringing them food and equipment, mail from home and gossip from the entire area, were eagerly awaited. For those just starting into the barren regions, Churchill provided the first breath of arctic atmosphere; for those returning South it opened the way to a long delayed normalcy. In Churchill people wore ordinary clothes instead of hides and furs, and one could set eyes on a few harried but carefully nursed trees.

When we arrived that July day in 1946, Churchill didn't look very impressive, with its forty houses scattered around on the narrow peninsula sticking out in the bay. What moved us more was the magnitude of the Churchill River which, flowing into open water at this point, provided an excellent natural harbor.

Churchill, Manitoba, gateway to the East Arctic. A part of the town is seen here with the Churchill River in the background.

As soon as the Muskeg Express pulled into the small station and slowed to a tired, wheezing stop, pandemonium broke loose. Shouting, slapping shoulders, pushing, joking, the whole motley trainload exploded onto the platform, there to be welcomed by even more rugged characters. Everyone seemed to know everyone else. The restraints of civilization were gratefully left behind and the most dignified officials behaved like barbarian extroverts.

Having lost our Hudson's Bay Company friend for the moment, we felt excluded from all the excitement until, through our repeated questioning, some of the Churchillians guessed who we were. This drew us instantly into the melee and we found ourselves engulfed in as warm a welcome as anybody could wish.

I must admit, though, that during our short stay in Churchill the place continued to look strange—even a bit inhospitable. It probably gives that impression to new arrivals just up from a softer life. Merely a matter of contrast, no doubt. As proof of this, I might add that later on at Chesterfield, when we gazed out across the inlet wondering whether the radio man would walk around his house from left to right that day or counterclockwise, we longed for noisy, booming Churchill and its cosmopolitan air.

Our wish at the moment was to leave Churchill behind and embark on the good ship *Severn* for our post at Chesterfield 300 miles farther north. We strolled down to the long dock for a look at the "royal yacht."

Presently, in answer to my question, a grizzled dock walloper pointed over his shoulder with a thumb: "I guess she's down there, guv'ner."

To us the large seagoing vessel moored next to one of the grain elevators looked quite satisfactory.

"She's bigger than I thought," I observed to Viola. Our grizzled friend, overhearing, swung around with a strange look. "That there's a grain boat. The Severn must be next to it," he said and walked off.

We looked around. Seeing no other ship of any kind, we approached the 5,000-ton grain carrier. The two might be tied up side by side. But there was no second one in sight. I asked a different man.

"*Severn?* Sure, she's here. Down the dock a piece, maybe."

It seemed indelicate to say I didn't see her this time, but I didn't. We strolled down to the spot he'd indicated, anyhow. Finally I yelled to a sailor high up on the deck of the grain boat: "The *Severn*—where is she?"

He expectorated over the side, drew the back of his hand across his mouth and pointed a finger—down.

It began to dawn on us that our ship might be somewhat smaller than a regular seagoing vessel. Following the sailor's gesture, I peered cautiously over the side of the dock—and saw only water. Then, casting all dignity aside, I got down on hands and knees, and with Viola holding on to my belt, leaned far over the edge. Below me, a tiny two masted sailing vessel rose and fell gently on the water fifteen feet below.

"See anything?" asked Viola.

"Yes," I answered.

Compared with the ship we had had in mind, the *Severn* reminded me of a sort of glorified dingy.

◆ 3 ◆

ON INTO THE ICE AGE

For an instant I could see us drifting around in icy Hudson Bay, hanging on to life preservers. But when with a mental wrench I adjusted to the new life we faced, the *Severn* began to look more like the sound little craft she was.

Equipped with a powerful auxiliary engine, she had served for years as one of the Hudson's Bay Company's coasters, carrying sixty or seventy tons of supplies to various trading posts. Besides this, she functioned as mail boat, rescue craft and passenger vessel. No other type of boat could navigate those treacherous waters safely and get into the small shallow ports that dot the northern shores of Hudson Bay.

Transportation in the arctic is precarious at best. Although large stretches of the bay remain open through the winter, one can encounter floating ice fields anywhere and at all times. Even Churchill in the subarctic, which can be serviced by large vessels two months of the year, about eight months of the year is surrounded by a huge slab of ice. And only 100 miles north of Churchill you'll find Hudson Bay frozen over for twenty miles out. This ice makes fine dog team travel, but blocks other access to the shore.

Since the northern waters are navigable only two and a half months out of twelve, fast action is required to get supplies to the outposts. Some 6,000 people depend, in one way or another,

on the timely arrival of small boats like the *Severn*. If they fail
to complete their summer rounds, trouble is in store for everyone the following winter.

When we went north in 1946 arctic flying was still a rarity.
"Mercy flights," taking patients away from their isolated
sickbeds, were, for the most part, still in the future. When they
proved, at cost of many lives, that flying was possible even in
winter, the picture began to change. A commercial airline now
stands ready to send chartered planes in any direction. But for
short distance winter travel the komatik, the dog drawn sled of
the Eskimos, is still the most practical way of getting about.

The Muskeg Express began our initiation into arctic informality. The *Severn* completed it. Captain Barber, veteran of the
northern seas, had some difficulty rounding up his crew from the
Churchillian bars to which all hands had gravitated. Assembled
at last, they reminded us strongly of a "B" motion picture
featuring an all pirate cast. When we discovered that our own
double bunk was separated from the "pirates' lair" only by the
flimsiest of curtains, we decided to save the effort of constantly
raising our eyebrows by leaving them permanently up.

Setting out into the bay and heading north, we began the easy
task of getting acquainted with our fellow passengers. A few
prospectors were aboard going after minerals. Scientists, too,
were there; among them a Dane, Svend Fredericksen, who had
been sent out by the Rockefeller Foundation. He was a graduate
of the University of Copenhagen, an Eskimologist, who was
going to study the art and culture of the natives and trace their
history. From him we learned much about Eskimo philosophy.
We were to see a lot of Svend on the trip.

In fact, we were destined to see much of all the passengers of
all the supply boats that ever put in at Chesterfield. It was
tradition, we learned, for most of the travelers touching our post
to make themselves at home in the doctor's house before
moving on to other regions. We were to have as many as fifteen
guests at a time. They'd roll up in sleeping bags all over the
house and keep Viola busy cooking. But they also furnished a
welcome diversion by supplying us with one of the staples of
snowbound life—arctic gossip.

Not far out from Churchill Viola grabbed my arms and
pointed to some bluish-white animals swimming and diving and

arching their backs gracefully before each dive. Captain Barber
grinned at our excitement.

End of trail. A bleak Eskimo cemetery is in the background with a "mudded" sled
runner in the foreground.

"White whales," he observed. "They're all over. The big
Greenland or Bowhead whales and the killers are practically
extinct—killed off by white whalers. Pretty tough on the
Eskimos, too. Takes more than fifteen of these little fellows to
give the amount of food the Eskimos used to get from one
sperm whale. A shame, ain't it?"

We agreed, without as yet realizing the extent to which Eskimo economy had been lowered by the absence of Bowhead and killer whales. A further hint of this appeared the second day out when we "sounded" our way into Eskimo Point, a small native settlement 180 miles north of Churchill. This, our first arctic community, gave an impression of complete desolation. A handful of huts in an endless wilderness of multicolored arctic growth! And in the background, miles and miles of rocky land punctuated by lakes, ponds and rivulets that went nowhere.

Viola's word for the settlement was "ominous"—a mild term for the place which later I came to recognize as one link in a deadly chain reaction of disease which stalked the country. The third day of "about a two-and-a-half-day trip" we spent fighting seasickness. The sight of Marble Island around noon was cheering because it meant an imminent change in our course—a change of any sort being desirable at the moment. The momentous piece of navigation was carried out with a minimum of complication. Captain Barber sent a sailor up the mast.

"See it, Jake?" he bellowed.

"Yep," came the answer.

Whereupon we changed our course so as to head in directly toward Chesterfield, our home for the next few years.

"Death Island," mused Svend the Eskimologist, pointing to Marble Island, still visible in the distance. "That's what the Eskimos call it."

The story of Marble Island was not a cheery one. About three quarters of a century ago a number of whaling crews were shipwrecked there in consecutive seasons. Some had been caught by the ice when they stayed north too long. Others were forced to land on account of sickness aboard. Few crew members survived this little known East Arctic tragedy. Some thirty or forty men and boys lie buried on the island.

"All quite typical of the arctic," Svend ended, with a weary shrug.

It was evening before Chesterfield came into sight. We saw it at its best. The sun was just disappearing for its short daily sojourn behind the hills. The few houses of the post stood silhouetted against a background of brilliant orange and pink, which fanned out into transparent blues and darker purples. Due

to the invariable absence of dust in the arctic, all colors were
brilliantly clear.

The Kazan Kayak has a creeping willow frame covered with caribou skin and is
an ageless and versatile craft.

I am still grateful that our first contact with Chesterfield took
place under such favorable circumstances. Otherwise we might
have been tempted to call off our whole adventure. There are
periods when some indefinable terror seems to exude from these
coastal outposts. Many times I was to see people turn pale after
being flown in to spend a few years out of a life that seemed so
sheltered when they boarded the plane at Winnipeg a few hours
before. In some cases that first shattering impact of a cold,
desolate future set off a chain reaction of creeping insanity. I
was forced as a doctor, in these cases, to fly them south to
institutions of a civilization which had sent them out but could
not take them back.

At low tide, the tiny harbor at Chesterfield is shallow.
Therefore, Captain Barber dropped anchor well out from shore.
Numerous canoes and kayaks took off from the beach at once.
Presently, the *Severn* was surrounded by fragile crafts manned
by grinning Eskimos and a few waving whites. We waved back,

recognizing the same flamboyant enthusiasm that had greeted us on a larger scale back at Churchill.

A moment later our welcomers piled over the rail and we were hailed by the manager of the Hudson's Bay Company trading post. Also present was the wife of the doctor whom I was to relieve. The doctor himself, she explained, was out on "a little patrol" 170 miles down the coast.

The Eskimos were gay and full of fun. They seemed perfectly at home on board and cheerfully set about unloading our luggage and supplies. This gave me a chance to study them at close quarters.

They differed in every respect from the Indians with whom we had mentally compared them. Ranging from five-feet-six to five-feet-eight inches in height, these Eskimos were stockily rather than heavily built, with small hands and feet, and little noses set in round faces that grinned easily. Their eyes were black, their teeth white, though often dirty. The men seemed very strong. They had little facial hair, but that on top of their heads was black, stiff and thick.

The darkness of their skins was more understandable after we learned that all became deeply sunburned in early spring, only to lose the darkest part of it during the following winter. We came to understand, too, their gift for music and clever mimicry; as well as the fact that personally they usually were brave, although fatalistic by nature and with a well defined native religion.

A few of the more prominent approached us to be introduced. They came grinning broadly, with outstretched hands. This first meeting with them seemed quite formal and fashionable, but when Viola felt prompted to say, "How do you do?," her politeness was lost on the Eskimos who merely grinned the harder. Finally, we lowered ourselves into one of the canoes and were put ashore a few minutes later—thus confronting the spot where we would spend several years.

The first thing that struck me about Chesterfield was a neat little path lined with whitewashed stones that led from the beach toward a handful of houses grouped around the small bay. That one little sign of orderliness, faintly reminiscent of the civilization we had left behind, seemed out of place. We had the impression of coming upon a fairytale puppet town making a desperate pretense at being real.

Chesterfield was situated at the entrance to Chesterfield Inlet, a long, narrow fiord that connects with freshwater Baker Lake, 140 miles inland. The importance of the settlement was due to its hospital, trading post, Royal Canadian Mounted Police post, and the fact that it contained one of the official radio stations of the Department of Transport.

We counted fifteen structures in all, including the storehouses of the Hudson's Bay Company, the church and a few permanent dwellings built by the government for Eskimo servants. The white population numbered twenty-six, with some 200 Eskimos living in tents in summer.

Our own house, it was hinted, was old and a bit "airy." But the doctor's wife was sure we could make out for a year, until the new one, promised by the government, was built. What an "airy" house could do to inside temperatures when a 70-mile gale was whipping across the frozen plains was left to our imaginations. Actually it meant snow in our beds, ice on the floor and icy whirlwinds everywhere.

So far as actual accommodations were concerned, however, the place wasn't too bad. Viola grew quite enthusiastic over the five downstairs rooms—especially the one with a bay window overlooking the water.

We mounted to the second floor.

"What on earth—" Viola began, slowly taking in the vast space. "This is your storeroom," said the doctor's wife.

"Our storeroom!"

"You have to order for two years at a time, you know."

"Of course," said Viola, weakly.

Later, I walked down another stone lined path, this one leading to my hospital, the largest building in Chesterfield. Downstairs it had facilities for old and crippled Eskimos. Upstairs I found an adequate dispensary and examining room, X-ray equipment, a developing room, a small laboratory, a surgery and space for about fourteen Eskimo patients. A small separate cubicle could be used for white patients. The supervising nurses belonged to the Order of the Grey Nuns.

Home and hospital! These formed my domain—the center of my existence in the arctic! Making some excuse to the others, I broke away and wandered off alone to organize my thoughts. Here we were, husband and wife and two-year-old baby, facing at least two years of solitary internment 1,000 miles from anything remotely resembling twentieth century civilization. The handful of whites and scores of Eskimos only accentuated our loneliness. Here I would practice my profession among people, some of whom doubtless had more faith in their own witch doctors than in the Kabloona medicine man. I'd have to make many "little patrols" into the barren stretches, leaving Viola to run a household without modern conveniences, each of us constantly meeting situations not in the books.

Chesterfield Inlet community 1946—center of photo is St. Theresea Hospital, haven for the ill and with its lighted cross, a saviour to many mariners.

As my thoughts ran on, I felt terribly inadequate. What did I know about medicine up here? I had yet to see my first sick Eskimo and begin to learn about the treatment of Eskimos. I had yet to discover what really was expected of me. This was a place where visiting a patient might mean a week's travel; where epidemics could blaze like forest fires; where people disappeared mysteriously; where men more experienced than I had tried— and failed. I remembered the fine red seals on my contract, and for one black moment wondered if I'd last longer than the ink in my signature.

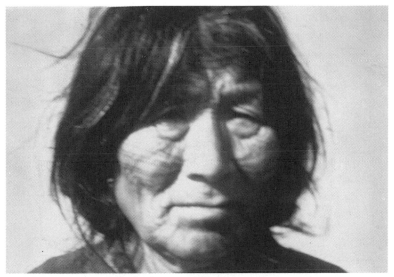

Facial tattooing is seen only in the oldest Inuit women.

♦ 4 ♦

DIAGNOSIS BY RADIO

By the time Dr. Rawson, my predecessor, had returned from his "little patrol", and departed for good, I was a little better acquainted with my duties. These included: first, justice of the peace and coroner—terms that still held no very clear definition; second, general practitioner for whatever was living and happened to be within reach—regardless of distance. It seemed immaterial whether "within reach" called for a 1,000-mile trip by canoe, plane or dog team, or meant merely opening my dispensary door while adjusting my stethoscope.

I learned from Dr. Rawson that the major diseases plaguing the Eskimos were tuberculosis, an inheritance from the whites; conjunctivitis, an eye infection caused by the glare of the arctic sun; frostbite; pleurisy and pneumonia; food poisoning; abdominal disturbances and a few other minor complaints to be found in any city practice. Those things I could have guessed or expected. Other matters were both new and startling.

For example, no one had made it clear that I would have to do a great part of my work by radio.

Admittedly, treating by radio was a comparatively recent development and perhaps Ottawa was not yet conscious of its scope or implications. An earlier doctor had received a few telegrams asking advice. When weather or distance kept him from organizing a patrol and seeing the patient himself, he used

26

to give instructions by wire. That was how it started. Dr. Rawson had elaborated on the practice. It was now considered a common thing to send a telegram to the medical officer hundreds of miles away, asking, for example, whether it was serious that junior kept vomiting blood and would the doctor please say what should be done.

In ordinary city practice a doctor may be confronted with a case of difficult diagnosis which gives him sleepless nights, even though he can have the patient on the examining table for hours on end. Under those circumstances he still is justified in having doubts and being pained by his moral responsibility. He may well end by being incorrect. But then he can always call in a specialist who is only too happy to tell him what he did wrong. I had nightmares after realizing that, together with my other duties, I would be living under the strain of having to prescribe the right thing on a long distance basis.

I am one of those doctors who takes his work very seriously, grieving if anything goes wrong, feeling a personal loss when death occurs. I imagined what it would mean to diagnose from the summing up of symptoms by an inexperienced layman, then by radio explain the steps that might lead to recuperation—or death. I dreaded the arrival of the first telegram asking me to get on the air.

The system itself worked simply enough. Throughout the arctic the Department of Transport had its radio transmitters. There also were the senders of the Royal Canadian Mounted Police. As in-between links, one could rely on the radio equipment of the Hudson's Bay Company trading centers. Besides all these were the weak senders of individual prospectors, trappers and research men who happened to be in the area. They were always ready to help.

Obviously, so vital a system could not have succeeded without teamwork; without the devoted cooperation of all the inhabitants of the region. Indeed, their very number was what gave me stage fright at first. The mere knowledge that, across miles and miles of barren land, people were breathlessly following every move I made, every word I spoke—every clearing of the throat even—was enough to scare me before I'd opened my mouth. But the help that I knew those same people could render me was reassuring and I took a certain comfort in knowing that I was not facing things quite alone.

Of greatest practical help was the fact that at nearly all posts and communities a supply of drugs and basic instruments had been cached, and my record of what was available enabled me to make the best use of the medication at hand.

There were, of course, mechanical difficulties caused by static, weather conditions, insufficient transmitter power and the inaccessibility of the area itself. I have often had to do everything by telegram, writing out long descriptions of methods, drugs and even of the containers in which they could be found.

Less frequently, I was able to conduct the whole matter by radio telephone, thus having the benefit of talking to somebody actually close to the patient—somebody who could report immediately on action and reaction. I much preferred radio telephoning even though it called for instant decision with the accompanying excitement that sometimes threw me off.

The wording of the brief telegram announcing my first case remains as clear in my mind today as when it arrived:

Baby Russel aged fifteen months temperature 103 pulse 120 headaches migraine type had a cold for week stiffness in shoulders and neck spine seems to curve stop looks bad mother desperate please contact by radio H.B. Co. Eskimo Point.

It was from Chesley Russel, manager of the Hudson's Bay Company post at desolate Eskimo Point, where the *Severn* had touched coming up. I had spoken to Chesley over the air quite a few times since then, and we had become friends. The patient was his little boy—an only child and one of the few white babies in the Canadian arctic.

The case sounded serious. I tried to think fast. There would be no time for me to call for a chartered plane and fly down to examine the boy myself. Instead, I sent a wire to Chesley telling him to get on the air at seven that evening so I could speak to him. The Hudson's Bay Company had a strong transmitter at Eskimo Point, and there seemed a good chance of treating by radio telephone.

I had little doubt what was wrong with the boy. There had been isolated cases of meningitis among the Eskimos in that section, and the symptoms given in the telegram were unmistakable. Meningitis is nasty, but there are cures. The crucial point was to determine how far the disease had progressed, and whether it was at all possible to save the child.

The curvature of the spine didn't seem right; it might be encephalitis. I checked the drug list and found to my satisfaction that at Eskimo Point they had soludiazine in ampules, the medication would have to be injected.

I got on the air at seven exactly, mind clear, nerves apparently well in hand. Then something happened. The instant I heard Chesley's voice, try as I would, I couldn't speak a word. The sound just wouldn't come. It was mike-fright to the nth degree. Hundreds of thoughts played tag through my brain. I felt cold in the overheated radio hut and was aware that my hands were shaking. Charley, the radio mechanic, sensing the situation, took the receiver away from me and made contact himself. When I heard him say, "What is that temperature?" I managed to get hold of myself and grab the horn from his hand.

"Hello there, how is it now?"

"Oh, Joe, it's real bad, the boy he . . . " the contact went dead.

"Hello, hello, Ches, are you there? Can you hear me?"

"Yes, Joe, reception okay here, you having trouble?"

"Not just now, go ahead."

"Doctor, it is like I wired this morning, he is stiff, arms don't move. Temperature is 104 now. He has terrible pains. Can't stop crying. What is it Joe, what is it?"

"Well, I think I know. But say, what about that spine?"

"I don't know, I really don't. This afternoon it curved terrifically, was way off the bed."

"Could it have been the pain. Straining to get relief?"

"Could be, Joe, could be. The wife said that. He seemed to control it. What can we do, Joe?"

"Have you got some soludiazine there?"

"What?"

"Do you have some soludiazine, the drug. And a hypodermic?"

"Hello, hello, are you there?"

"Yes, can you hear me?"

"Yes, what do you want me to do?"

"Do you have soludiazine and a hypodermic?"

"I don't know, Joe, what is that stuff?"

"It's a drug. You have to inject it."

"I . . . what . . . oh, wait . . . Carl here says that we have it."

"What kind of box is it in?"

"Yellow, yellow with red lettering, it is a La Roche product. Is that right?"

"Yes, that's right. It's a fluid, hey?"

"Yes, sure, in little, little, eh—"

"Ampules," I helped him along.

"Yes, that's it, it's in annodes."

"Good enough. Now listen, Ches, you take the top off that thing. You know how?"

"Yes, will do."

"Say, how much is in that ampule?"

"Hold it, let me see. It says two cc."

"OK, is your hypodermic clean?"

"Sure, comes out of the cotton."

"Fine, you take good care of things there."

"What?"

"Never mind. Now fill the hypo, the hypodermic, and get all the air out. You have the child right there, do you?"

"Yes, he's here."

"Good, now listen what you do, Ches. You know, on the child's head, right on top, is that soft spot, the fontanel."

"What do you want me to do there, Joe?"

"Can you find it?"

"Yes, I can."

"Now look for the spot closest to the center of the head."

"What?"

"Get it as far back as you can. Look for the spot closest to the center of the head. Right?"

"Check!"

"Now you inject . . . wait a minute. What kind of needle do you have on that hypo?"

"It's a thin one."

"OK, but what does it say on it?"

"It says . . . it says number twenty-four."

"Fine. How long is it?"

"It's real short, about an inch."

"That's all right. Now you must inject that needle into the soft spot, very gently. Not too deep. And straight down."

Silence. I didn't get an answer. My God, I thought, not now! "Hello, hello," I shouted.

Dead. Nothing happened. "Those damned sunspots," I said aloud.

"What was that, Joe?" He came through—must have heard me.

"Never mind, can you hear me?" I asked.

"You want me to inject in the soft spot?"

"Yes, that's what I said. Very careful, and keep the needle straight."

"I heard you, but Joe, that's dangerous."

"No it isn't . . . Just be careful."

"But Joe, I can't . . . I can't. You don't want me to do that, Joe."

"Yes, I want you to do that."

"But the soft spot is dangerous, Joe. They all say it. The wife says it, too."

"It isn't dangerous. You can do it. Just steady. I've done it hundreds of times." That was a lie, but I had to get him over his fear.

"He's my son, Joe, I could kill him," came the voice, plaintively.

"You want him to live, don't you?" I demanded, brutally.

"Yes but—"

"Then do it. Now listen carefully. As close to the center of the head as you can. Push it in very carefully. Not all the way, just about three-quarters of an inch. Do you hear me?"

"Yes, three-quarters of an inch."

"OK. Push it in and then empty the hypo slowly. And don't move it. Keep it perfectly still."

"I can't, Joe. I'm shaking."

"Then get yourself together. Go ahead now. Do it."

Bill, the mountie, took the receiver at the other end. "He's putting it in now, Joe."

"Does he actually have it in?"

"Yes."

"Then tell him to empty it. Keep him steady, Bill."

"Right." I could hear Bill relay my instructions.

"Is he very nervous, Bill?"

"Plenty, but it's all right."

I noticed that I was holding my right hand as if I were injecting the child myself. I moved my fingers and it hurt. I must have had them in that position for some time. I was shaking. I couldn't have done it now myself. I'd have made a mess of it. Oh, God, give him strength, I thought.

Bill's voice again: "He's got it empty, Joe."

"And the needle out?"

"Yes, it's out. One of the women fainted, Joe. Mary will look after her."

"Okay, never mind that. All the fluid is in. Right?"

"Yes, Joe, it's all over. How is the weather, Joe?"

"Oh, hell don't try to be funny. Give me Ches again . . . Are you all right, Ches?"

"I did it, Joe, It—it worked, I guess."

"Good for you, man. Now listen . . . This should help him. It's an antibiotic, it should take the fever away. Tomorrow he should be able to feel those arms again. Not move them, just feel. If anything happens in the next few hours, get me on. I'll ask the radio boys to keep the circuit open. OK?"

"Yes, Joe. I get you. God help me if the boy . . . " Something like a big man's sniffle reached my ears. Poor Ches, he'd had a tough time. "Joe, what do we do about that woman, she's out cold."

"Ice water . . . just ice water."

"Ha, ha, that's right, that's a good one. Will do, right now. You bet. Bye, Joe, and thank you, Joe."

"OK, Ches. Let me know if I can do more. Just keep me posted. I'll wire you in the morning. I'm signing off now."

"Yes, Joe, thank you, Joe."

I sat back and searched my pockets for a cigarette.

◆ 5 ◆

THE EXCITABLE TRAPPER

It was all over. I looked at my watch. The whole thing had taken scarcely half an hour. I hadn't done too badly. From now on everything ought to be. . . . My God!

I jumped up. The thought occurred that I'd forgotten to ask about any more symptoms such as vomiting, the legs, the neck, the eyes; about swallowing. I'd merely accepted the fact that it would be meningitis. What made me so sure? It could have been—well, no, but still . . . Sweat broke out all over me. I wanted to go back on the air but realized it would be useless. Right or wrong, the thing was done. I could only wait. If I showed the slightest doubt now, poor Ches would have a panic. I wouldn't know anything until morning, anyhow—unless, of course, things got worse. For an insane moment I almost hoped they would. Anything for an excuse to talk with Ches again; to find out what was going on. Well, no, of course I didn't want things to get worse. They wouldn't either.

Forcing a self-assuring, "You were all right, Joe. All *right!*" I finally left the radio hut and walked home through the snow-cold air. The moon threw its greenish light across the ice of the bay. A dog whined, then barked. I felt hot now and the snappy air refreshed me amazingly. I probably wouldn't sleep that night, but I was determined to lie down and rest, just the same. Steady nerves would be needed for whatever lay ahead.

33

Fortunately, my treatment worked. Ches gave his boy another injection the next day. Within a fortnight the baby was fine. If that first experience of diagnosing by radio had aged me ten years, Viola withheld comment. She is very tactful that way.

After treating a large number of these long distances cases, I began to wonder how successful the system really was.

"It's so hard to check up," I complained to Viola.

"With minor troubles, does that matter?" she asked.

"I'm thinking of the other kind, where I've had to send them out by plane to a hospital in Winnipeg or Montreal."

That was usually the last contact I had with a patient. Few big city hospitals thought of letting me know whether my conclusions had been correct, or even if the patient had survived. Sometimes it seemed about as satisfactory as tossing pebbles into a bottomless well.

Asking the government for a plane was a great responsibility, too. This meant requesting an expenditure of a few thousand dollars, sometimes more. It would be mighty embarrassing to send out an acute constipation case, for example, believing from my radio diagnosis that it was appendicitis. There was also the chance of leaving patients behind to die when I should have taken them out. Judgment was difficult. I never saw most of my radio patients anyhow. Some were in regions that I did not ordinarily cover.

There were the inevitable cases when the patient didn't make it. The old Eskimo with frostbite in his leg was typical. Gangrene had set in and it was apparent from my long distance diagnosis that the leg would have to be amputated at once, even though the old man might die from shock while this was being done. My next problem was to find a volunteer willing to perform the operation. The mountie on the post flatly refused and I could hardly blame him. While I was canvassing the air waves for someone else, that Eskimo died. I felt pretty badly.

At last I decided to try to accumulate enough figures to indicate what really was happening throughout my territory. It wasn't easy. In the end, though, the time spent gathering all possible statistics was worth it. Nearly 70 percent of my patients had recovered, about 23 percent had shown improvement and only some 7 percent had failed to make it for one reason or another. While not all of these last may have died, neither had they shown any improvement. So for statistical purposes I counted them out.

Viola had been watching the gathering of vital statistics week after week. When all possible reports were in, she took occasion to read me a lecture.

"After this"—she pointed to the figures—"don't ever let your radio diagnoses get you down, Joe Moody. Not *ever*—!"

With a clear conscience I began to promote the radio treatment as much as I could, suggesting various improvements and trying to regulate the transmitting schedule.

Another thing I liked about the system was that, when I went out on patrol, I found so many appreciative people. The fact that they could get on the air and reach a doctor in case of emergency, or just if they needed reassurance, gave them a tremendous amount of confidence. It was fun, too, to hear comments on difficult cases. Many people had listened in and followed the procedure step by step.

"Gee, Doctor, that sure was terrific. I could see it happen like I'd been there myself."

"That was really something, Doctor. Do you think he'd have made it if you hadn't ordered a plane for him?"

"That was one baby who'll never know what it took to bring him into the world. Pity about the mother, though, wasn't it? But you sure couldn't help that, Doc."

"You know, I never thought he'd get that finger off. He ain't so bright, is he?"

This last remark referred to the time when I directed a trapper to amputate a finger that had become gangrenous with frostbite. He was a fine man, but a little mixed up and certainly nervous at the time. I'll never forget that one. It was rather amusing. Went this way:

"Hello, Jim, which arm is it?"

"The right arm, Doc. No, no, I guess it's the left."

"Now which one, right or left?"

"It's left, Doc, sure it's left."

"What? Can't hear you."

"LEFT!" he yelled. Wow, that one came through. I had to shift the receiver to my other ear.

"Which finger is it?"

"The second."

"The second from where?"

"From the inside."

"What do you mean, nearer the thumb?"

"No, the one next to the little one."

"Why didn't you say so?"

"What? I did!"

"Never mind, do you have a scalpel?"

"A what?"

"Do you have a knife?"

"I've got a jack knife."

"Is it clean?"

"Well, I cut seal blubber with it."

"Boil it."

"What?"

"Boil it."

"But, Doc, it's a good knife."

"Boil it."

"But the wood, Doc, it'll ruin the handle."

"Boil it. We've got gangrene now. We don't want a few more infections."

"Ruin my knife," he muttered.

It went on for some time. This he didn't have. That he didn't understand. This he didn't want to do. That he couldn't find. The bandages had been used to clean his rifle and I strongly suspected that the antiseptic had disappeared in the manufacture of liquor.

But he finally made it! Did a fine job, too. Cut off a digit, tied off a couple of bleeders and sewed the whole thing up quite neatly. The story got all over the arctic.

I never knew what happened to the knife.

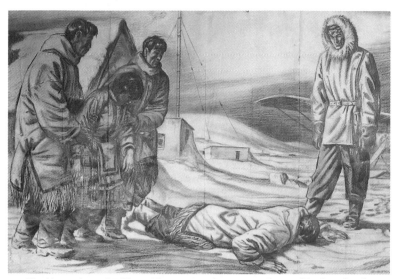

The Norwegian artist Giesen, has captured on canvas the combination of radio communication and air transport to fight epidemics.

◆ 6 ◆

BREATH OF WINTER

On rare days when things, domestic and professional, seemed to be getting nowhere with either of us, Viola and I could usually recapture perspective by comparing the present with our first few weeks in the settlement.

Our lives had fallen into a pattern sooner than we expected. What probably helped was my staying close by. Instead of venturing far outside the community, I thought it more important for a while to familiarize myself with the work at the hospital. Despite future patrols to far outposts, my professional headquarters would always be here in Chesterfield and I wanted to be able to use every hospital facility to best advantage.

Another reason for keeping near Chesterfield at first was its Eskimo settlement. In order to understand the nature of my future patients, I needed to mingle with them, and there was no better place than right there in Chesterfield.

At first they were friendly to me, but terribly reserved. Then the emergency of a broken arm played into my hands—literally and figuratively. After allowing me to treat some of their other immediate complaints, they began to give me more of their confidence. In time I found real pleasure in dealing with them.

The further I got into the work at Chesterfield, the more I found to do. There were always colds and intestinal troubles, wounds to be sewed up, eyes examined, broken bones to be set and a disturbingly high number of T.B. cases to be kept under observation.

So for some weeks my well beaten circuit comprised home, hospital and Eskimo settlement. In between I visited our white neighbors, whom I found eager and curious to get acquainted with us. Gradually it was borne in on me that the entire white populace of Chesterfield was a good deal like one big family. It had to be.

As Viola explained it: "There's no such thing as a self-contained family up here. We all need each other."

Cooperation was the keynote among the various officials, too. Beginning with my contact with the men in the radio hut, my acquaintanceship widened to include the mounted police, the trading post, the mission. Although each had its own particular duties, wherever administration of the Eskimos was concerned, these duties dovetailed. We *had* to consult and plan in unison.

Entering the house one day I found a disheveled Viola gripping the baby with one hand and stirring something on the stove with the other. All at once she let go of the little girl, sat down flat on the floor and burst out laughing. For a second I thought her hysterical, which wouldn't have surprised me much. Running an arctic household with no traditional grocery store around the corner wasn't easy, and Viola had to jump from one task to the next all day. But she wasn't hysterical now. Nor did she need sympathy.

"It's the knitting and crocheting, Joe!" she managed to say.

"Knitting and crocheting?"

She nodded, still laughing. "Don't you remember? Everybody back home insisted on my taking along a lot of knitting and crocheting *to fill my leisure time!*"

I sat down on the floor beside her and laughed too. Her knitting and crocheting! They were in the bottom of the trunk in which they had come. So far as we could see, there they would stay indefinitely.

Her hard, constant work paid off, though. She succeeded in making our home real cozy, at the same time keeping a watchful eye on little Gloria-May. The utter barrenness of our surroundings, which still awed and stifled Viola and me, had no such effect on our daughter. She was soon playing among the rocks with some new found playmates.

One day the clouds of mosquitoes, which had plagued us since the middle of July, left mysteriously, their sudden departure seeming to foretell a change of some sort. The weather was still nice. Temperatures reached the neighborhood of fifty degrees every day. Yet we were aware of a gradual chilling sensation hard to describe.

Perhaps the suspense laden atmosphere that settled over Chesterfield after the mosquitoes went was due, more than anything, to the increased activity on all sides.

We saw more fish drying on lines outside the Eskimo tents. Canoes and kayaks were hauled out of the water, wedged between boulders and roped down securely. Thick winter clothing was aired. Outside our homes the wind chargers were inspected and oiled with the greatest care lest we lack even artificial light in the dark months ahead.

"You know what impresses me most about all these preparations?" I said to Viola, as we stood watching one of the last kayaks being lifted from the water.

"What?"

"It's that everybody's so serious about it. I mean deadly serious. You'd think getting ready for winter was a matter of life or death."

She answered, lightly, "Maybe it is."

In later years we got hardened to the thought of winter, although it hung over us the entire year. Either we were living through one winter, or it was fall and we were getting ready for the next. Even in spring—while days lengthened and snow started to melt—there lingered in our minds the need to steel ourselves against the cold that would surely come.

But this was our first experience in the arctic and every impression, being new, sank doubly deep. A glance at the sick list told me that I'd be far too busy to get bored, as some friends back home thought likely when they advised me to start a diary.

Nevertheless, I had heard of winter boredom; even of the temporary insanity that overcame many during the months of total darkness. So I began a diary for its possible therapeutical effect. Soon I'd be making long patrols back into the snow covered barrens. That ought to furnish enough to write about to keep boredom away from me.

Snow was not yet with us, and ice covered only the shallowest puddles, when it became clear that some sort of magnet was drawing the white families together more and more. We grew to look forward to bridge evenings and impromptu parties. Hobbies sprang into being. Soon everyone was busy whittling or baking or sewing, anything to keep from getting bored. We met around at different houses; quite often at ours. But after a solid week of close propinquity it came over me with something of a shock that we could easily get bored with *one another.* There were only twenty-six whites at the post, and after the last supply boat had left, we'd be looking at the same faces every day for nine or ten months.

But that was in the future. For the moment the thoughts of everybody in Chesterfield were focused on the arrival of the last supply boat. She'd be due soon and the importance of her cargo could not be overestimated.

She'd bring the last fresh fruits and vegetables; the hundreds of pounds of canned, bagged, dried and condensed foods that must keep us going for many months. There would be fuel, blankets, pencils, nose drops, needles, light bulbs, socks, books; important and seemingly unimportant items to make a household function. I had prepared long lists myself—food and clothing for our family; medicine, bandages, glasses, X-ray film and vitamins for my patients.

Equally as important, in a way, would be packages from home, mysterious wrappings that would hold their secrets until Christmas; the things that had been ordered stealthily from department store catalogs for husband or wife, children or friends.

One day Chesterfield was thrown into an uproar by a radio man charging through the settlement yelling,

"*Severn! Severn!* just left Churchill! Ought to be here first of the week!"

People laughed, shouted to each other. Some of the women wept. Suspense rose to an almost unbearable pitch. The Eskimo "grapevine" must have carried it inland, for soon the first of the Eskimo hunters began to come back, eager to help unload the supply vessel and earn extra revenue.

"Look" I said to the manager of the Hudson's Bay Company post, "wouldn't it be better for them to finish their caribou hunt instead of cutting it short?"

"Oh, sure, Doc," he agreed, "but try to keep them away when the boat comes! Sometimes you can't get them to go out hunting at all. They'd rather sit around and wait for the last boat of the season."

The worst of it was, he went on, if the boat was late arriving the Eskimos might miss the vital caribou migration altogether.

"Then what?" I asked.

"Then they'll go hungry all winter, as well as lack furs for new clothing and bedding."

It was apparent that the Eskimos were becoming too dependent on white civilization. Even if they preferred buying their food and clothing to hunting them as of old, what little they could earn by unloading a ship would never support them all winter. It seemed pretty silly until I came to understand that the Eskimo is going through the lethargy of transition and doesn't much care.

Whether he could be taught to keep his own native ways of life was a question I had no time to mull over in the excitement of a sudden drop in temperature. The sun's trip above the horizon had grown quite short by now. This, coupled with the first real cold, suggested a frozen bay before long.

"She won't get here any too early," people remarked of the *Severn,* with a confidence justified by the nearness of her arrival.

Then came a radio message that knocked the props out from everybody's morale: The Severn *had sprung a leak a five miles out of Churchill and would not be able to make her trip at all!*

The little community was stunned. True, most of the supplies and the mail had been saved, we learned, but what good was that to us? Our lifeline had been broken. Presently, everyone turned desperately to checking his supplies, trying to estimate whether they might be made to last. Viola and I climbed to our big upstairs storeroom. There were still some staples left.

"Think we can stretch these over the winter?" I asked.

She wouldn't say. But, remembering what she had accomplished on a meager budget in our early married days, I believed we would make out at least as well as the neighbors. Most of them seemed badly discouraged by what their larders disclosed. It was not a very exuberant populace that settled down to await nine or ten months of ice and snow with no fresh foods and reduced staple rations.

Just as we'd got our belts pulled in and were adjusting our thinking to the coming challenge, the government and the Hudson's Bay Company joined forces to solve the problem. Most of our supplies they radioed, would be flown up to Baker Lake, 200 miles inland. The *Neophyte,* another Hudson's Bay Company supply boat, was there on its way out. She would load our stuff, head down through Chesterfield Inlet and drop it off when passing our settlement on the coast. Nothing sounded simpler.

On the surface, this play of emotions, raising us to the heights, dropping us to the depths and back again, brought a curious feeling of unreality. The "depths" was a nightmare; the "heights" too good to be true. Actually the news enabled us to loosen our belts again and face the slight delay with patience and revived good humor.

Snow fell a few days afterward. It averaged only ten inches, but in places piled up six and seven feet deep. I have been told that South Dakota actually registers more snowfall than Chesterfield—or than most of the Eastern Arctic, for that matter. What made it so bad with us was the wind. Gales came sweeping down across the endless open plains and wherever they met the slightest obstruction they piled up snow.

Our outhouses were soon buried and we had to dig tunnels to get some of the sparse light into our windows. The snow did us one good turn. It was such a fine insulator that, although our old house admitted some of the white stuff at the start, the first blizzard left us surprisingly warm and snug. That in itself was lucky. During the height of the storm no one was allowed out alone, as a man could get lost walking from one house to his neighbor's.

But while we rather enjoyed the novelty of those first storms, snow and ice were doing their work inland. Our hearts practically stopped when one of the radio men came wading through the drifts shouting,

"Neophyte's frozen in!"

"Where?" I yelled back. How close she had managed to get meant everything to the settlement.

His answer was garbled by the wind.

◆ 7 ◆

SHEENIKTOOK

The *Neophyte* was iced in between Chesterfield Inlet Community and Baker Lake, about five days' dog travel from Chesterfield.

I never knew bad news to spread so fast. Everyone in the settlement seemed to have heard at the same instant that our mail, food and medical supplies were stuck in the ice some 150 miles up the inlet. It was early October and at least seven more months must pass before another boat could possibly reach us.

But as I made my way about the settlement, it was clear that this latest misfortune came as less of a jolt than had the accident to the *Severn* a while before. (The *Severn,* with Captain Barber, are now both in retirement, which they certainly earned after many years of difficult arctic service in dangerous uncharted waters.) I wondered if people were becoming fatalists. What I failed to appreciate was that the old timers knew better than I that things now were more or less within our reach.

"If the weather lets up a little," they said, "a patrol can travel those 150 miles and bring back the mail and as much else as they can carry."

Like the other families, we rationed ourselves, just to play safe—and watched the weather. What worried me most was my medical supplies. I still had enough to carry on for a few weeks if all went well in the settlement. But let an epidemic once break out—!

Haunted by that possibility I radioed captain Eric Carlsen of the *Neophyte* and instructed him exactly how to preserve my medical supplies against freezing until our patrol could get through to the boat. He was a true old northener who had spent many years in the arctic and subarctic. He had captained many ships in arctic waters, and he drove the leading Caterpillar tractor over hundreds of miles of difficult arctic terrain in winter to map out the route for the Musk-Ox expedition. A nice fellow, be promised to follow my instructions carefully and was very apologetic about the whole misadventure.

"What are you and the crew going to do, Captain?" I asked, with an idea of having to bring them to Chesterfield along with the medicine.

Aksarnerk (Billy Brass), famous guide to many whaling expeditions, is seen here with his Cooke telescope.

"Oh, we're going back to Baker Lake by komatik," he answered, casually. "It's only seventy miles."

"Then what?"

"Then they'll fly us out from there. When the spring breakup comes we'll fly back to the *Neophyte* and bring her down to Chesterfield, the way we'd planned. See you then, Doctor."

"Well, good luck."

"Good luck to you."

Two weeks later Viola and I watched the start of a phenomenon that was mysterious, beautiful and (to us) very strange—the water of the bay gradually turning into ice!

This ageless episode began when the water took on a peculiar greenish hue and "cold smoke" in little wisps could be seen rising from the salty liquid. Gradually the water took on an oily appearance, and as the tides came and went the surface would undulate heavily to and fro in slow motion. "Getting lazy" expressed it best. The process was slow, steady, inexorable. Gradually the stones and sand about the shores became coated as with thick glass, and the lapping waters became slushy and then stiffened until all the land was surrounded by a glittering aura of ice stretched far out over the sea. Behind us, in the barren plains, the fresh water ice already had reached a thickness of twenty inches on even the biggest lakes. In a few weeks— maybe even days—some would be frozen solid to the bottom.

Sheeniktook, our Eskimo attendant and guide, had gone inland to one of the little fresh water lakes to "cut" our family water supply which he'd stacked in big blocks on the lake shore. As he hated menial work, it was with some reluctance that he announced the next step. As soon as the snow was more evenly distributed, he would go there with the komatik and restack the ice blocks nearer home. These we were to use for cooking and drinking. Melted snow was good enough for washing and cleaning clothes.

Except for the sickness of his wife, which kept him from wandering continuously around the country, Sheeniktook might never have appeared at our door that Sunday morning with the information that he'd come to work for the Kabloona doctor. We had heard about him before. "If you can get Sheeniktook," I was told, "he'll be a big help in all your work with the Eskimos. A good guide on your patrols too. But he won't hire out to many."

Sheeniktook proved to be a fine, husky man in his late thirties, dark after a spring and summer of exposure to the stinging sun. In time he became a good helper, although,

Eskimo-like, never my *servant*. He was a first rate companion, never completely a friend; a loyal adviser, never a partisan; a trusted addition to the family, yet always proud of being an Eskimo. To Sheeniktook, we whites were just a queer people who had money.

His name meant "The One Who Sleeps," but I never thought it appropriate. The name had been given him only because a long forgotten forefather had carried it. Now that his descendant bore his name the spirit of that forefather could live on.

Faithful huskies get a well deserved meal.

Originally a northern Eskimo, Sheeniktook was hardly full-blooded, yet he differed from the coastal Eskimos of the Chesterfield area. He had come there as a young child and been adopted by a highly respected Eskimo hunter called Billy Brass, Billy having come by his name while guiding prospectors' expeditions years before.

Now this Billy Brass, who seems to have been an outstanding man in the community, taught Sheeniktook more about life and the ways of his forefathers than was known to the average modern Eskimo. Too often white man's culture has trampled that of the Eskimo instead of complementing it. This was an exception. In Sheeniktook, to a greater extent than in any other,

I saw the solid old Eskimo culture smoothly blended into the white man's way. When men like Sheeniktook are gone, the disaster of white infiltration will have been completed.

It took adjustment on both sides before we managed to get along together. He was a good dog driver, an excellent guide and an expert igloo builder. Animals, ice formations, currents in the sea—this was the sort of thing about which he knew more than any other Eskimo I have ever met. But menial tasks around the house were below his dignity. These he performed with reluctance, bordering on the comic. When he came to us he knew little English, but he loved to learn and, particularly, to teach. He and Viola spent hours, each teaching his language to the other.

Overhearing Sheeniktook shoveling snow one day, I turned to Viola: "Where does he get all those 'damns' and 'hells'?"

"They just come naturally," she laughed, "whenever he does something he thinks beneath him."

It was true. The Eskimo language lacks words for interpreting those emotions which turn white men to expressions of heaven and hell. Besides, Sheeniktook aired his swearing mainly for our benefit, we discovered. Whenever we heard a muttered "damnhell," we knew it was to remind us that he was sacrificing dignity to our domestic comfort. He was in his proper element only when out on patrols. There nothing seemed undignified and he made himself indispensable. I foresaw so many of these patrols in my future work that I decided to keep him on, rather than send him away because of a few "damn hells."

Temperatures dropped down—down. Soon they were dipping between thirty and forty degrees below zero every day. Whether this was bearable depended entirely on the wind, or lack of it. Gales of eighty to ninety miles an hour, while certainly not commonplace, were normal enough to escape pointed comment. At such times it was all a man could do to zigzag from one house to the next through the sweeping turmoil.

To complete the insulation around our house, Sheeniktook had banked the house with snowblocks, covering everything but door and windows. In front of the door he built a half-igloo, its open side against the house. The entrance to this "vestibule" he cut at right angles to the house door, in this way keeping snow from drifting in during recurrent storms.

But while nature held us in its icy grip, it was putting on a marvelous show outside. With bay and lake now frozen solid, mysterious forces were still working under the surface, shaping the icy mass into weird forms—peaks, hummocks, rolling elevations, sharp breaks where ice had pushed across ice. But gradually this grotesque ice scape disappeared under layers of snow that stacked smoothly, soothingly, around every unevenness. The result was a stark unforgettable beauty whenever the sun painted the snow with many hues. Often the skies were a clean light blue streaked with white clouds. When more snow was coming the clouds showed dull gray.

All this was nothing compared with the spectacle of the northern lights flashing from horizon to horizon. I shall always remember one night in particular. It was late. Returning home from the hospital I stopped and gazed, enraptured at the great curtains and streamers waving back and forth as if moved by soft summer breezes.

Suddenly, long temporary arcs of light stretched over various lengths of the lines from the celestial pole to the horizon line. These vertical foci of light yellow multiplied into millions of fluttering, dancing arcs which fluoresced all the colors of the rainbow. Reds, yellows and greens were especially pronounced but all the spectral colors were faintly visible. Zones would break away from the main mass only to multiply themselves. Gradually half the sky became full of dazzling, dancing shafts of varicolored light pillars whose intensity was almost alarming, and whose reflection on the snow gave a quality of unreality to everything.

All at once, as if a celestial bond was released, the wavering lights leaped to the other sky segments, and the fabulous spectacle of northern lights stretching and vibrating from the horizon to the sky's peak could be seen in all directions. When this took place the brightness was unbelievable and the reflection on the ice and water caused both to glow with a strange smoldering fire of a golden, greenish hue. Sometimes horizontal bands would join and rejoin to form rings of controlled luminescence the vortices of which would invert and evert, causing an eye arresting display never to be forgotten.

Then, abruptly, the lights receded until a single lonely pillar was left dancing and vibrating in the velvet sky, and only the rustle of powdered snow blowing over the ice awakened me to reality from one of the world's most unusual phenomena.

The fantastic display gave me a curious feeling of smallness. Just before leaving the hospital I had been testing an Eskimo with a weak heart and no doubt had "heart" in my subconscious mind. This accounted, perhaps, for the dreamlike hallucination that crept over me and held me firm in its momentary grasp. I was no longer a man. In this vast space of nothingness I was a tiny heart beating amid overwhelming mysteries it could never comprehend. At the same moment I was conscious of new joy, new pride and a new satisfaction with life for being permitted to view such things. Nothing ever shook me more deeply than that experience. It made me understand how the arctic can so hypnotize people that they never want to leave it for good, once they've felt its pull.

Viola met me at the door. She looked worried. There had been talk of a small party starting out next day in the direction of the icebound *Neophyte.*

"Would you have to go along, Joe?" she asked, anxiously.

Still partly under the spell of the aurora borealis, I answered by dragging her out through the "vestibule" door, sweeping my arm triumphantly across the sky and uttering an awed, "Viola—LOOK!"

◆ 8 ◆

THE GRIP OF NIGHT

A round trip to the *Neophyte* would be perhaps 300 miles and, since no new snow had fallen for several days, this was a good time to leave. I looked forward to experiencing my first patrol.

At the last minute a full hospital kept me in Chesterfield, after all. The best I could do was describe to the members of the patrol which of the medical supplies they could bring back safely. Other medicines needed special handling and I preferred to get these myself later on.

But, as so often happens in the arctic, all this careful planning came to nothing. The day after our party left Chesterfield a number of strange Eskimos trudged in. They had our mail, Christmas packages and some of the more perishable stores. They had come from Baker Lake, the Hudson's Bay Company manager there having told them to stop at the *Neophyte* and remove as much as they could.

"You didn't meet our party?" we asked.

All shook their heads. "No see."

There was little use of sending after our own men because in the arctic everybody travels at the same speed—that is, as fast as weather permits.

"Well," we told ourselves, "they'll bring back at least something from the boat. We could do with a little more fresh food, anyhow."

We needn't have worried over our men going on a useless trip. Although the Baker Lake Eskimos had missed meeting them, our boys had stumbled on the others' tracks not too far along the route, and had turned back home at once. From tracks they find in the snow Eskimos often, as in this case, can tell who is traveling, and deduce where they have come from. So, two days after leaving Chesterfield for the *Neophyte,* our own crowd reappeared, grinning, in our midst.

Everyone was happy. With packages from home and enough food for a while more, we settled down to prepare for Christmas in a world where darkness already occupied a greater part of the day. Only between eleven in the morning and three in the afternoon was there any real daylight now.

Eulalie, an Arctic beauty, spring cleaning her igloo.

At about this time an unexpected remedy for boredom appeared. It seems that several white families had been malting a rather potent home brew. While officially its manufacture was forbidden, its consumption was condoned as the theory that where nature took such liberties with us, we might take a few ourselves. Along with these doubtful ethics was the practical advantage of social gatherings in which we could enjoy one another's company once more.

By the time we were down to two or three hours of daylight only—during which the sun rolled eerily along the horizon like a big orange-red ball—the long hours of darkness began to make me feel a bit queer. All household schedules were upset. Sleep was regulated by need, not habit; meals were apt to be irregular where time was no longer a factor.

That was when our wind charger, on which we depended for electric light became life's most important instrument. It required frequent checking. Although running most of the day, there was no guarantee that its oil wouldn't freeze at any moment. One night I was giving it a going over before turning in when, out of the corner of my eye, I dimly saw a huge animal sneaking away from our garbage pile. Examining its tracks later, Sheeniktook pronounced the animal a wolf. I thought it strange that none of our huskies had barked. Perhaps their relationship to the wolf was closer than I thought.

An Eskimo puts finishing touches on his "home," an Igloo. His whip is left on the dome, out of the reach of dogs, who take great pleasure in eating it.

For some reason this wolf incident, added to the almost continuous darkness, deepened my depression. Little things assumed monstrous proportions. Once we took off our storm windows long enough to scrape away the two-inch layer of ice on the inside. We thought this might give us something more nearly approaching daylight. But the scraped glass only let in more dull darkness. Instead of square patches of gray, our windows had turned into gaping black holes.

You could weigh the blackness! How much longer, I wondered, would these strange feelings of mine last!

Putting aside her own depression, Viola would try to cheer me up: "The crowd's getting together right next door tonight. Can you make it? Do us both good."

I'd try to make it—for her sake.

After a while, even the home brew parties lost their temporary lift. Then they went into reverse, so to speak. I discovered things about my closest friends that I hadn't seen before and didn't like at all. Physical characteristics, mostly. For example, the nose of a neighbor bothered me out of all reason. It was quite a normal nose, though rather large. I just didn't like that nose and took personal offense when he showed it around. He was a nice enough fellow, I had to admit, but he shouldn't have had that nose.

The dangling earrings which one of the women liked to wear at our parties made me nervous, too. I hoped fervently that somebody had sent her a new set in one of the Christmas packages hauled from the *Neophyte*.

Others fell under the influence of the arctic winter. Our evenings of bridge, to which we had all looked forward at first, became boring, then actually dangerous. Instead of feeling the warm, chatty coziness they used to bring, partners now glared at each other across the tables. This was unpleasant but hardly dangerous. What aroused us to the hair trigger nature of the situation occurred the night two of the radio boys got into an argument over a bid one of them had made.

"Is *that* all you raised me on?" rose one voice.

"All! What more d'y'want?" shrilled the other.

"A halfway decent hand, that's all. You're the damn rotten-est—"

"Listen! For a no-trump—"

"Oh, shut up!"

Both had risen and stood glaring at each other across the table. Next would come a first blow.

At this point the rest of us stepped in firmly. Even the women pushed forward, realizing that at last matters had gone far enough. It took some time to calm the pair down; to convince them that if fighting ever started among us it would be the end.

"It's this damned darkness closing in on you," one of them explained, almost tearfully, by way of apology. There was no need for apologies. Everyone understood. Instead of resuming our bridge that night we decided to break up "while we're all in one piece," as our hostess put it, with a mirthless laugh.

We trudged home silently through the snow.

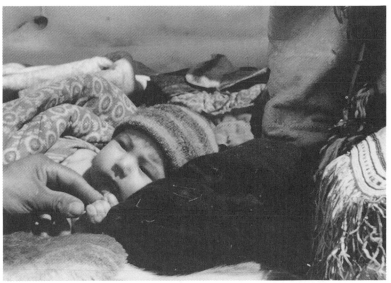

Baby Angote, although naked, is comfortable, and secure in her igloo home.

Fortunately, before our morale sank lower the nearness of Christmas shed a more peaceful light over the community. According to those who had spent Christmas there before, the advance signs would be unmistakable.

One day we saw these signs for ourselves—strange Eskimo families appearing from nowhere and building their igloos among those of their brothers. Distant Eskimos, it seemed, always converged on the settlement before Christmas to share in the festivities. Their advent had a remarkable effect on the whites. Activities picked up: people moved about busily, driven by a real purpose for the first time in weeks. Wives were making candy and baking weird concoctions culled from well thumbed cookbooks. Packages were being wrapped. Even the hobbyists were starting to turn out their masterpieces again.

The sudden restoration of a healthier outlook gave me vast relief. As a doctor, I had no wish to have more neurotic patients on my hands than is normal in the arctic. Besides, I had been feeling too much that way myself to handle them with proper objectivity. Now everything looked better. The spirit of Christmas was in the air.

Viola felt better, too, and the baby, continuing to take things in her stride, was showing an appreciative interest in her surroundings. In fact, our daughter's increasing alertness to everything was really the cause of a new worry for me; a worry inadvertently suggested by a passing remark of Viola's three days before Christmas.

"I wish we could make a better Christmas for Gloria-May," she said. "More like the Christmas she'd have had in the south."

"So do I," I answered. "Well, she'll have some presents, anyhow."

"I wish, Joe," Viola continued, "we could have a—*a tree.*"

"Tee, Daddy," lisped the small girl at her side.

A lump rose in my throat and I turned and stared out the window into the blackness.

There wasn't a tree of any sort in this part of the land. The nearest scraggy evergreens were 600 miles away!

◆ 9 ◆

WARMTH BENEATH THE SNOW

Gloria-May had her Christmas Tree after all—such as it was. The idea stayed in Viola's mind until her native ingenuity created a "tree" from the means at hand. Its backbone was a broomstick. For branches she fastened on small sticks and pipe cleaners, using tape. Then she covered the whole with strips of green crepe paper. Winter had either dulled or sharpened our imaginations—I'm not sure which—but to us the result looked remarkably like a real tree. She had painted small light bulbs different colors, and these she and I hung in series on her masterpiece. There were tree ornaments, too, made out of cotton, wood and cardboard. When all was done, we set the contraption in front of the living room window, turned on the bulbs and let them stay lighted day and night.

Soon the fame of Viola's Christmas tree spread through the settlement. Several Eskimo children, completely awed by the display, spread the word to the others. In almost no time a path was beaten to our window where these little Eskimos stood for hours, their brown faces all smiles. Viola and I looked at each other. There was no need to say anything. The Christmas spirit was here.

On Christmas Eve a special party at the radio station served to carry on a traditional event of several years' standing. Similar Christmas Eve parties were being held in other arctic settlements, their success depending largely on the fact that all were tied together by radio.

In Chesterfield the whites and a few Eskimos assembled in the tiny radio hut. Its atmosphere grew a bit thick, but all had a fine time. A special feature of this evening was permission to every one to speak over the radio and send greetings to friends around the arctic. Emotions were often controlled with difficulty, especially when voices began to be heard from the other posts. So near they seemed—yet actually so far away!

A program, broadcast by several gifted (more or less) members of our community, furnished needed diversity. Viola and one of the other women sang a duet. There were more duets and a solo or two. Some told their favorite stories. The nuns from the hospital had brought a small choir of Eskimo children, and it made us swallow hard to hear them sing carols and hymns in words they hardly understood but which held such deep meaning for us. Listening, we were only half-conscious of time or place, each sunk in his own thoughts.

Afterward it got gayer. One Eskimo played his mouth organ and another had brought his accordion. These furnished a decided change of pace. We also had records, and even swung into a few lively dances. Then the other radio stations made contact again, thanking us for our music and telling what was going on in their own little groups.

It was strange how those 200 or 300 people who had chosen the arctic for their home showed their awareness of this bond that united them. They lingered longingly around their far-flung microphones, loath, apparently, to break off the voices that came through the clear, cold skies.

Our party had a stabilizing, down-to-earth effect on all of us until, walking home, we were treated to a grandstand view of northern lights which undid all the stabilizing effect.

I thought I knew what northern lights were like from watching their varied performances night after night. Though never the same, they followed a basic pattern of sorts—at least to the extent of accustoming you to a kaleidoscope of grandeur. But grandeur was hardly the word for what we saw in the heavens that night. I'm sure there never was a manifestation of more unbelievable beauty; the kind that enters your soul and does things to you. It started with a band of multicolored light moving through the sky and finally rolling up into a tight ball. There were greens and reds and purples, soft yellows and oranges. As we looked, that ball of colored fire grew bigger —bigger—BIGGER! Then, with a noise that might have been a salvo from celestial artillery, it burst open, shooting out beams of light in the form of a giant star . . .

Several moments passed before we could so much as "Oh," or "Ah!" Then, as we turned toward home, someone murmured, in awed tones, "Star of Bethlehem."

The rest of the way Viola and I felt warm deep inside us; warm and very happy.

On Christmas Day, the mission put on its yearly "bean feast" for the Eskimos. It was exactly that—a festive occasion highlighted by the distribution of big bowls of cooked beans. How those Eskimos loved cooked beans! Just watching them eat was quite a sight. The recollection of other years had caused them to bring along a weird assortment of containers in which to carry away what could not *possibly* be eaten on the spot. This gay "gorge" led to considerable polite belching, and the whole affair culminated in square dancing "Eskimo style."

That evening all the whites of the settlement gathered at our home. We sat on the floor around Viola's improvised tree with the packages piled under it. She had made many different kinds of candy to munch on during the distribution of gifts. Everyone got a present of some kind which he or she pronounced "wonderful." But what excited everybody the most was opening the packages from home; the special presents, selected so many months in advance, that had finally reached us after their roundabout, disaster marked journey.

Earlier in the day we had brought over a small organ from the Hudson's Bay Company post. One of the mission Fathers now sat down at it and played until he had us joining in with our voices. Gradually the music faded out and we ended the evening with intimate talk of Christmases past. Somehow, it left us all quite happy with our little arctic world.

From Christmas through New Year's was something like a high plateau in the Chesterfield calendar. Because there was something different doing every day, it would seem particularly foolish to lose any part of that lively period. Yet that's exactly

what I did. I lost a day. It wasn't like the switching of days
when you cross the date line. This was my own fault.

"Well, we're getting close to 1947," I happened to remark to
Viola as we leafed through our day-by-day calendar. "Tomorrow's the twenty-seventh."

"The twenty-eighth," she corrected.

"Twenty-seventh. This is Friday, isn't it?"

"*Friday?*" She looked at me as if I'd gone out of my senses.
"Why, Joe, this is Saturday, the twenty-eighth, and you know
it!"

To convince her she was wrong I went over to the radio hut
for proof.

"This is Saturday, the twenty-eighth," they said, with a quick
glance at their log to make sure.

"Then Viola is *right?*"

"Of course, Doc. Isn't she always?"

With a silly grin, I left them to go home and assure Viola
that if either of us was off our reckoning, it wasn't she.

I don't know yet where I mislaid that day. The continuous
darkness probably was at the bottom of it.

New Year's Eve started off not exactly gloomily for Viola
and me. Rather, thoughtfully. We sat in the living room resting
and watching Gloria-May put her new "Eskimo" rag doll to bed.
Year's end is a time for reflection anywhere, but in the arctic
there seems more reason for nostalgic thoughts. Our region was
still practically unspoiled from the white man's invasion. It was
peaceful and remote from the world's turmoil—conditions that
led to solemn retrospection on the easy life left behind.

Our neighbors must have known from experience what goes
on in the minds of people spending their first New Year's Eve
in the arctic. A bit later that night our somewhat somber mood
was interrupted by people shouting outside. Then they were
crowding into the snow vestibule and pounding on our door.
With relief we discovered that it was only a party—not a fire or
an accident. They had come to cheer us up!

Home brew was soon much in evidence and the women made
potato chips. Ayranni, one of the Eskimos, came in with his
accordion, and we danced until late into the morning. It was all
very gay and confidential. I freely admitted how a while back I
had come to hate my neighbor's nose. We all laughed—including

the man with the nose. He immediately confessed to similar feelings about others in the group. We were like one big family and thought of our arctic life as a wild and fascinating adventure which couldn't be quite real but was fun while it lasted.

When finally we broke up, I walked out with our guests, then wandered through the settlement by myself, marveling that beneath all this cold could be so much warmth and happiness. A lone star near the horizon seemed to twinkle: "Welcome home."

◆10◆

ESKIMO CLOSE-UP

The first weeks of the new year I spent most of my time among our own coastal Eskimos around Chesterfield. They were different from their brothers inland because they depended for a living primarily on the sea. They hunted white whale, walrus, seal and polar bear, and naturally kept themselves well supplied with fish. Only during the short summer months did they travel inland to hunt caribou, which furnished their favorite meat and, more important, hides for bedding, tents and winter clothing.

The key to many ethnic as well as other scientific puzzles is locked up in the East Arctic. Some excellent work has been done in the various technical fields of natural science in the area, but it is most unfortunate that the many existing gaps in the realm of ethnology as well as geology and allied subjects show no signs of being closed for many years to come. In fact, "the surface has hardly been scratched" in any field of the East Arctic.

The Eskimo's origin is still cloaked in so much mystery that scientific research must rely on a good deal of guesswork to fill the gaps in his history. It seems most likely that the Eskimos migrated to the western hemisphere from northeast Asia by way of the Bering Strait, the great adventure taking place during the first years of the Christian era.

The original immigrants are believed to have come across Bering Strait and to have formed the following cultures: Those of the west were the old Bering Sea Panuk and Birnirk; the east had at least two groups, the Dorset and the Manitunik of the Belcher Islands; the Thule culture is believed to have originated from one of the western or Alaskan cultures, and to have preceded or to have given direct rise to our present day East Arctic Eskimos. Some ethnologists believe that some of the peoples under my jurisdiction were mixtures of the Thule and Dorset cultures supposedly from Greenland which, flourishing on the shores of Hudson Bay, were absorbed by other migrants.

By the time I came to Chesterfield, there were few pure-blooded coastal Eskimos left in Canada. Ever since the arrival of the white whalers a lot of white blood has been introduced to the Eskimo strain. The only true, or close to true, Eskimos of today are found in isolated areas such as the northern arctic islands, the Boothia Peninsula and the Back River region.

The Eskimos are a primitive race. More tactfully we call them "underdeveloped." But we can have only respect for a people who, before the white man destroyed what they built, were self-reliant and happy. Lacking any surging ambitions, nevertheless they have managed within the boundaries of their grim habitat to develop a comparatively high culture.

For example, their ivory and soapstone carvings, although lacking intricate design, are really works of art. The women who make the clothes are excellent seamstresses by any standard, even though the material may be skins. They can tailor each garment so that it fits the wearer exactly. The adornments, too, are tasteful.

Surrounding them in their snow houses, the Chesterfield Eskimos still had some of the simple tools and implements with which their race had fought for survival. But these they used side by side with many of our own imports. Their ancient seal-oil lamp, or kudlik, carved out of soapstone, still served in many igloos, forming a stove and source of light, yet the more fortunate used, instead, the white man's kerosene lamp.

The ooloo was their knife or scraper. Sometimes this useful implement was shaped out of bone or ivory, but in recent years more often of metal. Our steel knives had been widely adopted. Their dishes were small hoops of bone or wood, having one side covered with skin. Often they carved bowls from solid pieces of driftwood in which they placed their raw meat to be cut with a flint knife. Musk-ox horn supplied excellent cups, spoons or ladles. Stone and bone dishes were also used. As for weapons, they made their own spears, harpoons and bows from wood or bone, with points of stone or ivory.

I was particularly interested in the traditional sled, or komatik, they used, and in their amazingly graceful one man canoes, or kayaks. A pair of long wood, bone or skin runners joined by several crossbars of the same material formed the komatik. Their kayak was really a masterpiece of simple naval construction, delicate but tough, featherweight yet stable enough to be paddled anywhere by those acquiring the trick. The fact that all this native equipment had been supplemented by white man's modern tools undoubtedly made the Eskimo's life easier in one way. But since this made him less dependent on his former skills, it had the unfortunate effect also of corrupting his own culture.

The Eskimos, such as the Padleimiuts, Kazan River and Coppermine groups living at the tree line, had little trouble obtaining wood. The majority of the Eskimos, however, living far from wood, found it most difficult to obtain and a very useful and valuable commodity, until our own imports began to reshape their lives. That was why, before a young Eskimo could marry the girl of his choice, be had to make a trip south to the tree line to collect enough wood for tent poles and a komatik. Wisely, perhaps, the tribe considered it impossible to start a household without a supply of wood for its basic needs. The custom had another advantage too. It tested the young man's sincerity. For who, unless he meant business, would undertake a trip which weather and traveling conditions might easily drag out to more than a year?

Their culture, as expressed by their own music, is simple in the extreme. The drum is the only native musical instrument they know. Although they sing frequently, each song follows a monotonous pattern, melodious enough, but without much variation. On the other hand they have eagerly adopted the white man's musical instruments—especially our mouth organ and accordion. Since they have a natural ear, it is easy for them to duplicate or imitate our music.

Their best known native dance is the drum dance, which has a ceremonial origin. Other forms of dancing are practiced but are not spectacular—with one exception. They have taken enthusiastically to our own *square dance* and perform it with a vigor that might endanger an ordinary barn floor.

At play Eskimos show great skill and ability to concentrate. One of their favorite games is performed with a thirty-foot dog whip. They place small sticks in the snow, send the long whip lash spiraling through the air skillfully and flick them out one by one with a flip of the wrist. Contests in handling their kayaks are popular. Sometimes they like to race their dogs.

They are always eager to imitate games they see the white man play. One of the men belonging to the Royal Canadian Mounted Police at Chesterfield had a soccer ball. This the Eskimos adopted at once. Later, there was nothing more amusing than to see the Eskimos play their game of soccer with as many as thirty or forty people wildly running all over the place.

Long before coming north I had heard, of course, about the peculiar sex relationships among the Eskimos. So much has been written about this that one can hardly escape learning what certain authors consider interesting reading matter. In an effort to separate fact from fiction, I found that many wrong impressions have been created by ignorance, misrepresentation and a vulgar taste for sensationalism. It seems to me that few people have presented the facts within context and described the true causes and circumstances.

We should remember, first of all, that among all living creatures white man is practically the only one whose sexual behavior is in contrast with his nature. Governed by society and church, his code certainly has its place. But if people would abandon their bigotry and face the fact that their code does not reflect their natural instincts, they would have more tolerance for what goes on in the high latitudes of the Eskimo world.

Where people's very existence must be interwoven with the physical resources of their land, it is only natural that the laws of nature become the laws of man. In a country where all acts in contrast with our own codes are committed only because of dire need, is it hard to understand that need would dictate sexual behavior?

For example, it is true that a traveling Eskimo can depend on being offered the favors of his host's wife or daughters as a routine bit of hospitality. It is true, also, that reports of this custom cause us to raise our eyebrows; perhaps with a smirk besides. Yet there are logical explanations. In the first place, the Eskimo does not regard the urges of the flesh as an extracurricular pleasantry. He accepts it for what, to him, it really is—a natural instinct no more noteworthy than that man must eat to stay alive. Not having been exposed to pictures and "literature" that extol the physical relationship between men and women, he does not emphasize the matter. In fact, it has been my experience while working with Eskimos that, as a race, they are quite temperate in their sexual relationships.

While nature is the only force governing the Eskimo attitude toward sex, you can find other explanations for their behavior from the angle of need. For example, there long has been a shortage of women among them. This, in turn, stems from the fact that times of great distress have led to the practice of a certain amount of infanticide—with female children the first victims. Add to this loss the devastating influence of white men's diseases and the high sterility among both men and women, and the reason for the gradual shrinking of the Eskimo population becomes clear.

There is little doubt that their code of hospitality, inspired and carried out by practical considerations, has been of major importance to the survival of their race. Despite the fact of extramarital relationships, the average Eskimo family is a closely knit family and one free of any sense of perversion. The Eskimos want children badly, love them when they arrive and treat them with the greatest care and respect. If a child is born out of wedlock, it automatically is taken into the family and treated by the foster father as his own. Since the children of deceased relatives and friends are also adopted as a matter of course, this gives the Eskimo's the highest rate of adoption anywhere.

Inbreeding, of course, is prevalent but, so far as I have been able to determine, it has not weakened the surviving strain. At the same time one must take into consideration that abnormal persons rarely survive, whether on account of sheer hardship of environment or because of so-called assisted suicides. I may add that venereal disease, certainly carried there by the white man, does not appear to be present and, to the credit of the Eskimo, major abnormalities in sexual behavior are exceptionally rare.

• 11 •

TURNING POINT

In their relationship with the whites, Eskimos are careful not to become too friendly. Keeping aloof, they have a way of making you feel that you are just a visitor, after all. Blood brothership with the white man is quite unknown. Much as they may like you and help you and serve you, they are never anxious to approach you on an equal basis. They have seen too many white men come and go, influencing their lives in unfortunate ways. That, perhaps, is the "why" of their aloofness; the real reason for their lack of interest in learning from us.

But do not underestimate Eskimo intelligence. They show great respect for the modern machines and instruments we bring them and, with their knack for mechanics, they quickly learn how to use them. But their interest never reaches out beyond what you show them. Nor are they curious about what goes on outside of their own section of the world. The existence of other lands and peoples they accept by logic—but still do not quite believe.

They know what two- and four-engined aircraft are because they have seen them, but you'll waste your time trying to tell them there are eight-engined machines, and jets also. Even if shown pictures, they refuse to believe it. As for telling them about skyscrapers, trains and automobiles, they greet such tall tales with hearty laughter. No doubt this attitude springs from their own barren environment. Dwelling in an area that produces so little of lasting significance, they cannot grasp how we, in our world, can have so much.

My close contact with Sheeniktook taught me a good deal about Eskimo philosophy and psychology. The Eskimo usually hides his emotions so successfully that it is hard to decide if he is angry or insulted unless he actually commits a hostile act. He is stoic in the extreme. You never know what forces are at work behind the impassive mask of his face.

Mother is happy knowing that the drying Arctic char will provide many meals.

Yet his philosophy is very practical and, again, geared to his environment. Enjoy the present is his motto for living. But because time is a matter of only slight importance, the broader sense of "enjoy the present" is lost to him. He considers "yesterday" as too far away to be important, while "tomorrow" is too remote even to contemplate. He knows little of his own history. No one has taken pains to record it for him and little has been passed on verbally. Even the memory of his immediate forefathers means little and is preserved only methodically in given names. For it is in a name, he believes, that his forefather lives on.

Ask an Eskimo something about the past—some incident, perhaps, only a few days back—and you subject him to mental torture. The hardship of thinking contorts his face. Even after a display of the most painful grimaces he'll probably come up with a brief, "I don't know." Only if he thinks you really expect an answer will he take the trouble to produce one, and then it seldom has much bearing on your question.

Yet the Eskimos, as I found them, were not hard to like. If their faces were often masks, they displayed one emotion openly. That was joy. They loved a joke or prank. They laughed easily and hard. Their keen sense of humor was also shown in the aptness of their choice of nicknames. With their instinctive knowledge of human nature they often had a white man's character figured out long before he was able to size them up.

Going to the other extreme, their attitude toward death puzzled me until I understood a little more about them. At first I could detect no great grief at the loss of a loved one. Later, I knew that actually they mourned deeply. They seemed hardened against death and accepted it as a matter of course. This, too, resulted from an environment in which the life of man and beast follows the law of survival of the fittest.

Mercy killings are almost nonexistent. Assisted suicides are much fewer than formerly and only practiced occasionally in very isolated areas. Eskimo reasoning in the past, and sometimes in the present, dictated that there were times when old and disabled people—also infants, mainly girls—must be put to death because they consumed food that ought to go to those more useful to the family or band. Where the death of a hunter would be a major disaster, an old man or woman, unable longer to contribute to the group, would not be missed. Often these persons will themselves ask for death. It then becomes a case of assisted suicide, dire need giving the younger ones in the band the stern duty of helping these involuntary dependents to die.

The Eskimos' thoughts on life after death are not clearly defined and seem to differ somewhat from section to section. In some places all the deceased's possessions are buried with him. This certainly suggests belief in a life hereafter in which the departed will again need these things. Their reluctance to come near a grave also shows that they must think of the spirit as living on.

Wager Bay Inuit uses willow and heather for fuel to prepare a delightful meal of seal flipper stew and tea.

Still, it is significant that the Eskimo makes no attempt to communicate with his dead. That may be one reason why those passing on are so soon forgotten. Not the least of the uncertainties attached to Eskimology is whether those individuals who profess Christianity do so with real understanding, or merely as a gesture of politeness to their white teachers. To a race with its ancient "survival of the fittest" background, our Christian principles no doubt seem very strange.

Within the shelter of their snow-built domes and caribou skin tents, they have multiplied and survived over several thousand years. We ourselves could learn from their understanding of human values, their simple philosophy, their tolerance toward others. In this complicated world they lead an uncomplicated existence. Until the white man came, their life was more honest, more purposeful, more natural, richer, warmer and happier than that of the surrounding world.

The Eskimos around Chesterfield were slow to accept me. Fortunately, I didn't try to force myself on them. The turning point came with their realization that already I had begun to heal their wounds and relieve their pain. Then slowly their attitude changed until finally they received me in warm, genuine friendliness.

I found them generally honest, intelligent, admirable—a people perfectly adjusted to their environment. Moving from igloo to igloo, administering medicine, tying bandages, inoculating preventive serums and relieving distress where prevention had come too late, I took deep satisfaction in contributing at least a small part to the effort being made to bring a neglected race back to life.

◆12◆

NEOPHYTE PATROL

During the winter several small patrols took me to settlements south of Chesterfield. By the greatest of good luck, no upsurge of sickness hit us, and the meager stocks of medicine, serums and bandages that were in Chesterfield at the time of the *Neophyte* disaster held out miraculously. But I kept my fingers crossed night and day.

April arrived before a good excuse arose to set out northwest in the direction of my iced in supplies. It came with a radio message. An Eskimo living close to where the *Neophyte* lay was suffering severely from a frozen hand. Also, an Eskimo girl near the same place was showing such advanced symptoms of tuberculosis that she could no longer be allowed to stay with her family. As usual, such cases, far off in the wilderness, aroused my pity. But this time pity was mixed with relief at thought of visiting these unfortunates and at the same time getting hold at last of the rest of my medical supplies.

Because this patrol would be by far the longest I had made, it seemed a good time to have a dog team of my own. For previous patrols I had rented dogs from local Eskimos, since the distances had not been great. Even so, traveling with different sets of dogs had been difficult. Besides, my excursions would certainly grow in number as my work increased so that I was particularly anxious to have a team to which I could get accustomed.

I had long been impressed by the importance of the huskies to the life of people living in the arctic. Without his dogs the Eskimo is almost helpless. The husky is the only domesticated animal in those far regions. Naturally, the number a man owns is a measure of his wealth.

Resembling a wolf, the husky is a strong animal standing about two feet six inches high and weighing about eighty pounds. He can pull a load of around eighty pounds with great ease, and often keeps up a speed of four miles an hour with his 250-pound share of an overloaded komatik. In summer he carries a burden of up to forty pounds on his back. If let loose he can run at a speed of more than twenty miles an hour—even faster if he happens to be after a caribou. He can go without food for several days. He stays outside the igloo and sleeps unperturbed in blizzards, with temperatures of sixty below zero.

Appreciating their worth, Eskimos usually take good care of their dogs and are expert in breeding them. A lead dog, the one who habitually heads the pack, is particularly valuable, and therefore trained with great patience. He it is who selects the best route across melting ice, eases the strain for all by instinctively picking the best footing, dominates the rest of the pack. With your lead dog under control, you don't have to worry about the rest. If he is badly trained and unruly you will have endless trouble with every dog that follows his leadership.

What does his dog mean to an Eskimo? Some years ago, when the big grain elevator was being built there, a group of Eskimos were taken to Churchill. The whites accompanying them thought that of course their charges would be overawed by all the modern equipment amassed on the pier. The Eskimos didn't seem greatly impressed. Perhaps they didn't understand what it was all about. A little later they disappeared suddenly. A frantic search discovered them gazing, open mouthed, at a few dilapidated old horses used for hauling building material. Here really was something! This they could understand!

"Big dogs—big dogs!" they exclaimed.

These animals did the same kind of things their dogs did but on a much grander scale. They were much grander *dogs!*

Owning such fabulous beasts, how could the white man get so excited over dull, smelly machinery? Because I had learned to trust Sheeniktook's judgment and knew little about dogs myself, I asked him to select some good animals for me and buy them. The result gave me a new insight into Eskimo mentality. For when I walked over to get my huskies on the morning of our departure, I found two of the four dogs absolutely useless. One was lame, the other had an infected foot. I was surprised and pretty angry at Sheeniktook, and told him so. Then I realized that to him I was only the Kabloona doctor and that he saw no reason for not doing a good turn for a fellow Eskimo by helping him get rid of a couple of bad dogs. It was odd that Sheeniktook failed to realize that, as guide and dog driver on this trip, he would have more trouble with these dogs than I. Finally, I decided to leave the lame one behind and treat the one with the sore foot so that he would be at least partly useful.

That trip to the *Neophyte* was one of the most miserable patrols I can remember. By early afternoon Sheeniktook had lost his voice from shouting at the dogs. I took over until I too was producing no more than a whisper. On top of that, I acquired a nasty sunburn from powerful ultraviolet rays reflected by the snow. Because there is so little dust in the arctic, the sun has much more power and stings you viciously through the thin air. Sheeniktook should have warned me against that. But he was still sulking over my remarks to him concerning the dog buying fiasco. Within a few hours my face was swollen beyond recognition. I could hardly see because of puffed eyelids.

When evening came I began to feel more charitable toward Sheeniktook and a little later I stood watching in frank admiration while he built our igloo for the night.

Any doubts as to the Eskimo's intelligence, resourcefulness and ingenuity disappear in watching him construct one of his domed snowhouses. Though conveniently helped by the cementing qualities of subzero weather, he probably was the first human to build an unsupported dome by instinctively grasping the basic theories of mechanics which make a dome a dome.

Armed with a long stick and his invaluable snow knife, Sheeniktook searched for a three- or four-foot layer of solidly packed snow. Having found a suitable spot, he drew a crude, ten-foot diameter circle. This provided a "blueprint" for his foundation. Then, cutting blocks of snow within this outline, he began building.

The blocks were a foot wide, about two feet long and perhaps six inches thick. He placed them in a circle, following the foundation outline. Then, tilting them slightly inward, he smoothed down the edges so that each block fitted the next. After completing the first circle, he sliced the first two or three blocks diagonally, starting at the top of the third and ending at the bottom of the first. This gave him a sloping ledge on which the next row could be started in a slightly inclined position. In this manner he actually spiraled upward, each new layer increasing the inward slope at which the blocks were placed. This "coiled serpent" of icy bricks he finally completed with a wedge that closed the top of the dome. A freezing temperature glued the snowblocks together instantly. The result was that the entire spiral formed a solid wall.

When constructing something more permanent than an overnight shelter, Sheeniktook would build a thin slab of ice into the wall for a window. A low entrance was cut out on the side away from the prevailing winds and covered with an arch of snowblocks for extra protection against blizzards. About two-thirds of the floor area was left higher than the rest to form a sleeping and sitting platform, the part dug out deeper being toward the entrance, which itself sloped down from the outside ground level into the igloo. The temperature of an igloo varied with weather conditions. Near the source of the heat—the seal-oil lamp—it could get as high as forty or forty-five degrees. Closer to the walls it often didn't rise above zero. To control ventilation, you simply opened or closed a small wedge in the dome. I must admit, though, that the doorway usually provided enough fresh air—at least to meet Eskimo standards.

Sheeniktook could build a good sized igloo in about an hour; sometimes much faster. In bad weather he wasn't too particular but merely saw to it that we had some sort of shelter in the shortest possible time. That first night of our trip to the *Neophyte* he insisted on putting up a masterpiece. I don't know why, unless my rebuke to him about the dogs still rankled, and to get even he chose to prolong my discomfort. At any rate, he took his time. I was thankful—so, I suspect, was he—when finally we had the tea water boiling and, wrapped comfortably in our furs, could recline on the sleeping platform.

The second day my sunburn was less painful, and in better humor we both trudged along behind the komatik. We kept on in the general direction which Sheeniktook had nonchalantly indicated with a careless gesture. He seemed hardly to have given the matter a thought.

After several hours I said, "Sheeniktook, how long is this trip going to take, anyhow?"

He muttered some answer which meant nothing.

For Eskimos, travel days are separated by sleeps. Even if thcy sleep twice in twenty-four hours they will tell you that two days have elapsed since what really was yesterday. This interpretation of time is understandable, perhaps, in a country which has periods when either daylight or darkness—"day" or "night"—may last for nearly twenty-four hours. In winter, when the sun appears above the horizon for only a few hours, it is hard to define a travel day. The definition is equally hard in summer when darkness seems never to come.

"How long will this trip take?" I repeated, in a louder voice.

His answer this time was an uncertain, "Maybe another six sleeps."

I had to be satisfied with that.

◆13◆

SHEENIKTOOK REDEEMS HIMSELF

The picture changed on the third day. A snowstorm surprised us and enveloped us in a cloud of whiteness that stayed with us the rest of the trip.

Soon gales of forty miles an hour were lashing the snow across the barren plains. Our vision was limited to a few feet. I really learned to appreciate Sheeniktook then. He taught me the tricks of bucking the wind, of throwing up small half-igloos for protection when we rested. He taught me how to keep warm. Most of all, he continued to guide us in the right direction.

With everything obscured by streaking snow, with little humps in the terrain snow covered one moment and showing bare rock the next, with snowdrifts covering dangerous crevasses, with only a few hours of daylight to penetrate the darkness of the blizzard—under such conditions it was unbelievable to me that anyone could know where he was going. Yet Sheeniktook plodded confidently ahead, as unperturbed as the straining dogs.

The *Neophyte* had been described, over the radio, as frozen in somewhere near where that sharp curved point sticks out into the channel". . . Sheeniktook and I reached the ice of Chesterfield Inlet just half a mile short of our goal.

Exhausted and chilled, we finally clambered on board the deserted ship and, bending against the blasts, fought our way

78

along the deck to where we could get inside through frozen doors and hatches. Here in the black interior, between the frosted steel plates surrounding us, the cold was incredible. A galley stove, revealed by match light, loomed invitingly.

"We'll have a fire, anyhow," I promised Sheeniktook, striking another match and applying it to the ready laid fuel. We waited eagerly for the flame to catch and the deadly chill to be dispelled.

The flame caught, all right. But instead of warmth, a turbid cloud of smoke streamed out and so filled the galley with fumes that we stumbled back on deck to breathe. Happening to look up at the sky, Sheeniktook now discovered that all the pipes, including the galley smoke pipe, had been neatly covered with canvas. Without this protection, of course, the whole interior of the ship would have been filled with snow. Ten minutes after uncovering the galley pipe, we had a good fire going, a meal in process of cooking and a heavenly warmth permeating the place.

Later, a search disclosed my precious medical supplies, in not too bad shape, exactly where the captain had stored them nearly six months before.

From medicine, my thoughts turned to the two patients who were supposed to be in a camp not far from our ship. Tomorrow, I told Sheeniktook, we'd try to find them. He shook his head.

"I find now, bring to ship," he declared, turning toward the galley door.

"You'll never find that camp in the black wilderness around here," I said. "We've had a long, tiring trip today, anyhow. But tomorrow—"

The stubborn streak in Sheeniktook was never more pronounced. It was true, as he said, that I could treat them here under more favorable conditions, but I saw little chance of his running across the camp that night.

"I bring to ship," he insisted.

I finally gave in, suspecting that he might have some friends at the camp whom he wished to see for purposes of his own. Before disappearing into the darkness outside, he promised to be back as soon as he possibly could.

With Sheeniktook gone, the silence of the ship became frightening. I felt wholly deserted. The dismal howl of the wind outside only emphasized the desolate nakedness of the abandoned cabins and holds. For an hour I sat huddled on a bench, wrapped in my parka, waiting for him to return. But the silence continued. Then I added suspicion to my other worries. Had he deserted me in this icy wilderness? It might well be. He had taken the dogs and sled. I had heard plenty of stories like that. To what extent could an Eskimo be trusted, anyhow?

Dr. Moody in blizzard gear, unloads komatik in preparation for night's rest.

Worn out at last, I determined to try, at least, to get some sleep before facing what the morrow might hold. It didn't do much good. Every few minutes I awoke only to confirm the fact that I was still alone. By then I knew perfectly well that I had been left behind. I even planned to climb up to the radio hut in the morning and send out an SOS—that is, if the transmitter were working.

As I lay dozing, waking, twisting and turning in a bunk, suddenly a new fear brought me sitting up straight. *Would Sheeniktook come back and try to do away with me in order to get my equipment for himself?*

There had been stories along that line too. Our train trip north to Churchill came vividly to mind, when Viola and I sat listening to fearful tales of the arctic. As some of them now seemed more like than not to happen to me, I roused enough to lock all doors, and to place my pistol close to the bunk. After that I must have fallen asleep . . .

It was late when I awoke with the firm resolve, first of all, to climb to the radio hut in the faint hope of being able to send out an SOS. Next instant, all my accumulated worries slid off me like an unholy garment.

Folded up in front of the door lay Sheeniktook snoring lightly. The two patients lay at his feet. Finding the door locked, and unwilling or unable to wake me out of my exhaustion, all three had spent the night in the frozen passageway. It had taken Sheeniktook four hours, he explained, to find the camp and two hours to get back to the ship.

I felt ashamed of my earlier suspicions and, for recompense, hurried to make him and his companions a hot breakfast.

After that came the business of examining my patients. Frostbite in the man's hand was in an advanced stage. Since gangrene already had set in, there was nothing left but to amputate the hand. The man offered no objection. He probably had suffered enough with it already.

I turned to Sheeniktook: "You'll have to help me," I told him.

He winced a little, said nothing.

But when I was ready, he shakily assisted me all through an ordeal made doubly gruesome by performing the operation on the messroom table under a kerosene light.

With the Eskimo man made as comfortable as possible, I gave the girl a thorough examination. There was little to be done in her case but get her to Chesterfield and hope for an opportunity to ship her out to a sanitarium in the south.

She was only one of the many serious tuberculosis cases to come under my jurisdiction in the Canadian East Arctic, but the thought of this poor girl never left my mind. She had been victimized by a disease unknown to the Eskimos until white men came; a disease which was taking its toll from among 10 percent of the entire native population.

I pushed back the hatch and poked my head out for a few breaths of cold, clean air. The storm seemed to have abated a little; and, on the advice of Sheeniktook, all four of us left immediately for the return trip. I was thankful to get away. My night on the deserted *Neophyte* had been far from enjoyable. Sheeniktook and I loaded patients and medical supplies on the komatik and, though its weight overtaxed the strength of the badly trained dogs, we took off for Chesterfield at a fairly good pace. The weather really cleared while we were on our way.

When, after an absence of three weeks, we finally got back to "civilization," as Chesterfield now looked to me, tickets were already being sold for the great annual ice lottery.

This was no wicked gambling enterprise sponsored by some arctic gangster. It was a harmless game of guessing the one moment to which everyone looked forward—the moment of the ice breakup. Each year this pool was formed in which all white members of the settlement deposited a few dollars. Then all guessed when the bay ice would break up. The one guessing closest to the actual moment at which the blessed event occurred took the pot.

"They say it hardly ever happens here until about the middle of July," Viola coached me, as we walked over to purchase tickets and record our guess.

Middle of July! That would be a while yet, I thought, not knowing that I would soon be thrown into an adventure in which the ice breakup would feature most unpleasantly.

◆14◆

"FOGBOUND"

Some time before the theoretical breakup date, a radio message was handed to me. It seemed a routine affair, a couple of Eskimos having disappeared from a camp near Fullerton Point, some ninety miles to the northeast. To search for them looked like a job for the Royal Canadian Mounted Police rather than for me. Then I read the rest of the unpleasant news:

The two Eskimos were carriers of a dangerous and contagious disease! Frightened by their own illness, they had left their camp and were fleeing aimlessly from pains they couldn't understand. It was of the greatest importance that these people be located immediately. They must not be allowed to roam around the countryside endangering the health of that entire section of the arctic.

The weather was still unpredictable, with temperatures staying around forty below zero. Snowstorms and blizzards came up as quickly as they disappeared. The only safe way for me to travel would be by dog team. But how could I chase wandering Eskimos all over a few hundred square miles of rock, snow and ice? The mounted police sometimes took weeks to find elusive Eskimos, who can really make themselves scarce when they wish. If I could only scan the terrain from on high! If only—!

My thoughts turned to a man I'd never met, but who in time was to arouse my greatest admiration. He was one of the first

who dared take up a plane in midwinter into the East Arctic and
face the danger of unrecorded winds, sudden thunderstorms and
potluck landings on ice and snow. His name was Gunnar
Ingebrigtson, his nickname, Fogbound.

He had been a ground crew man in World War II; later, a
self-taught pilot. With his tiny Piper Cub airplane, he had
stationed himself at Churchill and started flying people into and
out of the great north. That was only a few years before, at a
time when arctic flying was rare and the maintenance of year
round service considered impossible by the experts.

Once, when I came to know him better, he wrote in our guest
book a single sentence that expressed his personal and business
credo:

> "We never stagger, we never fall,
> We fly at any excuse at all."

Between the scribbled names of friends, many of whom made
arctic history, Fogbound's signature stands out as recalling the
most adventures. Some of those friends who wrote in our guest
book and left our house after a cheerful farewell got lost and
were never seen again. Others staggered back to our door with
frozen limbs and tales of raging blizzards and attacking wolves.
Still others were killed within hours after the ink of their
autographs had dried, and while Viola was still washing the
dishes from which they had just eaten their final meal. But
Fogbound, bounced back by the elements he defied, always
returned. He lives on and will continue to take a prominent
place in the hearts of all true northerners until wind, snow and
ice build up a wall toward heaven—and he'll probably clear that
one, too.

In time he was to become my trusted companion on many
expeditions and patrols; one of the few fliers with whom I felt
safe in northern skies. He was the only one who would persist
when others quit, the only pilot whose ingenuity was always one
step ahead of the conniving elements. (Other pilots of East
Arctic fame are Weber, Bell, Bourassa, Coombes, Atkinson.)

At the time those two sick Eskimos disappeared from their
camp, Fogbound had replaced his Cub with a bigger Norseman,
was in process of building up "Arctic Wings," the first commercial airline of the arctic, and was teaching his own pilots the

Moody and Ingebrigtson refueling their aircraft before a flight into the Kazan River area for patients.

tricks of his exceptional trade. His nickname reflected the free-enterprise manner in which he conducted his business affairs. Whenever he considered his services not actually needed and

you asked him to fly you somewhere on a day when he happened to be having a good time "with the girls" in Churchill, he
would invariably radio back:

"Can't make it today. Fogbound."

I'd been hearing legends about this fabulous character ever
since we stopped off at Churchill in July. I'd never met the man;
didn't know then how much was legend, how much truth. But
with the sudden imperative need of finding two sick Eskimos
who might be spreading contagion, I wired Fogbound at
Churchill. I explained the situation and asked if he thought it
possible to land at Chesterfield at this time of year; if so, would
he be willing to fly me north over the Fullerton Point area?

Had I known him better, no thought of the derivation of his
nickname would have entered my head. I would have known
that this sort of crisis he never turned down.

My call for assistance he acknowledged immediately. When
I added a plea from the Hudson's Bay Company manager to
bring along some supplies to replace needed items frozen in on
the *Neophyte,* his decision was quick.

"Be there tomorrow morning with all she'll hold."

When he came dropping out of the sky next day, he brought
mail and the most desperately needed of the supplies. It was
almost like a dream—seeing his fragile ski-equipped craft appear
over the horizon like a speck of soot—circle above our little
community—come to a bumpy landing on the rough ice of the
bay.

Long after he landed, a phrase kept running through my
head: "Merciful miracle of arctic flight." I have not yet had
cause to alter that first impression.

Before we took off on our search, I thought it only fair to
make sure he fully realized what he was getting into.

"I just want to repeat," I said, motioning him aside, "that it's
a deadly disease these Eskimos have. I can't guarantee that you
won't catch it."

"Is *that* all, Doc?"

He brushed it aside lightly and acted more concerned over
the problem of finding the wanderers. That too bothered me.

Finally all was ready and Fogbound pulled me up into the
clear sky and turned the plane northeast to try to locate two
needles in a haystack. Approaching Fullerton Point and bearing

inland, we flew as low as seemed humanly possible, circling over miles and miles of rocky wilderness. Hours of this revealed only one sign of life—an isolated bear.

"According to all reports," I called out, "those Eskimos headed inland from their camp. At most, they can't be more than three day trips from the point."

Gunnar Ingebrigtson walks forward alongside his powerful and reliable Norseman.

Fogbound nodded agreement and skimmed lower than ever over the terrain, both of us straining our eyes in an effort to see two black specks. Darkness falling when the afternoon was partly gone ended the search—at least for that day. He swung the plane around and headed out over the sea. Presently, he turned inland again, and with unbroken sea ice still beneath us, swung southwest toward home, keeping the dimly seen coast line on our right.

With the day's work done, I was thinking of Viola and our little girl waiting to welcome us in the snugness of our home when suddenly Fogbound gave a whistle and pointed ahead. I jerked up straight and looked. A storm was making up and bearing down on us faster than I had thought any storm could travel.

Without a second's hesitation, Fogbound nosed the plane down, then straightened out for a landing on the ice. I could see that we would come down precariously close to the edge of the open water. I braced myself for what might be either a cold plunge into the sea or a shattering crash on the rough ice.

We hit ice. But the impact of our forced landing was so great that we bounced off again, nearly 300 feet into the air. All we could do was hang on and wait. After a series of gradually diminishing acrobatic jumps the plane came to a stop, still right side up.

"Quick—*get out!*" Fogbound yelled.

We tumbled out onto the ice.

◆15◆

DANCING AIRPLANE

For a few moments I struggled to keep my footing and at the same time breathe. The wind was slicing at us across the ice at what must have been sixty miles an hour. It flung dense streaks of snow in our faces and seemed to laugh uproariously at the joke it was playing on a couple of puny white men and their flimsy flying contraption. At times we were blinded. Then again we could see ahead momentarily for a distance of perhaps ten feet.

Fogbound was gesturing to me wildly, and I became aware that he held a length of rope and an ice chisel. He had made a grab for them just as we piled out of the plane. With this equipment we tied the plane to the ice as firmly as possible under the conditions.

"Can't pitch a tent in this mess, Doc," yelled Fogbound in my, ear, as we stood surveying the anchored plane. "Tear the canvas out of your hand."

The thought of putting up a tent on the ice was foolish, I well knew. But the alternative of climbing back for shelter into that straining, vibrating little aircraft seemed suicidal.

A quick drop in temperature made our decision easier. We climbed back.

As we didn't dare to start the engine on account of the lowness of our fuel, the cabin soon grew unbearably cold. We learned not to touch the metal with our bare hands. If we did, the frost glued flesh and steel together. We warmed our noses constantly with our hands for fear they would freeze. Finally we covered ourselves with the few hides we had and tried to settle down for the night.

Despite the physical discomfort, we slept. But not for long. The strange behavior of the plane shook us awake. It had started to *dance* on *the ice!* The tone of the gale was pitched even higher than before. A slight increase in wind velocity now would undoubtedly make the plane temporarily airborne and pound it to pieces on the ice many feet from where we were.

Once more Fogbound and I performed our act of scrambling out onto the ice. The fact that this time he insisted on our roping ourselves to the fuselage posed a problem which I never since have solved to my satisfaction. Would it have been better to get blown up into the sky dangling from a runaway plane, or, unattached, take a chance of staying on the ice by ourselves? Luckily, the aircraft continued icebound long enough for Fogbound to drag out a businesslike steel cable and a couple of ice chisels.

Still tethered to the fuselage, yet keeping our feet with difficulty, he and I constructed the most reliable airplane anchorage he knew anything about. We cut two deep, parallel slots in the ice, then dug out a connecting tunnel at least two feet below the surface. Through this tunnel we pulled our cable and fastened it securely to the runners on the plane. This performance was repeated four times until the wing struts and skis were all anchored to ice bridges. Now if the wind increased, our craft might be ripped apart, but it could not be carried bodily off. That was some satisfaction. We hadn't figured on other tricks the wind might play.

We had just made it back into the cabin when a thunderous roar, followed by a series of ear splitting explosions, brought us outside once more, this time dazed by the concussions and half expecting the end of the world.

For us the annual "breakup,"—on which chances sold in Chesterfield—had come early. In short, the ice on which we had landed had broken loose from the rest. We were separated from the main floe by a foot wide gap. Fogbound stared at that gap as though hypnotized. But when he saw it slowly widen, he made up his mind in a hurry.

"Our runners are five feet long," he screamed at me. "Maybe I can taxi her across. You don't have to get in, Doc. But if the impact of my take off pushes the ice further out to sea I can't pick you up again.

"I'm with you. Get in!" I shouted back, barely making myself heard through the bellowing organ tones now being produced by our vibrating anchor cables. We quickly released them and hoisted ourselves inside.

Fogbound worked desperately to start the engine. It was ice cold. But somewhere deep in its innards a little of the previous heat must have remained. After about a minute, just as both aircraft and ice pan began to rock ominously, the engine roared and we started to taxi slowly forward. Ahead of us the gap had become wider—some two feet, perhaps, of black water—and as we neared it, Fogbound gave our engine a full throttle . . . I shut my eyes . . .

A bump—and we were across!

The plane taxied to a stop. Instead of a shout of triumph from my companion, I was aware that he was sitting motionless in his seat, watching the whirling snow as if spellbound. Suddenly, he came to. We went outside and for the third time that endless night and anchored our plane to the ice.

"Probably won't have enough runway left to take off in the morning," he observed, with a grimace.

On that discomforting thought, we crawled wearily back into the frigid cabin and settled down to uneasy sleep.

Morning brought two surprises. The first was that we still had about two miles of level ice before us—enough for several takeoffs, should several be required.

But the second surprise contained so large an element of unreality that for a few moments I thought it the prolongation of a dream. It was no dream. Our taxiing during the night had brought us practically into a little snow covered tent pitched only a hundred yards or so away. And in it huddled our two sick Eskimos!

After purposely trying to evade us (with excellent success), they now piled gratefully into our plane to be flown to a hospital and recuperation.

By the end of May and the first part of June it looked as if nature was about ready to release the stiff-fingered grip in which she had held man and beast so long. First, the skies became clearer. Then they faded from their deep winter blue to a light, transparent azure. Millions of ducks, geese, swans, falcons and other bird species began winging their way over Chesterfield on their northward migration.

The bay ice turned gray and pappy. One morning we could see a wide blue gap in the ice a mile from shore. It was like a signal to the rest of the frozen surface. And the other ice obeyed the signal quickly, cracking all over like an old painting, then starting to move slowly out to sea. Less and less of it returned with each incoming tide, leaving more ice pans behind in open water to melt or be carried away by other currents.

On land the snow disappeared even more rapidly. Soon the tundra around us was transformed into a spongy mass—soggy beyond description but showing color at last; color which we had waited for during nine long leaden months. Flowers appeared miraculously and dotted the plains with bright reds and yellows-whites-oranges-purples. Everywhere life returned. Groups of Eskimos took off on trips into the interior to visit friends and relatives. Eskimo boats fanned out across the waters. A graceful sight!

But two more months passed before the great day arrived when, with her whistle tied down, the *Neophyte* proudly appeared before our shores. The roaring welcome we gave her was conclusive proof that summer had come at last.

◆ 16 ◆

"MERCY FLIGHT"

Our short, lively air search for the two sick Eskimos near Fullerton Point proved to be a dress rehearsal for the full-fledged "mercy flights" that became so celebrated later on.

Events leading to the first of these started on a day in late January with receipt of a carefully worded telegram from the Department of Transport post on Nottingham Island. One of the five radio operators there was sick. After detailing the symptoms from a layman's point of view, they asked for advice.

Everything pointed to a light case of heart trouble and general listlessness, so I instructed the boys at Nottingham simply to put the patient to bed and await developments. I failed to realize that putting someone to bed in an isolated radio station manned by five men would throw the whole schedule out and become a heavy burden on the patient's fellow workers.

This was soon made clear, however, by a series of follow-up telegrams from the island, each showing more uneasiness than the previous. The series ended with a blunt request to "do something drastic."

A glance at the chart showed Nottingham Island to be a small island well out in Hudson Strait, where the broad strait waters connect with the northern expanse of Hudson Bay. As the crow flies, it was some 400 miles northeast of Chesterfield. I knew that that was plagued by particularly high winds; also that the strait didn't freeze over in winter, but was filled with drifting bergs and ice pans which prevented ship navigation. I heard, too, that the high humidity area thus created caused frequent dense fogs or misty, low hanging clouds. Nottingham Island was not a place one would fly to just for the ride!

"But we can't let four healthy people go to pieces because a fifth can't keep his schedule," I pointed out to Viola. "Nottingham is too important a post to have anything go wrong."

"What can you do? You can't go there yourself," she said.

Fortunately, Nottingham Island lay less than fifty miles off the coast from the settlement of Wolstenholme, where the northern tip of Quebec juts out into Hudson Strait. "I can have Ottawa send a plane from Wolstenholme," I answered, glibly, "to bring that man out and take in a replacement."

"Why, of course," she agreed, after studying the chart. "But will Ottawa consider it possible?"

On second thought, I wondered a little, myself. No one had ever tried to land a plane on Nottingham in winter, and it was a question if the bravery of arctic pilots would extend that far—especially in a stormy January season, with little daylight and extremely low temperatures.

"It *has* to be possible to do something drastic," I declared.

I'm sure now that my boldness came partly, at least, from the fact that personally I felt somewhat aloof from the case and fully expected Ottawa to do whatever was done. So I wired the situation to the Department of Transport. Their reply came with reassuring speed:

"If you feel that it must be done we will proceed. But how?"

That gave me a chance to show them that I was not one to go off half cocked, but had the solution all figured out. I suggested that they send a plane to Nottingham Island from Wolstenholme.

This time their reply was so long coming that I supposed the necessary orders were being put through. Instead, an answer finally arrived which gave me quite a jolt. It was January, they pointed out, and the weather none too good. They had found no commercial airline willing to make that trip. *Would I undertake it myself?*

With such a challenge facing me, it was clear that my recom
mendations suddenly had become my responsibility! I had no
choice but to wire back a curt:

"Send R.C.A.F. via Chesterfield."

That started things moving. They immediately outlined to me
a detailed plan of operation. A Norseman aircraft of the Royal
Canadian Air Force would fly up from Winnipeg to Chesterfield
and take me aboard. We then would proceed to Nottingham—not
direct but by way of Coral Harbour on Southampton Island, with
its adequate air strip. Meantime, a big, two-engined Dakota would
fly direct to Coral Harbour, carrying the replacement and also a
doctor. There they would wait while we took the replacement in
our little Norseman and flew on to Nottingham for the patient.
After bringing him back to the big Dakota, which would fly him
straight to a hospital, we would return to Chesterfield. Our
Norseman, said the message, would be leaving Winnipeg for
Chesterfield in a few days to pick me up.

Since it was evident now that only small planes like the
Norseman could possibly land at Nottingham, the plan they had
worked out seemed a sound one. I knew that Coral Harbour had
been a radio station during the war and that a skeleton crew was
still there. Moreover, the distance from Coral Harbour to
Nottingham was less than 200 miles. Our Norseman aircraft
should be able to fly there from Coral Harbour, pick up the
patient and bring him back to the big plane at Coral Harbour,
all in an easy day. My responsibility would cease, of course,
once he was aboard the larger plane, headed south for a hospital.

Only if I lumped together in my mind all the possible
dangers from ice, fog and storm did I have any real doubt of the
successful outcome. But when the Norseman from Winnipeg
finally dropped down to take me on board, and I signed the
official papers exonerating pilot and crew from any responsibility,
I felt for the first time that this gesture might really mean
something. Indeed, had some clairvoyant power allowed me at
that moment to preview certain copy-hungry reporters' newspaper stories of this initial "mercy flight" into this arctic zone, I
might not have given my family so casual a farewell wave on
taking off.

The actual trip, though scary in spots, seemed less so at the
time than subsequent accounts implied. While living through an

event, you see it stripped of flowery imagination. You accept things that come. You cannot visualize how others, reading about your antics in faraway places, can add significance to your adventures merely because they take place under unusual circumstances.

It is true that to fly thousands of miles to take a patient from his isolated sick bed to a city hospital is no everyday operation. But all I can remember of that first trip is that we were pretty scared at moments when arctic hazards seemed to be getting the better of us. I can't recall any feeling of heroism; even of great drama.

Our pilot, an excellent flier, had had little experience in northern regions and, once we were out over the open sea on a course to Southampton Island, I saw that he felt uncomfortable. In those parts of Hudson Bay that don't freeze over in winter, the water becomes thick and slow and takes on a peculiar acid quality. Besides, it is so bitterly cold that one suffers severe frostbite if one comes into contact with it. Evidently, the pilot was well aware of these phenomena and doubtless was meditating on them instead of on his flying when, halfway on the first leg of our trip, something happened that threatened the entire "mercy flight."

From where I was sitting, huddled on a rubber boat in the back of the plane, I could see a red light begin to flash on the instrument panel. Since the pilot paid no attention, neither did I. My experience in flying was too limited to give me much understanding of what went on in the plane's cockpit. To the mechanic, seated beside me, the red light was invisible.

All at once our engine went dead and the overloaded plane started down at a steep angle.

"Fred!" shouted the mechanic.

At the same instant he leaped up like a jack-in-the-box, threw himself into the cockpit, grabbed a lever and began frantically to pump it up and down. Nobody spoke. The pilot and I sat tense, watching the mechanic work his pump up and down—up and down—faster, *faster.* I can still smell that faint odor of gas and rubber and remember how the sharp staccato of the pump strokes stood out in the silence of the cabin—the whole against the whining overtones of wind along the fuselage as we continued to dive toward the cold, green surface waiting below.

At almost the last second, it seemed, the engine grunted and sputtered into life. The pilot snapped out of his panic and, with a great effort, pulled us out of our dive and sent us climbing to safer altitudes.

The whole episode had lasted for perhaps one quarter of a minute, but in that time we had dropped to within 100 feet of Hudson Bay. The little red light that had failed to alarm me was a warning signal that fuel was running low and that the pilot had to switch tanks. Delay of another few seconds would have been fatal.

For the rest of the trip we maintained a lethargic silence, ears tuned to any unusual engine noises. Only after Coral Harbour came into view and we caught sight of the huge but nearly deserted post did our spirits surge upward in unexpressed relief.

◆ 17 ◆

FOUR FEET FROM ETERNITY

Coral Harbour, with its big air strip, had been an air base of great importance during the war but was practically abandoned when hostilities ceased. From the air it looked to me like a hopeful sign of mass infiltration into an area where men were as scarce as above zero temperatures. Actually, it was a deserted city in which human beings had given way to stronger forces.

The radio station was one small building out of a mass of prefabricated barracks, hangars, warehouses and other structures. Only ten persons manned the place—and all ten stood about in the snow, cheering and waving, as we managed a fairly smooth landing.

It was evident at once that the Dakota hadn't yet showed up, although expected. She'd be in later in the day, they said. Meanwhile, such facilities as they had were ours and we might as well make ourselves comfortable.

We did—and discovered that those who lived at Coral Harbour to man the radio station were enjoying a wonderful existence. The Pole-hopping planes, which occasionally stopped off, formed a steady source of supply for such luxuries as frozen fruits and vegetables; even frozen steaks. After months of canned food fare, I could hardly believe it real when an elaborate restaurant meal was served us that first evening.

Other special benefits turned the abandoned town into one of the most desirable arctic posts imaginable. Having been deserted

in typical postwar haste, numerous valuable assets had been left
behind. For example, with plenty of space available each man
could select a new sleeping room every night, if so inclined. More
important, each room contained a small ice box and a radio.

The pharmacist's store seemed to have held a tremendous
supply of cough mixture of very special quality, for it had lent
itself to the manufacture of a tasty liqueur, some of which was
served us that night with great ceremony. We couldn't have felt
more honored had we been offered the rarest product of some
famous distillery.

After dinner I wandered through the ghost town, no tinge of
jealousy marring my inspection of the empty buildings until I
came to the hospital. Here, innumerable items that I could have
used to advantage in my own Chesterfield establishment were
standing around collecting dust. The apothecary was a physician's dream. Naturally, the officials had removed all narcotics,
and the liqueur served us at dinner accounted for the fact that
no bottles of *cough medicine* remained in the place. But the
valuable collection of drugs which still lined the shelves caused
me to make a solemn vow: I'd stock up on what I needed most
before we went back to Chesterfield.

That evening the big Dakota, bringing another doctor and the
new radio man for Nottingham, appeared overhead and came
down for a safe landing. Coral Harbour got into communication
with Nottingham and remained in touch through the night.

"How's the weather there?" I asked at frequent intervals.

"Favorable," came the invariable reply.

When morning brought the same report, we decided to get
away early and complete our mission as quickly as possible.
Although it would not be able to land at Nottingham, the Dakota
carried orders to accompany us there and circle around to give
any assistance possible, should we get into trouble. Neither my
pilot, mechanic nor I saw much point in risking the big plane,
and we said so.

"Orders, Doctor," said the Dakota's pilot, evidently relishing
the novelty of giving orders to a doctor instead of receiving
them. However, we managed to maintain straight faces when the
pilot sheepishly informed us later that the Dakota's engines had
frozen up during the night and it would be impossible to get the

big craft off the ground. I could well believe it. The mercury
stood at fifty below zero.

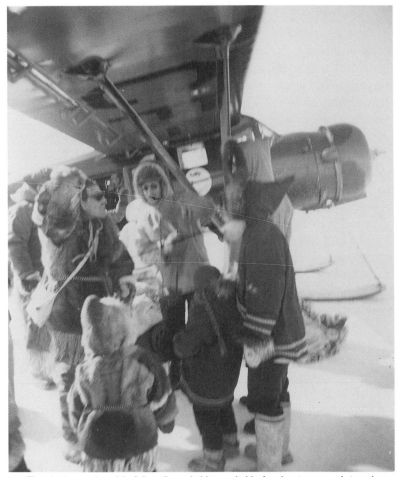

The doctor equipped in full caribou clothing, suitable for dog team or air travel
during difficult missions.

So we took off in our Norseman, adding to our crew of three
the man who would replace the sick radio operator. With the sky
so clear, we hoped for an easy trip. But by the time we reached
the vicinity of the small island in Hudson Strait, the weather
changed and Nottingham itself had disappeared in a dense fog.
It was necessary to drop to 100 feet in order to make out the

few scattered houses that had been erected in a sheltered valley between two huge cliffs.

As customary, our pilot began to fly over at a minimum altitude of some seventy-five feet in order to inspect the improvised runway which had been prepared for us, and get a general picture of the terrain. Such caution was commendable enough. The trouble was he became so engrossed in his scrutiny that, after veering off to return upwind for his landing, due to fog, he had not been able to note the true height of the towering cliffs on either side. I caught an instant flash of bare rock dead ahead, then found myself suspended diagonally in the cabin. The window, normally on my left, was now almost beneath me and through it came a terrifying closeup of boulders whizzing by.

I learned afterward that our wings cleared one of the cliffs by about *four feet,* and I distinctly remember feeling the plane vibrate violently when the pilot struggled to pull us out of the unexpected predicament which seemed bound to flatten us against the steep rocks. We held on, breathlessly, during the crisis, then shakily relaxed after the plane had safely cleared the top of the cliff.

"Fred," said the mechanic, solemnly, after we had rolled to a stop on the landing strip, "there are a few things you shouldn't do. One of them is holding me upside down when I've just had breakfast."

The pilot, pale and still shaky, didn't answer. I don't think anyone else was amused either.

We had barely landed when a man yelled and came running toward us from the radio hut, a slip of familiar yellow paper fluttering in his hand. It was a wire from Coral Harbour: "Southampton weather closing in return at once."

The pilot was starting back toward the plane when I reminded him that we had a patient to take along. I hurried into the building indicated and quickly examined the man.

Some heart trouble, yes, but not the main factor involved! After careful study one could see that the situation was a complex one and that isolation problems on the island probably played an important role in this man's condition. The question arose, was this the beginning of a form of arctic fever—a deadly depressive neurosis? Or was his weakened state due to a physical problem? Because of the arctic fever possibility and the man's organic condition he was immediately evacuated.

For a moment I stole a look at the replacement we had brought along with us. The young fellow stood in the snow taking in his surroundings, an uneasy fear in his eyes. This poor boy had just left the safety of a Montreal station and must have been appalled by the desolation of the isolated little island that he would be sharing with four companions for untold months. Would he become infected with arctic fever?

I had little time for speculation as our pilot was pacing the snow and calling loudly on me to hurry up. We took the sick man aboard immediately and gunned the engine. Our takeoff was as smooth as one could wish. But with a nervous pilot, two close calls behind us and an unstable patient, I didn't feel too happy over the prospect of landing at Coral Harbour in bad weather.

And it *was* bad. A fierce ground blow obscured the air strip completely. Luckily, the field was so large that we were able to make a blind landing which hardly jostled us. The trouble came later when we discovered that a series of storms would prevent either plane from taking off for several days. Considering the comparative luxury that ruled at the post, and the opportunity I had for leisurely selection of much needed medicines and laboratory equipment, I couldn't regret the weather too much, at that.

The army doctor confirmed my diagnosis and took the patient under his care. I had the satisfaction of watching the man start to improve even before the Dakota, after prolonged preheating, was able at last to take to the air.

We followed in our little Norseman, laying a straight course for Chesterfield. And while both pilot and mechanic kept an eye on the "low fuel" warning light, I sat on the rubber boat in the rear of the plane and reflected quietly upon the need for future "mercy flights."

◆18◆

ARCTIC FEVER

Long before sighting Chesterfield I had reached two conclusions. First, winter flying in the arctic, though precarious, was feasible. Second, arctic fever patients exemplified other cases that would make arctic winter flights a necessary part of medical service in order to avoid serious situations arising at isolated posts.

I knew that arctic fever was of two kinds. One type came from depression in people who couldn't bear the hardships of arctic life. It slowly drained their resistance and strength. They weren't able to adjust mentally to isolation and darkness, nor to the fact that in the arctic you are more alone with yourself than anywhere else. These people, unsuited to the life there, cracked up unless their temperament was discovered and they were shipped out in time. In the so-called barrens, it is referred to as getting "rocked," just as it is called "bushed" in the timber area.

That was where arctic flying could become invaluable.

Besides themselves, the condition of these unfortunates caused complications in others, endangering the health and safety of all with whom they came into contact. All trouble would be avoided, of course, if examining physicians could detect "anti-arctic" tendencies in a new man before he ever left for his isolated post.

Our experience at Nottingham impressed me so deeply that I resolved to make strong recommendations to Ottawa for more rigid medical standards. Later I did so, and have been delighted to note that more caution is now exercised in choosing new men for northern service.

Seated on my rubber boat in the returning plane, I recalled the symptoms of a second form of arctic fever. This too came as an obsession—but an obsession with an opposite urge. People were stricken with it by becoming hypnotized by the north. Even if they spent their holidays in more civilized parts, they showed signs of claustrophobia, and could hardly wait to get north again and bury themselves in the barren wilderness which had become their trusted refuge.

These were the men and women who, finding little satisfaction in the life they left behind, became overly impressed with the simple but honest existence of the northern natives. Gradually they identified themselves with the Eskimos until they actually took on the Eskimo way of life. Once this obsession had progressed beyond a "point of no return," they never willingly would go back to a civilization that seemed callous by comparison.

These were the people who disappeared from their posts and settlements just before they were to be relieved. Some succeeded in spending the rest of their lives with the Eskimos. Others just took off without plan or destination and eventually lost themselves in the snow and ice which exert such hypnotic powers over certain temperaments.

Such persons never should be allowed to travel into the north. Having little control of themselves, they must be protected from their own obsession. That type of case was extremely difficult to treat because, contrary to sufferers of the depressive kind of arctic fever, the obsession victim was drawn to the arctic again and again. Whereas depression cases usually improved quickly on leaving the arctic behind, the suffering of the obsession patients increased after they were taken out. Left to themselves, they would always turn up in the arctic again after having been forcibly removed. They were the people who "went native." One had to sympathize with them, too. For to them the rationalization behind their "back to nature" urge contained truths which could be crystallized only in the purifying atmosphere of the far north.

Just before landing at Chesterfield, my thoughts turned to finance. Not my own monetary condition. I was thinking of what this "mercy flight" must be costing the government. The result of a rapid mental calculation made me sit up very straight on my rubber boat and go over the figures again—this time with pencil and notebook. My first rough estimate had been about right, and the staggering sum reached remained a sobering influence with me in deciding on the need for future "mercy flights." The one I was just completing involved:

Two aircraft

Two aircraft crews

Two doctors

A great variety of emergency equipment

It took practically three weeks from conception to conclusion. But when I remembered that commercial airlines operating in the arctic charged over $100 an hour for single-engined aircraft, it didn't seem so fanciful that at least $40,000.00 must have been consumed in flying one arctic patient away from his doom.

As soon as it was proved that "mercy flights" could be made successfully in winter, other flying missions followed quickly. Many drew worldwide attention. The day-by-day newspaper reports of the case of Canon John Turner, for example, surpassed the most spellbinding mystery serials.

This Anglican missionary suffered a severe head wound at his almost inaccessible post near Moffet Inlet in the north part of Baffin Island. The terrain was rugged and landing an aircraft an impossibility at the time due to freeze up. Forming ice on the bays also prevented this area being used to land on.

Twice a multi-engined aircraft flew over the Canon, but due to bad weather, the pararescue group could not jump. Finally, after considerable delay, a team comprising a doctor and three technicians parachuted to the stricken man's aid. Because of high winds the team narrowly missed being dashed to pieces on the rocks, and the transmitter unfortunately was severely damaged. Later, more equipment was successfully parachuted. The team immediately set to work and did everything possible to aid the Canon.

Weeks passed before the ice was solid enough to land an aircraft at all. Unfortunately, by then the unavoidable delay had been too long and the missionary died soon after being hospitalized in Winnipeg, Manitoba.

Initially the news about Canon Turner had been wired to Chesterfield Inlet and Gunnar Ingebrigtson immediately offered to fly me to the man despite the unusual dangers involved. However, icing conditions were said to have been dangerous at the time and permission was refused.

John Turner, a practical and sincere arctic missionary, was known and beloved by thousands of Eskimos and whites. His stamina and the pararescue team battle to save his life will forever remain as one of the truly great epics of the East Arctic.

✦19✦

ODYSSEY OF DEATH

After nearly two years at our Chesterfield post we were promised Christmas vacation at home, and the news started us planning weeks in advance of the holidays. Fortunately, we knew nothing then of the odyssey taking place to the south and west of us. Indeed, it was months later when bits of information seeped in which, pieced together and motivated by what we had learned of Eskimo psychology, enabled us to trace that odyssey, clear as a road map, from start to tragic conclusion. Briefly, what happened was this.

Tutu, an Eskimo of "ominous" Eskimo Point, had completed his summer tasks. The caribou hunt had been successful and he had cached many a pile of good meat. When winter came he would take his komatik, assemble the contents of his caches and quickly carry the meat home to Eskimo Point. Furs had been good this year too. There would be new parkas and boots and sleeping bags. The spirits of his ancestors were good to Tutu.

He had sent his son back to camp with a promising load, but Tutu himself preferred to wait for the snow because he had decided to visit Churchill. There he would trade some ivory carvings at the Hudson's Bay Company store, or perhaps at the military camp where he might get better prices. He planned to bring his wife a few spools of thread; possibly one of those funny books with pictures that the Kabloona called catalogues.

Tutu's trip to Churchill was a great success. He stayed there quite a few days, trading his carvings with the soldiers. Then he hung around to help load one of the last boats bound north. September came before he decided to go home to Eskimo Point, where preparations must be made for the long winter ahead.

Tutu traveled slowly. Time was a factor, but not one of much importance. And, after all, there were many families he wished to visit on the way. Whenever he met a roving band of friends he stayed a while, telling them of his hunt, listening to their tales. They made him comfortable in their tents where, of course, he enjoyed all the privileges of Eskimo hospitality. Nunnulla was on the coast 100 miles north of Churchill. He arrived there just as his close friend, Akamalik, returned from his hunt. That was very good indeed. Akamalik had a nice daughter.

At another camp farther along, Tutu was delayed by an early fall storm, so that well over a month had elapsed before he reached his own camp at Eskimo Point. Festivities followed even then—including drinking tea and shaking hands with the crew of the *Neophyte* which was about to pull out for Chester-field on her last trip of the year. (She has since sunk in the Severn River.)

Tutu found new guests in his camp too. Because the priest was away, all held a fine drum dance to speed these guests on the journey back to their home at Padlei, some hundred miles farther inland. Touching at camp after camp, these Padlei Eskimos had hardly reached their home when they met a group of Eskimos from the great Kazan River district to the west. Once more great festivities took place. Huge quantities of fresh caribou meat were consumed. Numerous whip handling contests were held between hosts and guests. The Kazan River people eventually moved west to their own region and settled down for the winter.

From an epidemiologist view, this Inuit is the most likely first direct contact. However, there could have been other contacts and modes of transmission.

So, although Tutu himself had come home, others with whom he had intimate contact were still on the move, completing a circle of conquest that was to have memorable results. From camp to camp—tent to tent—Eskimo to Eskimo—a nasty little virus was wending its way into the arctic. He held the doubtful honor of being a pioneer, this little virus. None of his brothers had been there before. But with the help of Tutu who carried him around, the deadly penetration became a fact.

Since Tutu had been the protector of this pioneer virus, Tutu himself was spared. But the spread of disease caused by Tutu's leisurely trip was to create the fiercest epidemic the north had yet known.

Even before Tutu began this disastrous odysscy of death, Viola and I were turning our thoughts ahead to the pleasant subject of a Christmas trip home. Nothing seemed likely to prevent it. Nothing serious, that is. As cold weather approached, reports had come in from both Nunnulla and Eskimo Point of a few isolated cases of patients showing a type of residual paralysis. This was unusual but not particularly alarming. I was unable to see any of these cases myself because of a freeze up which prevented all travel. But at my request the department flew one of the Nunnulla victims to Winnipeg for an accurate diagnosis. The verdict came back: Guillain-Barré syndrome.

I never had heard of Guillain-Barré disease and looked it up at once. But books left me little wiser. A rare disease! Cause unknown! According to the books it had no connection with residual paralysis, but that didn't disturb me too much. I thought the specialists pretty certain to be correct. Besides, the symptoms had been reported to me only by radio—no guarantee of absolute accuracy.

Therefore, when other similar cases arose I based my radio given directions on what I had learned from the outside. Some recovered, others died. The weather was terrible and, though I claimed the bodies for autopsy, I could not organize a patrol to get them out. Frozen and awaiting my scalpel, the bodies remained in the various camps.

When several more cases of this mysterious disease were reported, in November, I decided to take Sheeniktook and try to reach Tavani, 150 miles down the coast from Chesterfield. I felt I must see some of those patients myself, if humanly possible. The season was marked by a sudden and most unusual change in weather. Up shot the temperature and everything started to melt.

Twice we had to give up the trip because the dogs were unable to drag the komatik through the soft snow. A third attempt succeeded. Even then ten days of rough going lay ahead. When we finally reached Tavani it turned out that they themselves had no cases of paralysis. I'd have to travel another 100 miles to find one to examine. The matter was put up to Sheeniktook. The Eskimo shook his head firmly.

"Snow too bad, and ice sticky and dangerous," he said.

I knew he was right and decided against trying to go on. However, while resting at Tavani I was able to sew up a few cuts, pull some teeth, treat eye infections and inject the children. This uninspired routine was interrupted by a provocative telegram from my nurses at Chesterfield:

"Several Eskimos from nearby camp taken ill showing sign of paralysis."

Since it would take too long to go back by dog team, I wired Fogbound, asking his help. He was in the south at the time getting his plane overhauled, but came as soon as he could. Only a few days elapsed before I was back at my post.

It seemed the height of irony to find, on arrival, that the sickness reported had struck a camp of Eskimos only fifteen miles inland from the exact route Sheeniktook and I had followed on our way to Tavani. I could easily have visited the place then and saved the trouble of a fruitless, ten-day trip to Tavani. There was some consolation in the thought that now at least I would set eyes on somebody who actually had this insidious Guillain-Barré disease.

As often happened in the north, I was wrong. Investigation showed that all the Eskimos in this nearby camp had been stricken a few hours after devouring a freshly caught seal. Some died and nearly all showed symptoms of respiratory paralysis. But further questioning also brought out the fact that the seal had been infected. From other Eskimos I learned that infected seals had caused similar deaths in the past. These, then, were plain cases of arctic food poisoning—unusual, but localized and not at all disturbing from an epidemic angle.

Then, just when I seemed fated never to see a real case of residual paralysis, Sergeant Paddy Hamilton brought in the body of an Eskimo who had died from the presumed Guillain-Barré infection. Although the whole affair was unpleasant, I got ready to perform an autopsy with considerable enthusiasm. Now we would see!

An arctic autopsy is different from that which one is accustomed to in a city hospital. Both call for the body to be frozen. But arctic temperatures provide a natural deep freeze far beyond that needed for preservation. It took several days before the body was even partly thawed, then I had to use blunt instruments to remove the specimens—a gruesome task in which the sergeant assisted. Every few minutes we would warm our hands, numbed by excessive cold. I managed to assemble the specimens and, although lacking the correct preservatives, carefully packed and refroze them for laboratory inspections in Winnipeg. Greatly relieved by having at last laid hands on material that could show us the true character of the disease—and because everything happened to be quiet in Chesterfield—I left the settlement with a clear conscience for our long Christmas journey home.

Southward bound, we stopped off at Winnipeg so that I could leave the specimens there for analysis. The technicians gave one look and announced that the material had been so badly preserved, due to lack of proper chemicals, that it was useless to the laboratory on which I had been depending for a clue.

Still hoping for an answer to the tantalizing mystery, I sat in on a few medical conferences dealing with the one patient who had been flown out from Nunnulla a while before and since returned to his camp. It seemed to be agreed that this was Guillain-Barré disease. Beyond that they could give me no help whatsoever in combating the strange illness still making its way among my charges.

"I'm sure it's a virus infection of *some* sort," I insisted.

"Better see Rhodes," they advised.

Dr. Rhodes, an internationally famous expert in this particular field, was sympathetic but not encouraging. He gave me much practical advice on how to treat virus cases with my limited equipment in Chesterfield, and how the clinical picture could be interpreted. Just as I left, he handed me several of his own technical papers on poliomyelitis.

"This, of course, is irrelevant," he admitted lightly, "but you might be interested in what we're doing."

I thanked him for his courtesy and promised to look the reprints over during the rest of the trip to our London, Ontario, home. Later, I'd add them to my library for reference.

Once we were home, everything about Chesterfield seemed infinitely remote as we greeted old friends and started to enjoy our brief contact with civilization. One afternoon, seated comfortably in front of the living room fire, I was handed a telegram.

Now, the ominous nature of a telegram has nothing to do with the length of the message. It can be disturbingly brief—like this one from Chesterfield:

"Several cases strange illness and death please return."

We had no choice.

◆ 20 ◆

RUNNING AN EPIDEMIC

We flew the last part of the trip with Fogbound, who picked us up at Churchill. His plane was overloaded with bulky supplies. There was no room for us to sit comfortably erect. But, sprawling atop the cargo, I tried to concentrate on the unidentified sickness which had taken hold in my district a second time—and of which, to date, I had seen no living example.

I was aware that Eskimos usually accepted illness for what it was. But when confronted by something they don't understand, they soon became frightened, sometimes even hostile—an experience the manager of the Hudson's Bay Company's most northern district had later.

On landing at Chesterfield, we found the atmosphere tense and unnatural. All the Eskimos seemed greatly upset by the sickness which had attacked many of their friends to the south. Each tale of bewilderment brought in by envoys from Eskimo Point filled them with new anxiety and fear.

Our nurses at the hospital were worried too. No cases had sprung up in the immediate vicinity but reports from the south were most alarming. Their own patients were growing more fidgety by the hour. After a quick survey of the situation, I asked Fogbound to stay overnight and fly me down to Tavani the next day . . . It was there that I saw my first paralysis patient.

Unconsciously I had been building myself up for this moment, hoping, expecting it to mark a sensational discovery. It would enable me to put my finger at last on the real origin of the infection and to determine the correct diagnosis.

None of these daydreams came true. Examination of some of the worst cases left me as ignorant of the exact nature of the trouble as I was before. It was some form of paralysis, no doubt, but the symptoms were strange. Maybe it was this Guillain-Barré thing, after all. Then again it might be meningitis or even—well frankly, it could be anything. But why so virulent? So *persistent?* Only one thing was definite. Whatever this disease, it was dangerous and demoralizing and had to be arrested at all costs.

Fogbound and I were preparing to swing inland and continue our flight to Padlei where more cases had been reported. However a wire from Chesterfield put all end to that notion. A man in Chesterfield had died during the night and more cases were coming in rapidly!

The hospital nurses did not ask me outright to return, but thought I should know what was taking place there. Lacking a direct appeal from them to go back, I was debating whether to do so or, now that I was this far, go on into the interior for further investigation. My uncertainty was brief. Only an hour or so later a second telegram from Chesterfield announced the death of more Eskimos. The picture painted was of a hospital packed to capacity and more patients trying to crowd in. It ended with the news that my daughter appeared to be stricken also.

An hour later, Fogbound and I took off for Chesterfield.

I shall never forget that "homecoming." Nor the curious reluctance that filled me as I walked dazedly from the landing strip to the settlement after a trip that had seemed endless.

The post presented a scene of gloomy chaos—bleak gray houses against the gray-white snow with a vast expanse of gray sky above. It occurred to me—as it had that first day long ago—that the houses had been put down without plan; that it showed a mighty poor attempt on the part of civilization to push into the realm of elemental nature.

The place seemed actually repulsive. No stone lined paths now were visible but a confused crisscross of footsteps, dog tracks and deep parallel lines drafted into the snow by patient bearing komatiks. My community was in dire distress and here was I standing, irresolute a hundred yards away overlooking the desolate scene and oddly loath to identify myself with it.

Some Eskimos came out to meet me, but stood back silently when I went near. One man fell down in the snow and could not move farther. Near the hospital two figures struggled forward carrying between them a seemingly lifeless girl. I bit my lip and walked on toward the house where my own girl lay sick.

Viola had spent a sleepless night with Gloria-May. The child's temperature had reached a peak of 105 degrees and strange muscle spasms had shot through her legs. For a while she had lost all control of them. However, the attack had passed. When I came in I found my wife asleep in a chair and our little girl sitting on the floor playing contentedly with a piece of walrus tusk. Whatever had been the trouble, her danger was over. I tried to make up my mind. Was it meningitis? Guillain-Barré disease? An acute neuritis? Telling Viola to send for me if necessary I rushed over to the hospital where dozens of moaning Eskimos awaited me.

There, a state of pandemonium ruled. All the beds were filled. Many patients were lying on the floor under caribou skins. Others hovered outside or had stretched themselves out on the entrance steps. The nurses were running around with thermometers, kidney basins, tongue depressors and hypodermics. Gradually the entire picture became clear. It seemed that Angote, an old and respected Eskimo, had died the previous night after being sick only six hours. Right afterward, others had fallen ill. Some of them appeared already to have recovered—or at least were recuperating—from the high fever. But many others had become paralyzed, and more deaths had occurred.

I examined two of the victims, then three, then six. After taking spinal fluids by puncture, I isolated myself in the laboratory and feverishly prepared tests. But although I spun the fluids and made stains, nothing definite developed. The fluids were clear; no bacteria. That ruled out meningitis. A virus, then? Maybe encephalitis? But why? How? Finally I hurried over to the radio station and wired Ottawa: "Some sort of virus disease epidemic of enormous proportions. Still testing for diagnosis."

By evening my laboratory had become a mess of tubes, smears, bottles of fluid, dishes of specimens. About ninety people were sick. Still no decisive conclusion. A virus—no doubt of that. But the symptoms didn't fit the clinical descriptions of any of the known virus infections.

By morning the number of patients had risen to 125—with two young Eskimo children dead. The illness had blazed completely out of control. Chesterfield was in a state of helpless panic. As I was rushing over to the hospital after an hour or two of restless sleep a voice shouting my name stopped me. It was Sergeant Hamilton.

"What's the matter, Paddy?" I asked, as he came up, his face wrinkled with worry.

"My constable has a sore leg. Don't know what it is, Joe, but maybe you could take a look at it later on when you have a minute. I really need the man."

I came near to laughing. "When you have a minute!" he'd said. For God's sake, don't bother me now with your constable, I thought to myself.

Aloud I said, "Sure, Paddy, I'll be over."

While examining rows and rows of patients, checking symptoms, trying to patch the symptoms together into something intelligible, I couldn't help thinking of that constable and his sore leg.

"A boil, probably," I told myself, "or maybe a sprained ankle."

No good. I couldn't get the constable out of my mind. Finally, to the amazement of the nurses, I abruptly deserted my patients in order to go over and have a look at the man.

I had just made ready to give him a routine sedative injection when suddenly I thrust the hypo into a nurse's hand and, after a quick second look, stumbled out the door and made for the radio hut.

I had seen the constable's limp foot—the muscle that had gone dead—!

There could be no mistake now, and immediately the full significance of my diagnosis hit me square in the face.

"Impossible," I kept telling myself. "Absolutely impossible. But *here it is.*"

I wired for help.

◆21◆

STRONG MEASURES

Polio in midwinter? Nonsense!

Those were not the exact words of the telegram that came back, but the implication was clear that I had gone crazy.

I hadn't. Later investigations and tests proved conclusively that my sudden inspirational diagnosis was correct. We had come upon the fiercest, most devastating polio epidemic yet to be recorded; an epidemic which to my knowledge has not been surpassed.

Polio had been known as a warm weather attacker. It hit Chesterfield during the longest recorded period of intense cold, when temperatures averaged thirty-eight degrees below zero for six consecutive weeks. Within ten days the characteristics of the outbreak changed medical history, and the impact of the disease left its mark on a whole generation of Canadian Eskimos.

For years polio had been considered a disease with a characteristic fifteen-day incubation period and a rather slow progress after onset. But in Chesterfield, people died within six hours of being attacked. Nor had polio commonly struck in the abdominal area. With us the percentage of abdominal paralysis covered nearly one-half of all cases. Most of these symptoms, in strict contravention to the accepted clinical picture of the infection, could only be attributed to the exceptional virulence of the attack.

117

Had an epidemic of this strength hit New York City under similar circumstances more than 4,000,000 people would have been laid up, 400,000 men, women and children would have been dead within ten days and 1,120,000 victims would have been left partly or wholly paralyzed for life. So deadly was the physical and economic effect of our epidemic in the arctic that any possible increase in the Eskimo population affected was set back more than thirty years.

No sooner had I noticed the constable's typical polio dropfoot and realized its meaning than a whirlwind of emotions engulfed me. My first clear thought was of the need to stop further spread of the disease. Within minutes I issued orders for complete isolation of all families in and around Chesterfield. No one was to leave his home, no contact could be made in any manner and extra precautions were ordered to enforce my ruling.

Food? A few Eskimos were charged with distributing food. They were instructed to set it in front of houses or igloos, and no inhabitant was allowed to carry it inside until the man who left it had gone away.

For days no one moved from his house. With the death toll mounting steadily in the hospital, the silent settlement took on an atmosphere of doom. I myself became a lonely figure plodding wearily from hospital to home; from igloo to igloo; from radio hut to the Hudson's Bay Company store—occasionally stopping to kick off attacks from famished dogs. At no time, I think, could more than five people be counted crossing the open space between the various buildings. But never were the frost-grayed windows free from anxious faces peering out at the ghostly community.

One thing I learned proved particularly valuable. At first, nearly everyone imagined he had muscle weakness, and I wasted a lot of time examining and reassuring frightened settlers and Eskimos. Later, I was able to spot from afar the symptoms of understandable but disturbing hypochondria. I dodged many a man who, even while he ran to catch me, kept shouting that his legs were paralyzed.

There was little doubt, though, that many of them had suffered actual minor attacks. Nearly everyone in the region was subject to contamination. Although the whites seemed to have

far more resistance than the Eskimos, several whites were
seriously ill and one or two were left with paralysis.

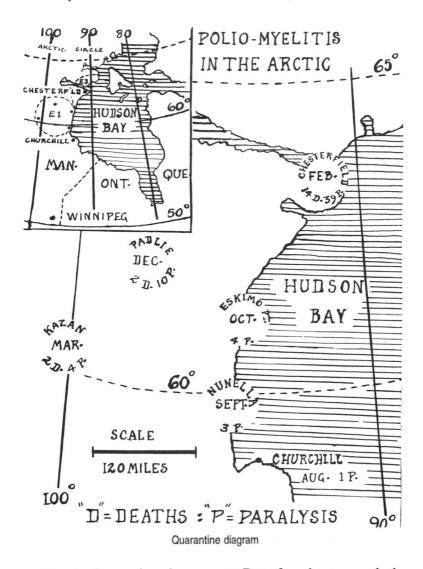

Quarantine diagram

The deaths continued to mount. But after about a week the
epidemic appeared to have passed its peak, after which we
entered the endless period of readjustment and analysis. The fact
that polio had struck during a period of almost unprecedented
cold weather remained the most puzzling aspect of the outbreak.

Aside from the situation at Chesterfield, who could tell how many Eskimos were roaming the country with the disease under their skins? How many carriers were visiting other camps, sleeping on the same snow platform as the host and his wife and family, eating from the same chunk of meat that passed from man to man? Where had the Eskimos gone who left the settlement yesterday or the day before? Or two weeks ago? How many virus were making their deadly way through the region unobstructed?

I looked at the map and realized that the disease had come to us from the south. Quite likely, then, dozens of earlier "mystery cases" that had eluded me like will-o'-the-wisps actually had been polio. How could I prevent the sweeping epidemic from enveloping the northern areas as well? If it ever spread to the north and west of Baker Lake—well, nothing could check the cycle of conquest. I went to see Sergeant Hamilton.

"Paddy," I began, "I'm going to quarantine the area."

"What area?"

"All over the place. Everywhere I think the disease may have struck. Here, hand me that map—"

I pulled out my pencil and, without hesitation, outlined the region within which all movement would have to be restricted; a region which nobody could enter, no one leave; where no two people could even shake hands. It included the south shore of Wager Bay and went as far west as Baker Lake; from there down through the Kazan River section and around the Ennadai settlements. Turning east, my projected quarantine ended on the shore of Hudson Bay, just south of Eskimo Point. The area to be shut off was huge. But so was my problem. The sergeant, who had been doing some rough estimating, whistled and said, "That's 40,000-near 50,000-square miles. You can't do *that!*"

"Then," I answered, "I can't be responsible for any of the 2,000 Eskimos in the far north. They're in my district, you know, Paddy."

"Will it work?"

"It should, if everybody cooperates. This thing has scared the hell out of the Eskimos and if you tell 'em to stay put I've a hunch they will."

A short silence fell. The sergeant walked over to a window, wheeled and faced me, his hands behind him. Suddenly he smiled, his eyes lighting up with an enthusiasm rarely exhibited by the even tempered sergeant.

"I'll be damned, Doc," he burst out, "if you can pull this off it'll be the biggest thing you've ever done—or ever will! . . . Where do we start?"

With Paddy firmly on my side, our strategy was quickly established. We wired and radioed orders to every police post and every Hudson's Bay Company store in the area; to every mission, to every trapper who could be reached. We radioed airplanes; later, ships. We printed fliers and announcements in Eskimo. Through radio and telegrams we lectured, explained, preached, begged, yelled, threatened—and inside of two days the largest regional quarantine in medical history had become a fact.

I had made a daring move. Just how daring I didn't begin to realize until I sat back from the microphone and wiped the sweat from my face after these first messages had been beamed out. I had virtually put myself and some 2,000 other persons on an island, cut off from civilization—from any contact with the outside world. From that moment, anyone venturing into my restricted area did so at his own risk, and could not leave without my permission.

I had no stomach for this necessary "dictator" role, particularly after the alarming scope of its effects occurred to me, one at a time. Supplies might run out, since Eskimos would not be allowed to hunt. Relief would probably have to be organized. Mass hysteria might well result. A dozen other disasters piled up in my mind. I couldn't sleep. I couldn't eat.

The complications that followed those first orders often made me wonder, at the time, whether I had done the right thing. For example, no ship was allowed to touch shore in the quarantined area and this became a vital problem with the approach of spring. Vessels bringing badly needed supplies, forbidden to land after visiting the more northern ports, could *approach* our coast, but that was all. The crews then loaded their cargoes on barges and lighters and deposited them on the beach. Only after the lighters had returned to the ship were our Eskimos permitted to pick up the goods and carry them to the settlement.

Airplanes had to land unassisted and dump their loads far away from the post. The export of furs and all other arctic products was stopped until it could be established that they carried no virus. In short, the quarantine violently disrupted the already shaky economy of the Eskimo. The languid routine of the arctic was no more.

But what might have turned into the greatest tragedy of my career became a really spectacular success—not to say personal triumph. Now that the facts are known, the unprecedented virulence of the epidemic recognized and documented, there are few who would not agree that my spontaneous move, conscientiously assisted by Sergeant Hamilton and the whole arctic family, saved hundreds from paralysis or death.

The disease did not move beyond the boundaries of the restricted area!

How well in general the quarantine worked was demonstrated much later when Fogbound and I, out on a patrol in the interior, were forced down by an oil leak. As we landed, an Eskimo saw us but refused to come near. I beckoned him to help us but it took a lot of talking and gesturing by both of us before he dared move in our direction. That happened more than a month after all restrictions had been lifted. Nearly *nine months* after the quarantine was established!

Yet within the closed area contamination was inevitable from the very start. How any of us survived just doesn't figure out on paper. In Chesterfield, which had become the center of the epidemic, the number of patients rose to 150—I worked feverishly, taking specimens, testing spinal fluids, giving drugs and consoling the dying.

One night, fighting off sleep and fatigue while working late in the laboratory, I started a test on a spinal fluid. It was a double check. I had already established that this fluid contained a count of more than 250 cell elements. I filled a glass tube and placed it in my centrifuge and pulled the switch. The machine started spinning around.

Suddenly the tube hit an obstruction and shattered, spraying a circle of death on the walls, on my face, on my clothes. It took a few moments before I fully grasped what had happened. That, I think, was when the epidemic came nearest to getting me down.

With the fluid dripping from my face, the centrifuge still whirling away madly, I just stood there like an idiot and stared dumbly at those splashes on the wall.

◆ 22 ◆

THE RECKONING

Had my mouth been open? No, it couldn't have been. I'm not one of those who always have their tongues out when concentrating. Still, it *might* have been—just then—just for a second—wetting my lips maybe or taking a deep breath in the close atmosphere of the tiny lab. Disjointed possibilities like that crowded through my mind.

Should I bother to go home or just walk over to the ward and flop down on a bed to await whatever might occur? But there were no beds empty. Then came the words, "If you can pull this off, it'll be the biggest thing you've ever done—or ever will!" Nice of Paddy to put it that way. Only now I might not be around to know if I'd pulled it off or not.

Then suddenly it struck me that all this time I had been staring at a map tacked on the wall; a map with a heavy red line encircling the quarantined area. Something was added to the map. The deadly fluid had stained a path across it and one big poisonous blot had all but obscured the name "Chesterfield," from which little drops kept dribbling down. The symbolism was ominous. But somehow the concentration required to separate symbolism from fact brought me back to reality.

I washed myself quickly and changed into a white coat that hung in the closet. It did something to my morale—that coat. Almost before I realized what I was doing—so automatic had

the motions become—I had another spinal fluid test on the way
. . . Days passed and nothing happened. I must already have
been immune.

Many were. Few, however, escaped the wave of hysteria that
swept the community. The Eskimos acted strangely. They grew
evasive. Some of them were far from cooperative. After the
hospital was filled, we had to treat many of them in their igloos.
They preferred it. Reason: the magnitude of the disaster that had
struck caused them to revert to their ancient habits. They wanted
to isolate themselves from the whites as much as possible.

I had asked Ottawa for help, and three days after my appeal
help came. Five doctors, all medical experts from the department, flew in on a special Dakota plane. They brought medical
supplies and all the necessary equipment, but were hardly
prepared for the vicious cold that met them as they stepped off
the plane.

With hardly a second's delay I escorted them to the hospital
to examine the patients. My colleagues observed the symptoms
closely as they walked through the ward, pausing at times to
consult among themselves. Then came the blow. One of them
turned to me and said:

"But Doctor, this isn't *polio!*"

Another, more tactful, added: "Whatever it is, it's serious and
we'd better give you whatever assistance you need."

I couldn't say a word. Horrible thoughts passed through my
mind. Was my reputation ruined? Here I'd been living with
polio for days, yet one of these specialists thought my diagnosis
incorrect! Had I really been wrong after all—made a fool of
myself? And *what about the quarantine?*

Finally I got a grip on myself.

"Will you follow me, gentlemen?" I asked, in a rather hollow
voice.

In the laboratory I confronted them with dozens of specimens, spinal fluid tests, clinical details, all records of paralytic
phenomena.

When we emerged from the little room, and after intensive
ward rounds, all of them were quick to agree that this was polio
and nothing else. They too had been misled by the unusual
characteristics of the epidemic.

Attwa and Sheeniktook at Chesterfield during the epidemic of 1949. The 'Dakota' has a special ski-wheel arrangement for difficult Arctic landings.

They set to work and greatly lightened the load I had been struggling under single handed. They examined every person in the community, prescribed therapeutical treatment, wrote long reports. They wholeheartedly backed up the quarantine and helped enforce it. Together we arranged that the more seriously paralyzed would be flown out for physiotherapy in Winnipeg —also that a trained physiotherapist would come to Chesterfield to treat others.

What impressed me most of all was the fine work of their epidemiologist. This specialist conducted an extensive survey to try to discover how the epidemic had started, and what had caused it to spread so alarmingly. But even he groped blindly for the answer until he started checking up on the history of Eskimo migrations and foraging trips during the preceding months. It was when he heard of the odyssey of Tutu that the whole picture snapped into focus.

One thing I hadn't known was this. Shortly before Tutu reached the army camp at Churchill, where he traded his ivory, an accurately diagnosed polio patient had been flown out of that camp. Why I wasn't informed of this will always be a mystery. The military authorities may have thought it only an isolated case or that it ought to be kept secret to prevent panic. Whatever their reason, not to report a polio case that occurred on the borderline of an area heretofore virgin to the disease seemed inconsiderate, to say the least. Since no other cases developed at the military camp, it is certain that Tutu, the Eskimo, carried the virus away with him and distributed it impartially among his brethren.

Most of those so called Guillain-Barré patients of the earlier months undoubtedly had suffered from polio, the disease being carried from camp to camp.

Plotting the course of the epidemic brought out a dramatic pattern. Wherever Tutu had been, a case had appeared there fifteen days later. Then all the Eskimos with whom he had come in contact had spread the virus, each to his own community. It was like setting up a chain reaction. Those first harbingers from Eskimo Point had started the Chesterfield epidemic which, because of the unusual concentration of our people, had taken the most lives.

In mapping the whole thing out, it was tragic to see how one more disease of the white man had followed in the wake of so many others—diseases against which the Eskimos had never built up immunities. We like to boast to the world that we bring civilization to the undeveloped areas. Yet even in my own day I have learned that our civilization can be an unwelcome gift.

The epidemic had taken so long for a correct diagnosis that most newspapers kept right on referring to the "mystery disease" and publishing columns bulging with pure speculation. The result was that well meaning citizens and crackpots from many countries came up with the most prepostcrous solutions.

Loading the critically ill aboard the aircraft requires all available assistance, including the nursing Sisters from the hospital.

By some I was advised to take more care in the preparation of caribou meat. Others told me frankly that I'd better go back to school because this definitely was cholera. I was still more confused on reading one letter marked "Very Urgent" from a kindly old lady who was good enough to tell me the truth at last. She wrote:

"I have already informed higher officials who, of course, took no notice of me. Their experiments with all kinds of bombs and rockets make holes in the ceiling of the earth. Unknown insects, surrounded by gas, come down through the holes and make way toward the coldest spot on earth, the North. People breathe these little bubbles of gas into themselves, the heat of the body dissolves the gases and the insect germs are then inside them.

"There is nothing you can do about these things except prevent them. However, I will try and suggest some remedy. These insects are breathed into the body and the heat of the body dispels the gases which protect the insects (heat kills the insects) but they raise the heat on the human body to tremendous pressures. Keep the patients cool. The insect without the protection of gas will eventually die of its own accord. Do not let them get hot (death) or use extreme cold, but cool temperatures. The extreme cold causes temperatures to rise to a death point. I hope this will help you to find the solution."

The medical team from the department left after five days, but not before the promised physiotherapist arrived from Toronto. This competent, cheerful assistant was a young nurse, Miss Beattie.

In a general recapitulation, we found that, out of some 300 people, 50 percent had been ill, 5 percent had died and close to 14 percent left paralyzed for life. In Chesterfield itself more than fifteen persons had died and forty been left with residual paralysis. These Miss Beattie went to work on immediately with her therapy.

When matters in our general vicinity seemed pretty well under control, my thoughts were turned to the far interior. From a mountie who had patrolled the Kazan River district, some 200 miles to the west of us, I learned that in three camps he had found three cases of paralysis among the handful of Caribou Eskimos who lived in those parts.

"What's more," he added, half in apology, "I took the liberty, Doc, of telling the group that the Kabloona doctor would come and take these patients away to be cured in a hospital. You were figuring on a patrol out that way, weren't you?"

I nodded. "I hope to take in the Nueltin Lake area, too, but if those Kazan people are expecting me, I'll arrange for Fogbound to fly me out there as soon as possible."

◆ 23 ◆

"POKATELLI HIM SAY THREE!"

The Kazan River is one of the biggest in the Canadian East Arctic. Flowing from the northernmost border of the tree line to Baker Lake, the Kazan is approximately 500 miles long. But like all arctic streams, it forms more of a connection between hundreds of small lakes than would a river in its own right. Some scientists even declare that there is no such thing as an arctic river; that they all serve merely as channels, draining and connecting the innumerable lakes, ponds and even the small puddles, thousands of which dot that northern terrain.

In summer the Kazan is immensely wide in places where it doesn't follow a definite bed. In other spots it takes on a different character, roaring and pounding through narrow gorges, and in one place forming a waterfall fifty feet high.

The few Eskimos left in the Kazan River region belong to the Caribou group, part of the once vast band of inland Eskimos who depended for their existence entirely on the caribou. However, because of wasteful hunting methods which thinned the herds and indirectly caused starvation, and because of white influence, with it resulting sicknesses, the past twenty years these great and admirable people have survived today as a small but irrepressible group. Today, hardly more than forty Caribou Eskimos are left in the entire area, and among them not more than half a dozen women of child bearing age.

Little hope remains that the colorful group will survive. In addition to hunger and ordinary illnesses, our polio epidemic also took its toll. Theirs is a life of the harshest poverty and since they must follow the caribou herds to exist, they are far more nomadic than Eskimos on the coast. Not only do they have little contact with their coastal brethren, they speak a dialect that sounds considerably different from the usual Eskimo language.

The Caribou people are also more primitive. For example, while they live in caribou skin tents in summer, in winter it is rare for a Kazan Eskimo to finish properly an igloo he has begun. He may pile up blocks of snow in the usual igloo building pattern but, rather than bother to complete the dome, will merely throw some skins over the open top and let it go at that. Some under even poorer circumstances, if imaginable, will dig a trench in the snow, build up the sides with a few rocks, stretch skins across the top and be "at home."

Their nomadic life and small number, which make them hard to find in their vast barren wastes, result also in the fact that they seldom see a white man. Naturally, they have held on to their old beliefs and customs, one of which is reflected in the great trust they still put in their witch doctors.

When I ventured into the Kazan River territory to find and take out three polio paralytics, I was the first "non-witch" doctor in many years to attempt to treat these people. As usual, Fogbound was at the controls of his Norseman plane when we took off for Padlei, the small post halfway between Chesterfield and Ennadai Lake. There we planned to pick up a guide and interpreter.

I knew quite a bit of Eskimo by now but realized that, because of their strange dialect, I'd need an interpreter to deal with the Kazan River folk. As for locating the three small scattered camps where the mountie had reported finding the paralysis cases, an Eskimo who could guide as well as interpret seemed imperative. According to rumor, Padlei contained just such a paragon. Spotting a coastal camp from the air isn't too difficult because the coast has many landmarks. But to uncover a Kazan Eskimo community by one's self in midwinter is practically impossible. You must come prepared to fly back and forth across a single small snow covered area for hours of intensive searching. Although the Eskimo whom we would pick up at Padlei would save us all this, Fogbound was realistic enough to have extra fuel on the plane—even though this meant carrying a belly tank, which is considered dangerous in this type of aircraft but an absolute necessity in those great stretches.

We reached Padlei in good time, picked up Apok, our primitive guide/interpreter, and took off in a westerly direction. Long before approaching the general vicinity of the Kazan, it became apparent to both Fogbound and me that our "expert," no doubt a good enough man for sled travel on the ground, was completely useless in the air. Unable to translate the speed of a plane into the speed of ground travel, Apok lost track of things as soon as we were on our way. The best he could do was gaze sadly through the small windows and, in answer to every question, give a monotonous, "Ahm—I," meaning "I don't know." Fogbound's restraint amazed me. It took four hours of flying before sheer luck revealed the first camp.

Between the heaving white ridges and windswept plains it showed up as a dirty spot. With a sharp, "hang on!" Fogbound slithered us to a landing on the only half-level place in sight.

"Where's everybody, d'y suppose?" I observed, as we made our way toward a few dilapidated snow houses. Most of them were empty. The present population numbered only seven persons—the other members of the tribe, including their leader, having moved away. A somewhat better linguist than guide, Apok found out that among the seven was a paralyzed woman. Explaining to her that I was the Kabloona doctor, he announced that she wanted to be taken out. We carried her aboard the plane and returned to ask the way to the next camp. The direction given was vague; somewhere to the northwest, I gathered from all the gesturing. How long since they had left was a question not even Apok could ascertain.

It took considerable time to locate this second camp. In fact, at one point in the search a remark by Fogbound nearly turned us back.

"I can't make it much farther today, Doc," he said. "Got to keep enough fuel in reserve to get us back to Padlei."

He had hardly spoken when we spotted a well frozen lake and a number of snow houses near by. Again he put the plane down without damage. The twenty-five or more Eskimos in camp made us welcome and Apok's guttural questioning brought the information that the Pokatelli, or mountie, had once said the Kabloona doctor would come. They had been waiting for him ever since. Now he had come. But my presence scarcely accounted for the tense air of expectancy that seemed to hang over everyone in the camp. I remembered then that there was supposed to be a witch doctor in the group, and decided to watch my step. Undoubtedly, they were anxious to see how I would shape up against their own "physician."

I looked the grinning crowd over and found only one person with residual paralysis—a middle aged woman. I tried to ask whether they were any more cases like hers, but Apok failed to get so technical a questions across and I forgot it for the time being. It was obvious that more medical work had to be done. I should have liked to vaccinate them against other disease, but didn't know how they would take it and decided to let vaccination wait until spring. I was reluctant to do any major medical work until I came to an old lady, apparently the matriarch of the group. She had a loose tooth. That was something I could safely take care of.

"The exact thing," I told myself, "to impress their witch doctor and show them how the Kabloona doctor can do his work without pain."

I planned, of course, to anesthetize the tooth and extract it without the slightest trouble. As the igloo was too dark and cramped to perform the operation inside, I had them move my patient outdoors and set her down on a caribou skin in the snow. I hadn't figured on the really vicious cold.

When I tried to inject her in order to "freeze" the nerve and thus insure a painless extraction, the fluid congealed in my needle. I tried again. No luck! Each time I pushed it into her gum the stuff would thicken and refuse to go in. While I knelt there in the snow, literally sweating in my frantic endeavors to get the hypodermic working, I was aware that all the Eskimos had gathered around and were watching me wonderingly. When they saw that I was having trouble, they grew fidgety. At last in desperation I seized my forceps and yanked that tooth out in the good old fashioned way. The procedure was far from gentle, but the old lady seemed quite well satisfied and the Eskimos grumbled approval.

I treated a few other persons for minor complaints and handed out tea and tobacco to keep them friendly and pave the way, so to speak, for the next time I'd visit them. They had had a bad hunting season and seemed to be starved, so we gave them food also. I might have doled out still more had not Fogbound spoken firmly:

"Come on, Doc. Time I got you out of here!"

The weather was closing in and he was anxious to get back. We loaded the paralyzed woman onto the caribou skin and, waving friendly goodby's, started toward the plane. Then the trouble began. Showing sudden signs of anger, the crowd followed after us on our march to the plane. Fogbound led the procession, followed by our mechanic carrying the front of the improvised stretcher, with Apok struggling manfully with the other end. I closed the rear of the parade.

As we neared the plane, our pursuers' behavior became ominous. The men were talking excitedly among themselves and gesticulating in our direction. All at once, as on a signal, they moved ahead quickly, overtook us and placed themselves squarely in our path. We stopped. Speaking as calmly as I could, I told Apok to find out what was wrong. He entered into a long conversation with them, and came away, looking more worried than before.

"What is it? What do they want?" I asked.

"Me not know. But him big boss. Him mad!"

"Well, find out, Don't just stand there. Talk with them again," I urged sharply.

More discussion—getting nowhere. It ended in what I took to be a complete deadlock.

"What do they say?" I yelled.

Apok turned to me with a helpless shrug. He was too scared to utter a word. I watched his dark face a moment as he struggled to express himself. Then I turned to the rest of our party.

"Oh, the hell!" I said. "Go ahead, Fogbound. Forget about it!"

Again we tried to move on, but this turned the attitude of our "hosts" into something really hostile. They formed a line—in order of importance, no doubt—and tried again to stop us. But as we pushed ahead, the chief motioned to someone down the line and his man disappeared into one of the igloos.

By now Fogbound had forced his way through to the plane and climbed in to warm up. The rest of us, somewhat hampered with carrying the paralyzed woman, were following cautiously, when glancing behind, I saw the Eskimo coming back from his igloo. Whatever may have been the misunderstanding before, I knew now that our lives were in danger. The fellow was carrying a rifle.

◆ 24 ◆

THREATS AND MISUNDERSTANDINGS

I hadn't encountered hostile Eskimos before and didn't know what to do. Without weapons we could hardly get away.

The instant he saw the rifle, our assistant dropped his end of the skin and made for the plane. Our patient tumbled into the snow. I found myself standing alone with Apok, who looked as if he was going to run any second. Grabbing him by the arm, I said,

"See here, you've got to find out what they want. You've *got* to. Do you understand?"

"They mad. Don't know," he muttered, and closed up for good.

I tried to use my imagination. What on earth could they want? Why did they get so upset all of a sudden? How could we calm them down? That, after all, was the important thing.

The man with the gun came closer and, although he didn't point it directly at us, he looked dangerous enough. When I took a step forward, my action caused an instant reflex in the whole group. They meant business. We were trapped and they knew it. Something would have to be done. We couldn't afford to offend these strange people, but of one thing I was sure: if they attempted to prevent me from taking that sick woman away they would have a hard time. I decided to try to find out myself what the trouble was all about.

Carefully I approached the head man or witch doctor and questioned him in the best Eskimo I knew. At times I fancied that he was catching the general drift of my speech.

"We take this woman because she is ill," I tried to explain, with appropriate gestures. "We will make her better. We have come hundreds of miles to get her. We cannot leave without her. There is another woman in the plane and she came from your other camp."

He gave me a blank look and just nodded.

"Listen," I continued, raising my voice, "didn't the Pokatelli say that I would come to help your sick people?"

That seemed to mean something to him. I couldn't be sure, though, until I heard him grumble.

"Pokatelli—him—say—three!"

I must have smiled in relief, for the chief's face wrinkled into a sort of answering grin. I knew at last what the trouble was. The mountie who had reported the paralysis cases to me had promised these people that I would take three out. Yes, Pokatelli had said three, and three it had to be. The true purpose of our visit meant nothing at all. They were not going to let me leave without taking a third patient. There was only the one case of paralysis in camp. We had another in the plane. Where I wondered, could I find a third!

I drew Apok into the conversation and learned that there was another woman polio patient in a small camp "three sleeps" away.

"Tell them we can't go for her this time," I directed Apok. "The weather looks bad and we have to turn back at once."

I knew from his anxious face that Fogbound wouldn't stand for much more delay. Still, if they wouldn't let us go unless we took a third . . .

Acting on a sudden hunch, I asked, "Where is this woman's husband?" indicating the patient lying on the caribou skin.

When the chief heard Apok translate this, he gestured and a strapping Eskimo man stepped out of the line.

"Him," said Apok, "woman's husband."

"We'll take him," I decided.

The crisis was over. Everybody smiled. Some even danced a little for joy. They didn't care who it was so long as we took *three*.

As they stood around shouting their profuse thanks, we quickly loaded the woman with paralysis, together with her husky husband, into the plane before they had time to change their minds.

The 300-mile trip back to Padlei was more tedious than eventful. At this point the perfectly healthy husband of one of the polio cases decided he would remain. We were relieved to leave him as we picked up more polio cases here and had quite a load by the time we arrived at Chesterfield Inlet, another 300 miles northeast. The healthy man I had left at Padlei was my responsibility, and I worried as to what I should do about him.

A couple of days went by. Then, no other plan occurring to me, I went to Paddy Hamilton to see if he could issue our visitor a ration so that the man might stay a while longer. "Later," I explained to Paddy, "I'll probably be able to fly him back to the Kazan on another patrol."

"A ration for the Kazan fellow?" asked Paddy. "That won't be necessary."

"Why not?"

"He's gone."

"Gone?"

"Sure. Didn't you know, Doc? He left yesterday for his camp. Said it was better for him to go back."

"You mean he just up and went—*alone?"*

"Yes."

"Did he have any food with him?"

"Very little as he couldn't carry much. Henry Voisey, the Hudson's Bay Company manager, offered him food but he only wanted a little tea and tobacco."

I took a deep breath. This Eskimo, for whom I felt responsible, had taken off on a journey of some 300 miles through unknown terrain, with nothing but tobacco and a little tea. He hadn't given any thought to food. Since it was still very cold, although spring was approaching, I had no idea the man would get through. It worried me for weeks.

Two months later a trapper in the Kazan region radioed that the Eskimo had arrived back at camp, apparently no worse for his solitary grand tour.

The news brought relief and gave me new respect for the rugged independence of the Caribou Eskimo.

We had gradually assembled quite a few paralysis cases in Chesterfield, some of whom were being treated by Miss Beattie, the young physiotherapist from Toronto. Most of them, however, would have to be flown out for more intensive treatment in big city hospitals. This meant delay because a plane big enough to carry them all couldn't land at Chesterfield until the ice broke up. I decided to utilize this interval of waiting by calling on Fogbound to fly me back to the domain of the Caribous for another patient or two if we could locate them.

Again we picked up Apok, the interpreter, at Padlei, then went on west, this time heading for a small camp I'd been told about which seemed ripe for immunization. It was near a landmark known throughout that part of the arctic as Schraeder's Cabin, an old trapper's hut presently occupied by Andy Lawrie, a government biologist doing research on the caribou and their fawns.

"Good," exclaimed Fogbound, observing that the ice of a nearby fresh water lake had already melted, "there's where I'm landing."

Despite the absence of any solid lake ice, landing was rough enough to damage one of the pontoons. As a result, Fogbound had to spend most of his time in the camp trying to get the pontoon into shape for a take off. The delay was not wholly wasted. Andy was a nice fellow and, knowing a great deal about the Caribou Eskimos, he gave me information that I might never have acquired otherwise.

I was particularly interested to hear that many of them still adhered to their old pagan religion, with its trio of gods. There was a good god who took the form of a tall, powerful Eskimo. There was a partly bad, partly good god who, said Andy, with a solemn wink, resembled a white man. Their third and worst god was really a goddess. She was a horrible old woman with one eye. Her specialty, it seemed, was flying through the air headfirst. Occasionally she appeared to the Eskimos as a warning, making terrible sounds and scaring them nearly to death. By piecing together bits of information he had heard from the people, Andy was of the opinion that their three gods represented the three vital influences in their lives—the Sun, the Sea, the Wind.

"But this one-eyed woman," I observed. "Do they really believe in the existence of such a thing, Andy?"

"*Do* they? Listen, Doctor . . . "

He told of having traveled with an Eskimo guide, who, one storm swept night, had actually been confronted with the frightful airborne woman on the trip.

"He'd left the tent to tie up the dogs," Andy recalled. "A moment later he came tumbling in again, pale as a bucket of snow and shivering all over."

"What did you do, Andy?" I inquired.

"As you know, Doctor, I'm no medical man. Just a biologist. But, I've as much curiosity as anyone and I did what you might have done yourself. I felt that Eskimo's pulse to see if he was putting on a show. Well, sir, his pulse was racing so fast I couldn't count the beats. That's the shape he was in."

"Couldn't he talk?" I wanted to know.

Andy shook his bald head. "Never a word. To get his mind on something else I suggested that he go out and finish tying up the dogs. You know what happened?"

"He fainted on the spot. The idea of going out there again, I suppose. Took three hours of shivering and shaking before he could speak; then it was only a whisper in my ear. Seems he'd met the one eyed woman face to face. She'd come swooping at him headfirst and he'd turned and barely made it back to the tent."

Now, Andy Lawrie, government biologist, was not the man to believe in horrible women who flew through the air headfirst. But the abject fear that he once saw in the face of his guide had demonstrated to Andy how deep rooted was the Caribou Eskimo's belief in this evil spirit.

After learning from Andy that the camp contained one woman victim of the recent polio epidemic, and arranging to take her out, I was anxious to immunize the people in that camp. In order to prepare them for what to them might appear a frightening experience, I asked Apok to say that I was going to keep them from getting sick. As the interpreter talked, I saw the faces of his listeners show sudden interest, then joy.

"No trouble this time," I said to Fogbound, at my side.

He returned a cautious, "Maybe."

I was sterilizing the arm of one of the women picked at random when a commotion rippled through the group around me, turning into a show of excitement that I didn't like.

"Hold it," Fogbound advised, with an I-told-you-so inflection.

A needless warning! With our experience among the people of that other camp fresh in mind, I stopped instantly and turned to Apok.

"What's wrong this time?"

Plenty, he reported. I had insulted these people by not vaccinating their witch doctor first.

Fact was, it had occurred to me that this man might prefer not be vaccinated at all, since he evidently considered himself above the ordinary members of the human race. That's why I was starting in with the woman. Now, changing tactics, I gave the chief the first injection with all the ceremony I could muster for the occasion. He was very cooperative. The instant I had finished with him he marshaled everyone in line and, directing the vaccinations that followed, turned the whole thing into a social affair. The Eskimos thought it great fun. So, for once, did I.

After accepting from us all the supplies we could spare, they decided to put on a celebration of their own.

◆25◆

THROB OF A DRUM

First they used what daylight was left to put on a demonstration of kayak handling, inviting us to join the fun. I refused, smiling but very firm. Paddy Hamilton had once warned me that among the Eskimos' favorite jokes was getting an unskilled white man to try paddling a kayak. They know he will probably capsize immediately.

This nimble little one man canoe is a featherweight craft consisting of skin covering a frame of wood or bone. The Caribou Eskimos of the Kazan River region use caribou skins, stitched together with sinew. They make a double seam that renders the skins absolutely watertight. The kayak is completely decked over except for a round central hole or cockpit, into which the owner lowers himself and which fits snugly around his waist.

These boats are used by the inland Eskimos for lake and river travel as well as for hunting and fishing. They are indispensable to their owners in summer as are his dogs in winter. It is no exaggeration to say that without caribou, dogs or kayaks, the Kazan River Eskimos would not long survive.

We looked on with growing admiration as our hosts maneuvered their kayaks with incredible speed, chasing one another all over the lake. For a climax each paddler rolled completely over in his kayak and came up laughing—all without taking aboard a single drop of water. They put on quite a show.

Evening came, however, before the real festivities began. These started with a tremendous meal of caribou meat. Fogbound agreed with me that each Eskimo gulped down at least five pounds, and some of them much more—all this to the accompaniment of tearing and gnawing noise, the cracking of bones and a continuous barrage of unrestrained burping.

As a physician, I looked for them to fall asleep after such a gorge. They did no such thing. From Apok, who had consumed a fair amount of meat himself, I learned that they were now going to put on a drum dance, one of their oldest ceremonial dances and one of the few remaining expressions of an Eskimo folklore.

Inklings of this mysterious ritual and the hypnotic influence it could have on the dancers had filtered out to us at Chesterfield. While some of the reports seemed absurdly exaggerated, they had made me curious without ever really expecting to satisfy that curiosity. Here, apparently, was my chance. I hardly hoped to come close to participating myself.

"Watch out, Doc," whispered Fogbound, as we seated ourselves on the ground among the overfed Eskimos.

"What for?"

"Nothing. Just watch out."

They hauled into view a big hand drum made of caribou skin stretched over a wooden hoop. The skin could be tightened or released by the drummer. In this way it produced different tones when beaten with a stick. I noticed that the drummer struck it on the rim where it gave a more "nasal" sound than it would have if beaten in the center where the full expanse of skin could have its play.

After a short incantation, doubtless destined for the gods, and in which everyone took part, the chief got to his feet and started a shuffling dance in front of the group. Presently, his mouth opened and, in a monotonous monotone that followed the rhythm of the drum, he sang with long drawn out words. Following each stanza, the whole crowd would come in with a high pitched refrain that sounded like "Ahhh yai, ahh yai, aye aye aye."

It seemed the chief was modestly singing of his own accomplishments.

"I am the greatest chief of the Inuit, Ahh yai ahh yai yai!" the song went on. Then "I am the best hunter in the land, Ahh yai, aye aye aye yai! I have three beautiful wives, I paddle the kayak faster than anyone, Ahh yai yai ayi!"

R.C.A.F. Canso # 11057, loading polio and T.B. patients at Chesterfield Inlet, August 21, 1949.

He might have added that he ate more caribou meat than anyone. But if that particular gift was omitted from his self praise, I am certain nothing else was left out. He took a long time to sing his way through the list.

Finally another man jumped up to tell about himself. He used the same monotonous monotone as the chief, but his achievements were different. He was the best guide—he had seen the big sea—he had killed twenty caribous in one day.

During the song listing his attainments, those in the audience had started slowly swaying from side to side, following the rhythm of the refrain. After a few minutes they appeared completely engrossed. They had forgotten everything in the world except that pounding rhythm.

Not all got up to brag about themselves. Some man would tell about a hunt, for example; how he had sighted the herd; how he had stalked and shot them; how many caribou had fallen; how richly he had stocked his caches.

For some reason the women either were not allowed, or were unwilling, to take part in the dance. They sat among the onlookers, their high voices wailing the refrain, their bodies rocking back and forth. No famous musical conductor, had one been there, could have welded an orchestra into greater rhythmic unity.

At first I found it not only boring but completely inartistic. After a while, though, a curious thing happened. I came under the spell of the drum myself. I could actually feel its throbbing beat inside my head, while a steady undertone zoomed in my ears. To my surprise, I had to suppress a sudden urge to start rocking and swaying. Why I suppressed it wasn't clear because, although I had a sense of falling into a hypnotic state, I didn't care a bit.

Gradually the tempo quickened until it whipped up to a violent staccato. Each dancer became wilder. Now more than one of them performed at the same time. Those looking on clapped their hands and fairly yelled the refrain. I watched a miracle happen. Old men, scarcely able to hobble, leaped up and danced fanatically, while in their singing they turned to challenging each other and boasting of their own impossible deeds . . . A dog barked, and I snapped out of it.

Dazed, I looked around. The rest of the audience appeared not to have heard the dog, but remained in a sort of trance, many swinging back and forth with their eyes shut tight. The dancers seemed to have lost control of their movements entirely. The performance had gotten out of hand!

I nudged Fogbound, rocking along with the rest. He awoke from his trance and realized the danger at once. Walking to the front, he calmly shook the chief's hand and thanked him for the celebration. We were tired, he said, and would stop now and go to bed.

That casual matter-of-fact action on the part of Fogbound put an end to the party. Some of the performers fell down, panting. Others stumbled away. Still others simply gaped in bewilderment. Gradually the group dispersed.

I don't think we were in any real danger. Not up to that point. But if what I was told later was true, we were fast approaching the fringe of possible disaster. In some drum dances the performers get so excited and so soundly hypnotized by that soft terrible rhythm that they lose all contact with reality. They will walk through fires. They will challenge one another to *prove* their boasts. Sometimes such a dance will last for days and after it is well under way none of the dancers has the slightest control of his actions. In our case, if that dog hadn't barked, the affair might well have degenerated to a tragic level.

The following morning the sound of the drum was still throbbing in my head. It kept on pounding and throbbing until long after we took leave of our friendly, well meaning hosts and flew our polio patient back to my hospital in Chesterfield.

We had grown very fond of Miss Beattie. She had done remarkable therapeutic work among my patients since flying in from Toronto during the epidemic. Besides, she had been a nice companion for Viola when I was out on patrols, and there was no doubt at all that every child in the community adored her. Even though her tour of duty was completed in the arctic, we dreaded having her go back to civilization. At last it was arranged that she would leave Chesterfield with eight of our most serious cases as soon as the plane could land. She would be invaluable for looking after them on the trip.

A day arrived when the big air force Canso appeared and caused a commotion by splashing to a landing on the bay. Viola organized a farewell dinner and Miss Beattie and the plane's crew enjoyed a grand meal of arctic trout.

That part was fine. But the evacuation of eight paralyzed Eskimos was a pitiful sight. Many young men, formerly great hunters, were carried out with arms and legs dangling helplessly.

Viewed with imagination, the sight was even sadder. Who, one wondered, would take care of their families now? Or, with father dead and son lame, who would hunt the caribou? Who would replace the dead infants with new babies, now that the wife was a helpless cripple? Who would carve walrus tusks, now that the nimble hands were limp?

All this was evidently passing through the minds of the other Eskimos as, grieving silently, they watched their friends being carried aboard the plane. Tragic end to the great epidemic, it drove home more than anything else could have, the fact that an entire section of the Eskimo race had been crippled. But we waved a cheery farewell. Miss Beattie waved back bravely and laughed and called out something about seeing us again.

On board Canso is flight crew under command of First Lieutenant Rush. In mid-canoe position is Constance Beattie, physical-therapist. Six hours later this mercy flight crashed in N. Manitoba. All 21 on board perished.

A few hours after they took off, we received news that ground contact with the plane had been lost. This was bad, but not necessarily fatal. We waited all night for a report of the plane's safe arrival at Winnipeg.

No word of any sort came until next day. We knew then that neither Miss Beattie nor any of her twenty companions and patients would ever come back. Scores of searching planes from two countries finally spotted the wreckage of the big Canso, which had been caught in a violent thunderstorm between Churchill and Winnipeg . . . The passengers' remains could hardly be identified.

The impact of that crash sent ramifications all through my district. The difficulty of explaining to the Eskimos just what had happened led to their refusing for a long time to ride in any plane. This, in turn, made necessary the abandonment of pending plans for a mass evacuation of critical T.B. patients—a plan that would have saved countless lives, could we have carried it into effect promptly.

Looking back at the results of the epidemic, Viola and I marveled at the way the great disaster pursued the Eskimos like a nemesis. By direct action, it had crippled a race. Indirectly, it had been responsible for a plane crash that added another blow to the thinning ranks of the coastal and Caribou Eskimos. Then, in final revenge, it had reached out beyond the realm of my quarantine and, by preventing prompt evacuation of critical T.B. victims, contributed to the death of countless more.

Why these three major catastrophes? Any two should have satisfied the Eskimos' evil gods—even the flying, one eyed woman.

"What was it the Caribou chief kept harping on?" asked Viola.

I knew what she meant. I'd thought of that myself. But it had struck me as too silly a fancy to be mentioned aloud. Now, for a moment, I wasn't so sure.

"Pokatelli," I answered slowly, with a half-smile, "Him —say—*three.*"

◆ 26 ◆

HIS MAJESTY, TUCTU

Although the mother gives life to her Eskimo child, it is Tuctu, the caribou, that keeps the flame of life burning during his stay on earth by providing nearly all his necessities.

From the moment the Eskimo baby is wrapped in a small piece of caribou fur after birth to the time his hunting implements of bone and horn accompany him into the grave, the Eskimo is fed, clothed, housed and equipped with articles the caribou supplies. You can scarcely think of the Eskimo without thinking of this remarkable animal on which his very existence depends.

Unfortunately, the precarious future of his race is all too closely linked with the equally depressing outlook for the survival of Tuctu.

In some coastal and far northern areas certain tribes have already had to adapt their lives to the use of sea animals for food and clothing. This is especially true of the last century as whalers wiped out most of the coastal and far northern herds.

The caribou is believed to have originated in Asia. It may have migrated to the North American continent with, or preceding, the great movement of Eskimos across Bering Strait. Although differing in appearance, nevertheless, the caribou is related to the reindeer of Alaska and of the European and

Asiatic arctic; also to the jumping deer of more southern regions.

Female caribou weigh between 150 and 200 pounds, while the male weights from 200 to 300 pounds. He is a migratory animal, and has never been domesticated like the reindeer. This, of course, rules out his usefulness as a supplier of milk and a carrier of loads.

Early spring finds Tuctu moving north to the muskeg plains of the arctic. In September and October, except for small groups that often stay behind in the arctic during winter months, they retrace their steps to well south of the tree line, where they spend the rest of the year. Caribou breed in the north and have their young there when they return the following spring. Sets of twins have been reported. In traveling, their progress is slow but steady and occasionally disorganized. Their habitual migratory routes seem to be gradually shifting to the west.

Because an Eskimo must shoot at least thirty a year to survive, missing a caribou hunt is an economic catastrophe. From the skin, either with or without the fur, he makes his clothes, tents, sleeping bags and the covering for his kayak. In winter he wears two jackets. One, the attigi, goes over his bare skin with the fur turned inside. The outer jacket, called the kulitah, is pulled on over the attigi and has the fur on the outside. Neither jacket contains pockets or overlapping closings, but both are slipped on over the head like a sweater. Quite often the kulitah is given a three-quarters or full length tail fringed with small strips of skin, while the hood is occasionally trimmed with wolverine and fox fur to keep the wearer's face warm and to slow down the breath frosting which occurs in intensely cold areas. Wolverine fur is better suited for this than is, for example, the fur of the caribou, which quickly becomes covered with a layer of frost in cold weather.

Long stockings or leggings—the fur inside and reaching to the hips—are worn under trousers which have straight, stovepipe legs extending to within a few inches below the knee. Boots and mitts of caribou skin complete the Eskimo's clothing outfit. His sleeping bags and covers are, of course, fashioned of this same furry material, while tent and kayak coverings have the fur scraped off.

He makes his kayak waterproof by sewing the skin coverings together with thread of caribou sinews or ligaments, which conveniently *swell up when wet.* So far as I know, these sinews are the only natural waterproofing thread. A double seam is both safe and lasting.

The meat of the caribou is eaten raw, cooked, smoked or dried. It is very tasty. The steaks especially are a great delicacy. Bone marrow provides extra vitamins. Eskimos often drink the rich blood of a freshly killed animal. If no wood can be found, the rib bones are used for kayak frames; other bones are made into spears, lances, harpoon points, drying racks, ice scoops and eating utensils.

Since the Eskimo's life centers so completely on the caribou, his very mode of living is dictated by the movements of this migratory animal. For example, the need for hunting the caribou by following him on his trek causes many Eskimo bands to turn into nomads themselves.

Little is really known about Eskimo beliefs, there is no doubt in my mind that the caribou plays an important role in his religion. Formerly, strict taboos—and occasionally strict even today—laid down by native witch doctors, existed against eating certain parts of the animal. Whatever their purpose, if any, such restrictions were without real sense because nearly all caribou meat can be eaten. Often the very best cuts came under the witch doctor's ban.

Eskimos will shoot a caribou wherever and whenever they see one. They do most of their organized hunting, however, the last of August and on through September and October, when the caribou is migrating southward. Then is when the animals are heaviest and their fur in top condition. Besides, this is the time of year when the Eskimo himself gets restless; when a feeling comes over him that the one worthwhile thing in life is to hunt Tuctu.

My observation is that the caribou hunt has important significance to the Eskimo. Not only is it an economic necessity for him, but it appears to satisfy one of the more complex impulses of his race. You can't say he looks at it as a sport exactly, yet so urgent is his need for the excitement it furnishes that you can only liken his action to that of an alcoholic craving strong drink. If anything prevents his going off hunting after the first signs of restlessness are evident, he is likely to lose his usual good humor and become difficult to handle. I have seen this phenomenon too many times to doubt that the hunt expresses some profound racial trait.

Because I always enjoyed a caribou hunt myself—though the slaughter was no attraction—I usually got ready at the first report of the fall migration, hoping no medical work would turn up to keep me in Chesterfield. Another thing, the sight of a herd of caribou invariable threw the Eskimos into such excitement that they paid little attention to where they were shooting. It wasn't hard to convince myself that a doctor ought to go along in case of accidents.

I well remember the first time I accompanied a hunt. It was late summer and a period when Sheeniktooks' grouchiness, suddenly growing acute, had its compensation. For all I had to do was diagnose it as a bad case of caribou fever—and appoint myself his physician to accompany him on his "cure."

One beautiful morning early in September he and I took off for my first hunt with a large party of Chesterfield Eskimos. Men and young boys—some of them mere children—carried old fashioned guns that looked as if they held greater danger for the hunter than the hunted. Dogs, too, went along, each bearing twenty to thirty pounds of supplies. We made most of the journey inland by water, walking the rest of the way, a distance of sixty miles.

Snow had not yet fallen. The yellowish-brown growth of muskeg was splashed in innumerable places with the brighter oranges and reds of fall vegetation. The arctic flowers were almost done. Occasionally we would stop to pick the last of the blueberries and tiny arctic "apples." The lakes and pools were now a denser and more relaxing blue, while the smaller ones had a layer of micaceous ice on their surfaces. The sky, now pale blue, had become the stage for dense, eye holding cloud formations which looked so detached from the sky itself that one had the impression that they might fall any moment. The sun had lost its summer sting, and as it swung past the noontime mark, it bathed the already colorful land with a strange golden hue. The air felt nippy. This was the fleeting arctic fall, and cold weather soon would be with us. Already my small thermometer registered a snappy thirty-five degrees above zero.

Next morning all started roaming through the country, each man and boy alert for Tuctu. Some small pools of water could be seen three miles away and the Eskimos hoped to find caribou there. Only three miles! But since the caribou always flees against the wind, we had to walk at least five miles to get above the wind and so into position. He also had a very keen sense of smell; for which reason, the Eskimos spread out before approaching the little valley and formed a semicircle in which the animals would be quite certain to be caught.

Two of the most experienced hunters went ahead to spot the herd, if any, and shoot the first few animals. As Sheeniktook explained the hunting technique to me, each herd had its leaders and these were the ones you must shoot first if humanly possible. Miss, or start blazing away at just any animal, and the leaders would organize the group and all take off at great speed. But if you killed the leaders, the rest of the herd would mill about without aim and fall an easy prey to the hunters.

We were lucky. The two men ahead of us had come on to a herd and were signaling the good news. I saw both men spread their arms and raise them level with the head. In the clear arctic air I could even make out each hand with fingers parted wide. I glanced sidewise at Sheeniktook, who translated the age old Eskimo hunting signal by a cryptic, "Him say antlers sighted!"

◆ 27 ◆

RIVER OF FUR

Tension gripped the Eskimos. All moved carefully ahead and in dead silence took up positions behind boulders. My gaze followed Sheeniktook's trembling finger and I peered into the valley.

About 200 caribou were visible. Some stood in the water, drinking. Others grazed on the surrounding muskeg. A few were lying down. A peaceful scene! Their coloring blended with the terrain. The brown and black fur, with lighter legs and a few white spots, formed a prefect protective camouflage. Every moment I discovered another animal by noticing movement where my eye had expected only muskeg and rocks.

Two shots, well aimed, brought down the first animals and stirred up a commotion in the herd only equaled by the commotion among the hunters themselves. Suddenly, shots cracked all around me. Men leaped up from behind their hiding places. Small boys started running about from rock to rock, firing blindly into that mass of brown fur. Bullets whizzed through the air dangerously close and ricocheted off the rocks. I dropped to cover, mentally counting the wounds I'd have to dress after it was all over.

The poor confused animals ran around in panic, tripping over fallen comrades, searching desperately for a way out. They were dropping so fast that it seemed none would survive the volleys which crashed through the valley. Yet they did manage to form into some sort of organized group and finally came stampeding straight through the cordon of Eskimos who kept firing away at close range. Every man and boy was on his feet by now, all trying by yells and gesticulations to divert the fleeing caribou from their course. They succeeded only partly. My feelings were all for the animals. While Sheeniktook laughed and shouted and pointed to the dead and wounded, I exulted inwardly to see a lucky few escape the barrage and, antlers high, race off into the distance with scornful elegance.

It had been a good hunt. Over 100 animals lay scattered among the rocks; a few had to be dragged from the water. The Eskimos then got busy dressing their victims. Knives flashed while the animals were being skinned and cut into pieces. The skin was scraped roughly, the cut of meat lined up, the sinews and ligaments that lie close to the backbone carefully cleaned and spread out on rocks. Only a few choice cuts were taken off the carcass for immediate consumption, and for the women in Chesterfield who liked their fresh caribou steak.

The rest was piled up, some of which were covered with the stomach contents for preservation, then buried under a layer of heavy stones. Presently all I could see were heaps of stones with antlers sticking out to identify ownership of each cache.

The stones had to be heavy and built up carefully, and all the crevices filled in with small stones or gravel. If one left so much as a small crack open a wolf or wolverine would worm its way into the cache, eat a considerable part of the meat and spoil the rest for human use. When a wolverine contaminates a meat cache even the dogs hesitate to eat the meat. According to Sheeniktook, some Caribou Eskimos will spread the stomach contents of the caribou over the meat, which they claim discourages animals from raiding their caches. Thus it serves a dual purpose—helping preserve the meat and lending a very special flavor. Sometimes the Eskimo will eat the bowel and stomach contents of the caribou as a salad. This, and arctic berries, were probably the only type of vegetable foods included in their diets before the white man came.

The caches were left just as they were. In a few months when travel by komatik was possible, the Eskimos would come back to where the antlers stuck out above the snow and remove the rest of the meat. How they were able to tell their own caches from others' has always been a mystery to me. But they have their ways. It is important that they make no mistake because taking someone else's meat can cause that person to starve, or even die if he has patrolled a long distance to get it and then finds it gone. Intentional pillage of caches is very rare and the punishment is then severe.

An antler marks the carefully cached caribou meat which may not be retrieved for months.

A great celebration meal was served that evening. The Eskimos devoured tremendous quantities of meat, eating it raw or roasted over a muskeg fire. Their excited talk of the hunt was not marked by understatement. Each recounted his personal accomplishments with a rare appreciation for drama—if not always for strict fact.

The day's work, I gathered, had been merely an *initial* expedition. Tomorrow the main hunt would get under way.

Now, the best place to hunt caribou is where they cross a river for, although good swimmers, they make slow progress in the water and so become easier victims for the men with guns. It was decided that a certain traditional fording place in the Kazan River would be visited next day. There was a chance that the Kazan River Eskimos of this region would be there too. But that didn't matter, said Sheeniktook confidently, as there would be enough for all.

The Kazan Eskimos prefer to hunt from their kayaks. Until recently they rarely used rifles but used spears to kill or wound the animal as he was swimming rivers or lakes. Caribou spearing is still engaged in, however, and even the bow and arrow may be used in some areas when a shortage of ammunition occurs. When spearing they try to hit near the spinal cord and sever the aorta. While it certainly takes more skill to hunt from a frail kayak—which makes this method seem more sporty—it is being discouraged by the authorities. Their reason: many animals fail to die on the spot and stagger ahead to bleed to death a few miles farther. Since some Eskimos never follow their wounded victims, the meat is wasted and will be eaten by wolves.

The recent slaughter had given me my fill of blood and death, and I made up my mind not to accompany the hunters the following day. When they left camp early in the morning I wandered off by myself. I wanted to see the animals, not in panic, but moving peacefully along in the great herds about which I had been told.

Walking a few miles, I came across a caribou path. There are many in the arctic—routes along which the animals return each year, moving along in single file, trampling a narrow line across the brown landscape.

I found myself near one and waited. I stood there more than an hour without seeing a caribou and, disappointed, decided to go back to join the hunters, after all. Just then I heard a noise. Straining my eyes, I watched for an approaching herd. Not an animal appeared. The noise grew stronger, however; no doubt of that. It was a rhythmic cadence that reverberated in my ears until I could almost feel the vibrations in the soil under my feet. "They're coming closer!" I thought with growing excitement.

All at once the strange noise seemed coming from behind me instead of in front. I quickly walked a few hundred yards to where a little hill obscured a fold in the land. I crawled to the top on my stomach and cautiously peeked over. The sight was one I shall never forget—hundreds of caribou moving by with gentle haste. Mingled with the sound of the hoofs one could hear the grunting of the mature caribou and the occasional calf bawling. They surged forward, not singly, as I had expected, but *more than twenty abreast,* and the long procession seemed to extend from one horizon to the other.

They traveled along swiftly, lightly, barely touching the ground with their hoofs. They appeared to *glide* over the spongy soil. Such breathtaking grace compared startlingly with the ludicrous way I had been dragging along for days, trudging clumsily through the difficult footing.

Generally, muskeg is soft and spongy so that animals running over it do not produce the pounding noise one gets on the plains. The caribou hoof is especially adapted for walking and running over this spongy mass, and when he walks it is almost silently. However, when he runs you hear the "squish" of the muskeg and the rustle of vegetation as the animal gains speed. An immense herd multiplies these noises many times. When a herd of caribou travels over a gravel ridge and over rocky dry zones or hard snow one can hear the hoofs pounding, of course. Also the caribou is very light in weight and fleet-footed, so that he doesn't have the pounding effect cattle and buffalo have.

I saw a spot where a rock must have been in their path. One by one, supple brown backs would arch up above the waves of fur that rolled forward like the corrugated ocean swells one sees from a plane. That measured jump became a focusing point, and I began to count. They traveled about seven miles an hour, an unending parade of bouncing life. Jump—264; jump—265; jump—266 (that was a beauty); jump—267. When I came to the four hundreds I lost count and was satisfied to keep my hypnotized gaze wandering over the river of moving caribou. The antlers, somewhat darker than the stream of fur, seemed to float on top of an animal river as if separate from the proud head that carried them. I moved over a little so that I could see them standing out against the blue sky—thousands of fingers pointing to heaven.

For three hours I watched, never tiring of the magnificent sight. Then gradually the river of fur began to thin out, until it became a trickle of stragglers; a few old ones, a few young, some crippled, and occasional mother stopping to nurse her offspring. I was still standing there watching these last when five or six wolves came sneaking by in pursuit of this legion of juicy prey. It made me sick. I knew the innumerable deaths the wolves have on their record, killing a straggler, eating little in order to hurry on to new victims. For the first time, I wished heartily that I'd brought my gun.

But, walking back to camp, I forgot these slinking omens of death in the movement of the herd still pulsating in my blood. Again I saw those leaping figures, pointing antlers, light colored breasts heaving with the stream. How many animals had I seen? Ten thousand? Many more, Twenty thousand, then? That was closer; perhaps a bit too high. Who could tell? I felt happy and singularly pleased with world that could casually display such stirring magnificence.

In the evening the hunters came back to camp with incredible tales of success. But when, later that night, I heard wolves howling in the distance I began to wonder about the future of Tuctu.

A long while back as many as 5,000,000 caribou are estimated to have occupied the arctic. At the turn of the last century there were still about two million left. In those days Eskimos hunted them mainly at river crossings. On hills near fording places along the Kazan, Dubawnt and Back Rivers, you can still find ancient blinds built out of rocks. Behind these lurked the expert hunters of old who killed with arrows, harpoons and spears—and rarely missed. But since they lived under the pressure of witch doctors' taboos, there is no doubt that the long history of waste and destruction dates back to those times. Through following decades the Eskimos lost much of their hunting skill. They wounded animals without killing them, thus furthering the waste that left abandoned, blown up carcasses scattered across the land.

Then the whalers came and brought firearms which intrigued the Eskimos. But because the Eskimos were not good shots, more animals were killed and wounded uselessly. By the time they learned how to fire guns properly, they had forgotten how to use bows and arrows. On learning to shoot better, they shot too many caribou, often killing many more than were needed.

Finally the diseases arrived, and with the diseases the wolves have become a real factor. No one knows how many caribou are killed by wolves each year. It is likely that these animals, added to accidents, diseases and inclement weather, take a greater toll than does the modern Eskimo.

Although the caribou have been seriously depleted, the story is not so disgusting as that of the buffalo and musk ox. The musk ox, once close to 1,000,000 strong in the subarctic and arctic, now numbers 500 on the mainland and a few hundred more on the arctic islands.

Ayranni carefully smooths out caribou back sinew to dry. This is the thread Eskimo use to sew boots and garments.

Only about 650,000 caribou are now left in the eastern arctic and there is little doubt that their number is steadily decreasing. Diseases cannot be stopped. Wolves cannot be stopped. If the species is dying out from natural causes, that cannot be stopped, either. But waste *can* be stopped and all efforts are not being exerted in this direction. The government and the missions try to overrule the old taboos and, in the more accessible regions at least, have succeeded. The export of caribou fur has been forbidden. That, too, has halted an important killer. Inexpert shooting and spearing is being stopped as much as possible.

A restricted season aimed at protecting the northward migration when the does are carrying their young has been instituted. No white man can hunt the caribou without a permit and even Eskimos are officially limited in their kills a year. This last, however, is difficult to enforce, particularly because a small number fails to cover their actual needs. The diseases too are constantly being studied but it will take many years before results are known.

Meanwhile Eskimos go hungry and inadequately dressed because they cannot find Tuctu. Many have to travel weeks before sighting a herd; others find that the herds are thinning dangerously and that the animals seem to be taking new routes. Because of the migratory habits of the caribou it would be difficult, perhaps impossible, to create reservations where they could roam in peace. Nevertheless, something like that must be tried out to insure their preservation.

The herd that I saw surging across from horizon to horizon was fantastic. That one herd should be sufficient to feed, clothe and house the Eskimos for several years, even though more may perish with the coming of advanced hunting techniques.

But if it is true that herds, on the whole, are being depleted and cannot be built up, the future is grim. On the white man, who has shaped the destiny of the Eskimo, rests the responsibility. He must somehow solve the problem of the disappearing caribou—or the whole race may go down with its provider.

◆28◆

TOUGH PROBLEM, TOUGH SOLUTION

Together, the United States and Canada possess close to 5,000 miles of arctic coast line—*virtually unprotected!*

Of this, Canada alone has a 3,500-mile stretch which, except for Alaska, lies nearer Russia than any other territory on the North American continent. Ninety-nine and nine-tenths of this natural front is uninhabited and barely accessible.

But the fact that many thousands of square miles have never even been explored by white men does not preclude the possibility of landings being made there by people with a purpose not hard to guess. For this coast line stands guard over a few million square miles of land containing coal, iron, oil, copper, nickel, lead, cobalt, asbestos, silver and gold—not to mention high-percentage uranium composites.

A really effective defense of this vast frontier by permanent garrisons would take an army of 500,000 men, with a standby reserve of as many more. No soldier on active duty in these icy regions could serve for more than three consecutive months at a time.

Were troops dispensed with, an air force of at least 150 fighter and bomber wings would be needed to patrol the shores of the mainland, and of the hundreds of islands which reach out to within 600 miles of the pole. These planes would need perhaps sixty air bases from which to operate. If one chooses to maintain neither adequate troops nor a man sized air force, a third alternative would be a string of extremely powerful radar stations spaced every 500 miles, with at least two weaker stations in between each pair. That would be no defense; merely a *warning* system.

Needed, of course, is a combination of troops, planes and radar stations. Since this is impossible at the present time, what our defense departments are striving for is a patrolling air force of a few wings, aided by sporadic radar posts in the most strategic places.

It would doubtless be possible right now for small raiding parties to enter the arctic by water or through the air and go unnoticed. A disturbing thought in the light of possible germ warfare! Perhaps my experience with polio has made me particularly sensitive on this point. If our epidemic proved anything, it is that germs can survive and get around in subzero temperatures.

Whether the defense of this great area is a strategic "must" has long been debated among even high military officials. Few would deny, however, that its actual possession would be vital to an aggressive enemy. There is too much at stake to think otherwise.

For example, with the shortest air route between our nations and Asia arching over the North Pole, our present important transatlantic routes could be controlled from a few bases in the north. Another consideration: our eyes may not be the only ones focused on the strategic mineral resources of the area. Then, too, a well equipped foreign army accustomed to the problems presented by our terrain would not have too much difficulty transgressing the arctic plains; indeed it might find much to its liking. Important as this region is to us as a potential source of vital materials, it remains a precariously weak link in our national defense.

During the past twenty-five or thirty years many arctic explorers have pointed out the strategic importance of the north. It was not until the beginning of World War II that military officials began to take real interest in the matter. During the war, aircraft were flown across the arctic to Russian bases in Asia and American bases in Europe. Huge but temporary airfields were built near subarctic Churchill and, as Fogbound and I had occasion to know, on Southampton Island. Smaller emergency fields were laid out farther north, and a few more radio stations established along the way. But all this was insufficient. The arctic was considered merely a steppingstone, with no thought that some day the stone might not be there for us to use. Few attempts were made to integrate this area into a future line of defense.

No arctic training, other than that of a "survival course" nature, was inaugurated, and even this applied only to fliers. There was no thought of bringing in troops. When the war ended, the huge airfields were left to disintegrate, like the one we visited at Coral Harbour on Southampton Island.

When the international situation again grew tense, interest revived. But only since 1948 have we been trying—feverishly —to make up for lost time. A weak frontier of some 5,000 miles would have to be strengthened. Installations, equipment and men would have to be adapted to temperatures of sixty-five degrees below zero and hundred-mile-an-hour gales. Problems of transportation, housing, supply, clothing and armament would have to be figured out. A long road lay ahead. We still have a long way to go. But we're learning every step of the way.

At first, lack of research hampered the operations. Structures were erroneously anchored above the permafrost. As a result, foundations broke up, steel beams twisted and houses came tumbling down. The surface layer of soil, consisting mainly of muskeg, is constantly in motion and an arctic house must be floated on top of the permafrost or anchored into it. Also, it should be built as a flexible unit so that it can shift with the soil. Concrete must be of a waterproof type, and the house must be practically airtight to keep out cold and fine drifting snow.

Heating and insulation require much attention. Latest developments show that aluminum foil provides one of the best insulations because it reflects the cold on the outside and bounces back the heat on the inside. All fuel, of course, has to be brought in from the south. Considering that it cost the government $100 to send me one ton of coal in Chesterfield, you can imagine what that involves. Water supply is another problem. Fresh water lakes, not more than eight feet deep, freeze to the bottom in midwinter. Only the deeper lakes can supply water for an army, unless ice is utilized in winter. The use of ice blocks for water is a tedious method, especially for a large group. Nor has the sewage problem been solved satisfactorily, as yet. From all this you can understand that the cost of supplying an army, or even a token force, is staggering. Even more important, it has yet to be proved that a steady flow of supply can be maintained, since there is no possibility of year-round transportation by ship, and air transport can be halted for weeks by arctic storms.

Land transportation of men and machines, which is out of the question on the soggy muskeg of the summer months, isn't so simple in winter either. A few years back, tests were made during operation Musk Ox, when a column of heavy machines and equipment such as bulldozers, snowmobiles and carriers set out for a trip across the snowbound land. Most engines broke down within the first few hundred miles; the snowmobiles were often too short to bridge the gaps in rocks and ice; oil casings froze; caterpillar tractors were smashed; equipment was snowed in during the night and the men suffered immeasurably from the cold. If air support had not been available to fly in supplies and spare engines and parts, the column would have broken down before reaching the real arctic. As it was, operation Musk Ox was abandoned after a few weeks, and much of the equipment left stranded in the arctic wilderness. Although the army learned much from this failure, many of the results could have been predicted by experienced arctic dwellers.

After this, on-the-spot experiments were preceded by more intense research. Scientists in all fields are now actively investigating the area. Bugs are studied to determine whether they carry diseases. Plants are being tested for edibility. Cosmic radiation and meteorology are subject to constant research. Unknown areas are being mapped from the air and uncharted waters slowly explored. In the matter of clothing and equipment, experts are waking up to the fact that laboratory cold chambers cannot accurately reproduce arctic conditions.

More and more field tests are now carried out in the arctic itself. New radar stations draw the warning net slowly tighter. But sunspots often hamper radar and radio transmission. Each year contains several periods of ten or twelve days during which the air waves are useless.

New airfields and landing strips are laid out in many corners of the far north, Resources of the region are under development. Because the Laurentian Shield, which covers most of the arctic, has yielded important uranium finds in more southern regions, mining companies are fast reaching out toward the new mineral wealth.

Training has become essential. When you go into the region as a lonely individual, you have to learn the hard way, slowly adapting yourself to the peculiarities of the surroundings. You learn to accept the ways of the Eskimo who has so many generations of experience behind him. But you must know the tricks before you can take the responsibility of sending an army of inexperienced boys into one of the most forbidding territories in the world. Arctic training courses are now in full swing and special selective standards have been developed for arctic service. Men have to be strong and stable to withstand the depressing influence of the long northern night. There are still problems of camouflage to be whipped. Camps and bases are hard to hide, for, in the wide flat spaces of nothingness, structures stand out and can be spotted easily from land or air.

But the jigsaw puzzle of arctic military operation is slowly fitting together. I am still proud that unexpectedly, I was able to contribute to this development.

◆29◆

SHEENIKTOOK INSTRUCTS THE BRASS

Shortly after the year of military awakening in the arctic, Sheeniktook and I made a patrol from Chesterfield to Baker Lake. From there we were flown—dog team and all—to Churchill by the Royal Canadian Air Force. After landing at the military airfield, we hurried into town to dig up supplies for the rest of our trip to Eskimo Point and beyond.

I had no idea that I was the object of an intense search until the following morning. Leaving Sheeniktook to do some trading of his own, I was walking down the street when a shout of, "Oh, *Doctor!*" swung me around. An army major caught up with me and grabbed my hand.

"Doctor," he exclaimed, "we've been looking for you all over town."

I was puzzled. He introduced himself and explained, "We were expecting you to stay at the camp. There's an arctic training course going on, you know, and we'd mighty well like your help."

"Why, of course, but—"

"Our experts had hoped to get some firsthand information from you and your Eskimo."

Whereupon he formally invited us and I agreed to come "as soon as I can locate Sheeniktook."

Together the major and I hunted the elusive Eskimo, whom we finally discovered trading some furs for an alarm clock to bring his invalid wife. I explained what was wanted of us and his quick nod implied that he was taking the new turn of events in stride. We packed our belongings, collected the dogs and moved to the military base.

It seemed that an extensive program had been planned for us. I described his part to Sheeniktook. "You show them how Eskimo builds igloo and does other things," I said.

"What you do?" he asked.

"Talk."

Sheeniktook seemed a bit scornful of my part in the program, which was to consist of lectures on various aspects of arctic life as I had experienced them.

I was apprehensive about these "lectures" myself until I found that what simple information I could give was eagerly absorbed by my uniformed audience. Sheeniktook reveled in the privilege of eating in the officers' mess. As a desirable substitute for his smelly caribou clothing, they allowed him to wear the army dress except for tie, which he voluntarily left off. The novelty of this pleased him immensely. What thrilled him still more was the promise of sleeping in a real bed in the base hospital.

At our first meeting with the program committee it was decided that Sheeniktook would build an igloo for an audience of high military officials. They set an exact time for this feature and, as Sheeniktook had a watch of which he was proud, I showed him the hour and minute for him to begin on his igloo. Considerably impressed by the importance of the role he was to play, he nodded agreement and went off, grinning, to look for some good building snow—a material not too easy to find in subarctic Churchill at any time of year.

I was pleasantly cocktailing with the medical officers when an orderly stormed in to ask where Sheeniktook was. It seemed that nearly 100 officers—including an admiral, not to mention the press and numerous photographers—all were waiting for his demonstration. But he was nowhere in sight.

We jumped up and started a search of the immediate vicinity. No luck! We inquired of everyone we met. No one had seen a uniformed Eskimo without a tie. Expanding our operating radius, we finally found Sheeniktook far out on the other side of the settlement patiently testing snow with a stick.

I boiled over, then simmered down enough for a curt, "But, Sheeniktook, you promised to be back there for the igloo demonstration. What the devil—?"

"I am here," he announced, placidly, explaining that only the snow here was suitable, and now he was ready to give his demonstration of igloo building.

We had to take him back to the camp, where the snow was inferior but the operation within range of the cameras. He was not at all pleased but gloomily started cutting the inferior snow and stacking the blocks as best he could. He cheered up a little on noticing how closely his audience was watching. It ended with his putting on a real show, with movie cameras grinding, reporters and officers taking notes and a staff painter reproducing his every move.

But after a while, being the center of attraction failed to compensate for the extreme brittleness of the snow. When his dome fell apart several times, the officers began to look skeptical. I arose in my place.

"The snow, gentlemen," I said, "has to be just right for a good igloo. I can vouch for that."

The poor man got it finished after a time and was generously applauded.

An argument then arose between the officers. Who was going to sleep in the thing that night? Sheeniktook stared at them in amazement. Who would want to sleep in an igloo when good beds were close by? The officers looked at the matter differently. The admiral and a couple of others won out. That was when Sheeniktook got worried for fear his handiwork would cave in on top of the Big Brass.

For Sheeniktook and me, at least, the igloo would have been the better choice. After a few hours in the hospital ward I awoke in a sweat. Not used to sleeping in a thoroughly heated, closed room—Viola likes cold, fresh air at night even in the arctic—I felt near suffocation. Something drastic had to be done. Then I noticed that Sheeniktook already had done it. Seated on a chair next to his narrow bed, head in hands, and utterly miserable, he looked so ludicrous in a pair of hospital pajamas that I broke out in a guffaw. He grinned a little himself. Without further hesitation, I opened the windows wide and turned off the radiator. We woke up in the morning feeling so refreshed that we paid little attention to the basic English hurled at us by the hospital engineer. He had come to find out what had happened to his thermostats and had discovered our two radiators frozen and leaking all over the floor.

We wandered outside. The igloo inhabitants had not met with disaster during the night. Instead, everyone was practicing cutting snow blocks. While Sheeniktook gave further demonstrations, dramatically tampering with the snow, I found myself pampered by fetes and cocktails and playing the role of a willing authority on arctic affairs.

I answered questions, backing my answers with firsthand experiences and findings. Did cold affect the lungs? The laboratories said no. I said yes, having found that if a person were suddenly exposed to very low temperature, after spending a few hours inside, he invariably had a terrific coughing spell and sometimes coughed up blood.

There was the matter of eyes. I had established beyond doubt that the usual polaroid goggles gave too little protection; that anyone using them more than a few months in the arctic was likely to damage his eyesight for life. Points like these were of practical value and I had a hopeful feeling that my suggestions would be put to good use.

After a few days of this—and having been treated lavishly with camp luxuries—it seemed time to continue our patrol back to Chesterfield by way of Nunnulla and Eskimo Point. When, in an unguarded moment, I suggested that some officers accompany us in order to experience arctic life in the more—or less—raw, and test instruments and equipment, they seemed to have been waiting for just such an invitation.

"Delighted, Doctor!"

"Of course. The very thing!"

So Major Smillie and Captain O'Connel became part of my patrol.

Before leaving next day, the commanding officer of the post called me aside with a worried, "Will you need air support, Doctor?"

On seeing that he was in deadly earnest, I explained tactfully that, having traveled thousands of miles without it, I thought we could take care of ourselves this time without air support. Nevertheless, the question made me realize how few of these officers had ventured into the real arctic. I was the first, perhaps, to offer them a chance to conduct much needed tests in the colder regions of the north. It was surprising to find them so little ready for a journey into the area they were preparing to defend.

Our komatik could hardly carry all the army equipment they assembled for the trip. "Fred Buccolz him travel north," Sheeniktook suggested, indicating a trapper from Nunnulla, whom he had met in Churchill buying supplies. I explained the situation to Fred and found him happy to join our party and share the load with his komatik.

On leaving, we ended our series of demonstrations— Sheeniktook's and mine—in an embarrassing manner. We wanted to show an example of the semi-fan hitch used in the treeless barrens for attaching dogs to a komatik. But we overlooked the scrub spruce and tamarack that cluttered the immediate terrain.

Now, while the semi-fan hitch is practical enough in open spaces where a dog is free to seek his own footing, in a country like this with more vegetation, they must be hitched in a single line. The result of our thoughtlessness was a confused mass of tangled ropes and dogs before we had covered thirty feet. After straightening things out and calling back to the semicircle of amused watchers some inane remarks about "showing you how not to do it," we were on our way.

◆ 30 ◆

THE ROUGH ROAD TO LEARNING

That trip turned out to be most enlightening—at least to me. I have reason to believe that the army men found it worthwhile too. I was impressed again, as I had been many times before, by the ingenuity the Eskimo uses in adapting his mode of living to the climate and physical characteristics of his harsh environment. What impressed me equally was the ignorance the white man shows in trying to adjust himself to arctic conditions by means of newfangled and supposedly "better" ideas.

If our trip demonstrated nothing else, it must have hammered into the army men how impractical some of their desk top theories could be when tested in actual use; and how much had yet to be done if the army was to be adequately prepared for its appointed task.

Their course of instruction was not long starting. The first truth, of which the officers felt painful physical proof, might have been entitled, "Dangers of Misjudging Ice." This lesson took place our first day out, and only a few miles from Churchill at Button Bay.

In order to survive, any traveler in the north must be well acquainted with the peculiarities of the ground he passes over—particularly if that "ground" is ice. I liked to think I had become something of an ice expert myself, yet I usually left final decisions to Sheeniktook. He had an instinct, or hunch, which reinforced his profound knowledge of ice conditions, making it doubly valuable.

Now, after one look at Button Bay, he swung the lead dog around so as to skirt the shore rather than head across the frozen bay.

"Look, Doctor," one of the officers called, "why go so far out of our way. This ice seems at least fifteen inches thick. What more do you want?"

"Ice him bad," Sheeniktook interposed, and stuck to it.

I tried to explain that the ice was probably soft and treacherous; that, although it might be even more than fifteen inches thick it was the kind of ice that contained slushy layers where a man could get trapped. Much better, I said, to travel a few more miles and avoid the risk of breaking through. The ice looked so solid that my argument must have sounded silly to the officers. It would have seemed rather senseless to me when I first arrived at Chesterfield. Since then I had acquired great respect for Sheeniktook's intuitive judgment. But one of the men was hard to convince. He felt it a great loss of time to hug the shore, and asked somewhat curtly why we couldn't cross the bay and be done with it. And I—well, the officers were our guests, in a sense, and I didn't want to appear too arbitrary.

"We'll take a chance, if you like," I said, after some hesitation. With a sullen look, Sheeniktook turned the dogs back onto the ice and we started out. We went along all right for a mile, the two officers wearing jaunty didn't-we-tell-you expressions.

Suddenly I sank into the bay to my hips. Simultaneously, three of the dogs plunged through the thin layer of covering ice and had to swim. That really scared the army men. Cursing myself for having given in, I told them to climb onto the nearer komatik where they would be comparatively safe. Meanwhile, Sheeniktook, grimfaced, had yanked the dogs out, untangled the traces and headed for shore. I felt as relieved as did the officers when we all had solid ground under foot once more. They pressed no further ice suggestions on us the rest of the trip. Which was just as well for my peace of mind because I felt more and more responsibility the farther we got from Churchillian civilization. What would have happened if an entire army had taken that "short cut" across the ice was something I hoped was bothering the officers as it was me.

That afternoon the major sprained his ankle slightly and had to ride on a komatik. He wanted to walk but the going was getting rougher and I advised against it. The weather was much colder now, and both officers were shivering in their new army snowsuits. Despite all the personal discomfort this entailed, no more convincing argument against unsuitable clothing could have been advanced.

The trouble was—and any practical arctic man could have pointed it out, that their specially designed garments contained pockets and zipper closings. If there is one feature to be avoided in the arctic where sharp winds penetrate everything, it is pockets or any other openings in outer clothing. I had already criticized these same garments, as well as newer designs shown me during my talks at the military camp. If many of the listeners doubted my words at the time, I was pretty sure that these two shivering officers would confirm them when they got back.

We camped that night on the open flats and Sheeniktook had a hard time finding good snow for an igloo. In the level plains where high winds often sweep all snow off the bare rocks, this can be a serious problem. Many an Eskimo has died when unable to get snow to build himself a temporary shelter. Whether our two guests believed me when I told them this I do not know, but I noticed that both helped most enthusiastically when at last Sheeniktook found enough snow for an igloo. It was crumbly, though, and not much good. After crawling into the finished igloo and settling down comfortably in our sleeping bags, Sheeniktook glanced up and announced,

"Roof him no good."

The dome did look a little weak. I thought, however, that the constantly lowering temperature would take care of that. Besides, Sheeniktook didn't appear too alarmed. I should have remembered that that was a typical Eskimo trait. He was worried, all right, but didn't feel that the time had come yet to do anything about it.

We had all reached the point where we felt deliciously warm and snug, when he spoke up again:

"Roof not good. Maybe him fall. Better get out!"

We glanced up. The top of the igloo was sagging jeeringly down at us. Grabbing instruments, equipment and supplies, we scrambled out in a hurry and stood miserably in the snow while the Eskimo cut the dome away and covered the top with canvas. Whereupon we piled in once more, nobody feeling very cheerful.

The next arctic lesson began when it appeared that the special sleeping bags of the officers weren't warm enough. Otherwise they were beautiful bags, designed to permit the occupant to jump out of them hastily in case of emergency. But they gave so little protection against the cold that Sheeniktook and I ended up taking the two men in between us to keep them warm.

They suffered a good deal during the trip, yet remained good sports, seriously interested in all the new ideas encountered. They made notes about every move; they sketched and measured and asked hundreds of questions. In the morning when Sheeniktook kneaded some mud balls with which to replace the mud on the runner, inadvertently knocked off by rocks, the captain came running up to measure the exact diameter of the balls.

For winter travel the sled runner of whalebone or wood is coated with a layer of mud about three inches thick and four to six inches wide. Often this mud is hard to find on a trip. The mud is heated in a tub, molded into balls and pushed onto the runner, where it freezes. It is then planed to give a smooth, flexible surface, but a very hard one. After this, many layers of water are run onto the mud and rubbed along it by means of a bit of bearskin. The water, of course, freezes onto the mud, giving a slippery, smooth surface. This is called "mudding" and "icing" a sled and is necessary in midwinter. During a hard trip some mud may fall off and must be replaced. It was the replacing of this mud that brought the captain running.

Fortunately, Sheeniktook kept a sober face, though I could see he was amused at the officers' interest in what to him seemed so insignificant a detail. The captain then proceeded to take elaborate notes on the entire runner/icing problem.

The zeal of these men really surprised me. I felt now that there was no question of their appreciating the things our trip was demonstrating, however unpleasant some of the experiences might be. What disturbed me was that so many basic techniques of arctic survival were not unknown to them but were still overlooked.

Later that day I noticed the major limping more than usual.

"It's nothing, Doctor. The leg feels a bit cold, that's all."

"Let's have a look."

"But—"

"You don't want to lose a leg, do you?" I shot back, with a touch of military harshness which seemed to impress him. When I removed the boot his leg was a dead white. If the flesh turns white that way it usually takes only a few minutes before severe freezing sets in. I had to act quickly. We finally succeeded in restoring the blood circulation, then gave the major boots and leggings of caribou skin.

His army boots, however fine the quality and cut, had been a bit too tight for rugged work—a particularly dangerous condition in the arctic; one that conceivably might render a large body of men wholly useless. I also persuaded the officers to accept other caribou clothing for better protection. I was quite firm now, refusing to take further chances.

Our tests, worked out in conjunction with the army men, uncovered many shortcomings in the instruments and implements they had brought along. For example, their fine army pressure cookers proved impractical because the plastic handles became brittle and broke off in extreme cold. The valves froze up after the steam condensed, causing considerable difficulty in using them and limiting their utility. Preparing one meal was the extent of their usefulness. Then we used other equipment.

Another mistake unexpectedly disclosed was the new gasoline stoves. Beautiful, intricate contraptions, those stoves! But their practical operation was most inefficient. They were typical examples of vital items that failed under strenuous arctic conditions. Many gimmicks and gadgets do not work where there is no mechanic at hand to repair them or replace delicate parts. Equipment must be blunt and simple and foolproof to stand up. So we put one thing after another to severe but normal arctic use. Some of these the officers quickly ruled out. Others they set aside for future study and improvement.

That night a howling wind made the mere thought of an igloo shelter comforting. Such protection would be far more desirable than the tents we carried. But an igloo was out of the question due to lack of snow. Instead, we came at last to a small tumbled down church or chapel, long abandoned and looking strangely out of place on those barren wastes. But by pitching our tents inside the dilapidated structure, we would enjoy the advantages of a double shelter, so to speak. Having put our guests to considerable hardships in the interest of science, I thought a cozy, quiet, long sleep that night would be a real treat.

Next morning, both the captain and major were ready to give up the whole trip and get back to Churchill the best way they could. Anything, they intimated, would be preferable to what they had just been through.

"Not a wink of sleep all night," one of them growled.

"Nor I," the other agreed, red eyed and yawning. "Those damn noises—horrible—simply terrifying! What sort of animals do you raise in these parts, Doctor, anyway?"

Having slept exhaustedly myself, I had heard nothing. Their efforts to imitate the animal cries they had heard stirred some memory in my brain. Then suddenly I knew.

But for the good of the expedition I kept the knowledge of Sheeniktook's incredible snoring strictly to myself.

◆31◆

NOTEBOOK AMMUNITION

That day, however, turned out to be more enjoyable than had seemed likely earlier. The men, better adjusted to the low temperatures by now, could hardly help being impressed by the harsh beauty of the terrain. On the wide plains near Nunnulla, bailiwick of our trapper companion, Fred Buccolz, the fantastic blue of the snow, the serene magnitude of the heaving, endless stretches of wind swept barrenness—all this drew deep breathed admiration from the officers. They never had seen anything quite like this.

All of a sudden they became vitally aware of our dogs. Apparently, it hadn't occurred to them before how efficiently these animals had been doing their job the preceding days. On being informed that the dogs had been towing some 200 pounds apiece for ten-hour periods, they grabbed their notebooks and really went to it.

Toward noon the appearance of a caribou brought further excitement. He was too distant for shooting yet close enough to give the men their first good look at this regal animal. Later, the sight of a wolverine following our caravan made them apprehensive. One moment we saw the wolverine half a mile behind us; an hour later he crossed only a *few hundred yards* in front of us. I told how these vicious creatures could sneak into your tent or igloo during the night and slash your throat with one snap of their powerful jaws.

That evening we reached the camp of Fred Buccolz, near Nunnulla, but not without inadvertently giving the army men an example of how easy it is for even an old timer to get lost up there. When it was apparent to the officers that Fred didn't know just where he was, one of them grew slightly sarcastic.

"I thought they said you trapped around this region, Buccolz," he observed.

"Yep. Had years of it."

"And you can't locate your camp?"

Fred stopped and faced the army man. "Listen, mister. Sounds foolish, maybe. But have you noticed a single identifying landmark for miles back?"

"That's right, I haven't. It's all amazingly monotonous. I'd think you'd have to use your compass."

"Did you ever use one so close to the magnetic pole?"

"Oh, of course. But only as useful as the nearness of the magnetic pole and local ore bodies let it be, eh? I never really thought of that."

The officer said no more because of Fred's growing embarrassment. I was beginning to wonder myself if he'd ever pick up a familiar clue to our whereabouts, when the dark, geometrical form of some sort of man made structure ahead of us stood out against an organdy sky. This was Fred Buccolz' hut and he discovered it just in time to save himself a nervous breakdown due to embarrassment.

Instead, he turned at once into a generous host and insisted on celebrating our arrival with a bottle of rum that he'd been cherishing for a long time.

After supper he showed us his traps and explained the technique of catching the elusive fox. He had been most successful some years back but, like the Eskimos, had felt the impact of decreasing fur prices. Now, no more trapping licenses were being given out to whites, he said, and if a trapper failed to renew his "permission" he lost his trapping privilege for life.

Fred had his license and had always renewed on time, in spite of which the situation was bad—very bad.

"Prices getting lower and foxes getting scarcer," was the way he summed things up.

"Doesn't sound sensible to me," the major broke out, after a pause. "A scarcity of foxes should hold prices up, shouldn't it?"

I couldn't answer that paradox, either. Fred's only solution was a hopeless shrug. All he knew was that nowadays he was having a hard time making a living.

We glanced about the scantily furnished little hut, and appreciated his gift of rum all the more.

The fourth day rose full of new expectation. The two officers were to see their first real Eskimo camp. It was occupied by a rather small band whose chief welcomed us when we reached the place late in the afternoon. Our arrival wasn't exactly unexpected, the mysterious grapevine having projected news of our coming. The result was that a sturdy igloo, just completed, awaited us.

Fortunately, the major had brought tea, tobacco and trinkets, and the gratitude of these friendly folk seemed to assure a warm reception for all army personnel that might follow. Being hungry, Sheeniktook and I appreciated particularly the heaping dishes of fresh caribou meat the Eskimos offered us.

The officers had brought their own army food, mostly in tins, and thereby made another discovery to report back to headquarters. The discovery was that their food, frozen solidly, refused to leave the cans. They dug it out in time but not without convincing themselves that here was something in the line of rations to which no army in the field should be subjected. Previously, they had been favorably impressed with our cooking methods. Now they asked for details—something constructive to offer in their report.

"Well, it was my wife's idea," I told them. "Viola always makes a special stew for us to take out on patrols. What it is is mainly caribou broth with minced caribou meat and dehydrated vegetables added. She puts in a few other nutritious items if she has them. She lets it freeze rock hard"—and I waited for their scribbling pencils to pause—"then with an ax we chop the whole thing into serving size chunks. These we carry along with us in canvas bags—"

"Canvas, you say, Doctor?"

"To save the weight of heavy metal containers."

"There's a point," the major looked at the captain and nodded. "Then how do you prepare a meal on the trail?"

"All we have to do is boil some water, throw the blocks of food in and wait a few minutes. I can assure you it makes a hearty, well balanced meal. This method," I added, "might not be practical for a whole army, but it certainly would solve the food question for small patrols."

I left the officers with their notebooks and went out to see if there was any sickness in camp.

Later that evening our hosts put on a drum dance and delighted the army men with this mysterious ceremony. Still later I rounded up some medical cases that needed looking after and found the major, himself a medical officer, eager to assist. He became much interested not only in the simple methods of treatment I had learned to use up there, but especially in the patience of the Eskimos, and the blind trust they put in the Kabloona doctor.

In fact, the major would have stayed longer had not the army arranged to send a plane to Eskimo Point next day, pick up the two officers there and fly them back to Churchill. We were still about fifty miles south of the rendezvous—which meant a strenuous day's work ahead. The trip was made rougher by leading us through the beginnings of a formidable storm, despite which we made our fifty miles and arrived at Eskimo Point with army accuracy. I think I heard sighs of both relief and regret as the two officers climbed aboard the transport plane to report on their trip "into the arctic" with the Kabloona doctor and his temperamental Eskimo.

I felt that the expedition was really quite a success, providing the army—or a part of it—with a chance to experience some of the hardships and basic techniques of arctic travel. It had been possible to test and evaluate a great deal of equipment. The recommendations made by the two officers on the basis of their firsthand experiences already has changed numerous important items that had been accepted erroneously as suited to service in the north. There is no doubt that that hastily planned little expedition helped to improve the equipment and general preparation of the untold legions of soldiers now secretly roaming those frigid wastes.

The vital importance of the region has at last been fully recognized. A long neglected line of defense is now uppermost in everyone's mind. So the army continues to plan, prepare, and learn.

Progress is slow and much has yet to be accomplished in order effectively to defend that strategic outpost of North American civilization. The frontier is still 5,000 miles long; still virtually unprotected. For the next few years we can only hope that those who argued against the case for arctic defense can afford to keep on saying, "We told you so!"

✦ 32 ✦

MAGISTRATE'S DIARY

That the arctic is a land of unsolved mysteries is reflected in these random sections taken from my diary. Oolik and Jim Farrel are typical of the characters with whom a medical health officer deals if his job, like mine, includes justice of the peace and coroner.

February 8

Today Sergeant Hamilton reported rumors among the Eskimos that Oolik's second wife was dead. Oolik is the Eskimo whose first wife "disappeared" under peculiar circumstances last year, and the sergeant has been keeping a suspicious eye on him. A few months ago, he (Oolik) remarried Eskimo fashion—without registration or religious ceremony. He lives about sixty miles from here and because we've had a snowstorm for three days, I'll not be able to do much about it before next week.

February 14

As medical health officer I received a radio telegram from Jim Farrel, a white trapper in the Kazan River district. Said he was gravely ill and feared he might "go mad." He gave a number of symptoms not indicative of mental illness. He also seemed to speak of a blood disease. However, there were many

183

cosmic disturbances today and I'm not sure the message came over correctly.

I mention his fears only because insanity was brought into the picture. If complications develop later, our records will carry this information.

I hear that one of the Fathers visited Oolik's camp. He should be back soon. Then I will verify the rumors about Oolik's wife.

February 20

It is true, Oolik's second wife is dead. Cause of death not ascertained. The matter calls for further investigation.

March 6

Weather permitting, I will make a patrol with Sergeant Hamilton to investigate the Oolik death. We leave tomorrow.

Another radiogram from Jim Farrel. This time it really sounds like a serious blood disease. I must take steps to have him removed from the area. He married an Eskimo girl several years back and has, I believe, six children.

March 9

After a difficult trip we reached Oolik's camp. Couldn't find out where grave was. Eskimos hate to come near graves and refuse to assist in disinterment. Finally found body, frozen and well preserved, under a great deal of snow. The woman was bruised and scratched, which indicates maltreatment. Also very thin, probably due to neglect. However, an initial autopsy showed that she may have died from T.B.

Decided to send body to Winnipeg for further autopsy pending possible criminal investigation. Oolik, calm and reserved under it all, will be taken along to Chesterfield and kept busy around the community so that he can't get away.

March 19

An Eskimo has been killed near Wager Bay, apparently during or following a drum dance. The R.C.M.P. will investigate. Obviously one of those cases of murder inspired under the hypnosis of the dance. Little can be done. If police discover murderer they will undoubtedly bring him in for trial.

I have asked that Jim Farrel be removed from his camp. He must be sent to Churchill or Winnipeg for medical care.

April 15

The police returned today from Wager Bay with the Eskimo who has admitted killing that other man during a drum dance. As far as they have been able to establish, the murdered man challenged him to shoot, claiming that it would not hurt him. Such boasts are common during these ceremonial dances and they can often be fatal. This is a typical case of conditional hypnosis. These drum dances are dangerous. I will make a formal request to Ottawa, asking that a court be sent in this summer, to try the case. The murderer will be employed by the R.C.M.P. during the rest of the winter. He has been forbidden to leave the community. I don't see how the man can be convicted. What is justice in a case like this? He barely understands what happened. I don't know what the Eskimos themselves would do under the circumstances.

April 26

A white man has disappeared from a Hudson's Bay Company trading post in the Back River district. No explanation offered. Local R.C.M.P. investigating.

May 5

Eskimos say that one of Jim Farrel's small daughters is gone. Farrel came through a few weeks ago and went south to The Pas where, I understand, he found work. I definitely established his illness and recommended that he be treated in a hospital on the outside. His daughter disappeared shortly after he left his camp. I had wanted him taken away by mounted police, but no one could go and he came here to Chesterfield under his own steam, although medical service paid for his trip. Beside my above mentioned diagnosis I could not find much wrong with him. Since he seemingly has settled down in The Pas, I believe that he became obsessed with the dark winter months, as happens so often. If so, his previous claim of madness carries more weight and this must be investigated immediately. The R.C.M.P. will make a patrol to Farrel's camp and try to find the girl, although I don't know whether they should look for a girl or a *body*. Maybe the Eskimos know more about this. Farrel's wife is a native.

May 16

I have learned that another attempt to find an escaped criminal has failed. An Eskimo killed a man thirty years ago and was arrested, but escaped in a storm. Several patrols have since been sent out to find him. He is believed to be roaming around near Beverly Lake. The last patrol searched that area but did not find him. Yet, the Eskimos know that he's alive and speak of him among themselves. The Eskimo grapevine may warn him whenever a patrol sets out.

May 26

Now a *second* man has disappeared from the Hudson's Bay Company Back River post. A bad area! This time it was an Eskimo, which seems to rule out the possibility of the first man who vanished having been murdered by a native—unless this Eskimo himself was the criminal. No explanation so far, and no trace of either man. They have had terrific blizzards up there, but no one travels alone in a storm and it seems strange that single persons would get lost. The local police continue investigating.

June 4

A small time explorer named Andrew Milford had come to Chesterfield and reported some of his gasoline and implements stolen by small group of Eskimos up in the Repulse Bay area. Coming on them while exploring the Rae Isthmus, he camped with them two days. Third morning Eskimos were gone—and so were two barrels of gasoline, some food supplies and a few implements. Milford asks that no action be taken; says they were very poor and certainly had great need for what they took. He just wanted to report the incident so others could be warned. It is not known that bands of Eskimos reside in this area. These people may have come from farther north in search of caribou.

Some of these Eskimos are very poor and have inadequate clothes or housing. If they miss the caribou migration they starve. I have suggested that we try to find this little band and help them with relief.

June 7

The Eskimos now say Jim Farrel's wife and baby have also disappeared. Impossible so far for a police patrol to go in and investigate, but now it must be done. I have reported this and asked that Farrel be kept under observation.

June 10

Well, Oolik has married again; at least, is living with an Eskimo girl in the igloo village here. Autopsy reports from laboratory indicated nothing definite so that, like the death of his first wife, that of his second remains unsolved. The police will keep an eye on him here. He is still not allowed to leave.

June 19

I think that the R.C.M.P. of the arctic has an anniversary this year. The first mounted police post in this area was established in 1908 near Fullerton Point. Because of shifting concentrations of Eskimos, this post has been abandoned. However, I can imagine what it was like when the first mounties came to live in the arctic. In later years the force established posts all through the arctic, many in completely isolated areas where the mounties live for months without contact with the outside world.

There has been a marked decrease in crime in this area. The force has contributed considerably to our knowledge of the region, and its official record is dotted with instances of individual heroism.

As a magistrate, I want to report here how much I appreciate the cooperation of this force. The individual members are men of exceptional standing who add to their keen sense of duty a real human interest in the region. As sole "arm of the law" in the arctic, they are charged with varied responsibilities and always perform their duties with the greatest care. That's why they get favorable results.

June 21

A police patrol, visiting Jim Farrel's camp, found no traces of any member of Jim's family. They looked for graves, but the ground was too hard for digging. Weather getting milder now, I'll go there myself next week. Hope the ground will have thawed partially. Because these people seldom get lost, what we must now look for are *graves*.

June 28

Accompanied by Constable Anderson of the R.C.M.P., I have been at the site of Farrel's camp since yesterday. We searched the countryside for graves, found none. Before leaving Chesterfield, I received a report that Farrel's daughter was supposed to have drowned in the lake nearby. Don't know whether this information came from the father himself or from the Eskimos. We will continue search tomorrow but must return if not successful.

June 29

This afternoon, digging deep, we hit a small wooden box, too small, I thought, to hold a body. The box was disinterred from a depth of about six feet. Whoever buried it must have had a job digging down that far in the frozen ground. Witnessed by Constable Anderson I opened the box. Found the partly decomposed body of a little girl. The head and limbs had been severed from the torso. Bruises and scratches visible. Box closed in presence of the constable and sealed. It will be taken to Chesterfield, then sent south for police autopsy.

Difficult to say what happened. If child drowned, body could have been bruised by ice. Wolves may have torn it apart before it was found. Unless knife or bullet wounds are detected there will be no proof of violence. But why was it buried *far deeper than customary?* The graves of Farrel's wife and/or baby have never been found. Return to Chesterfield tomorrow.

July 10

The wreckage of an airplane, lost six months ago, has been found on Melville Peninsula. The aircraft, a Norseman, was piloted by Frank Vaughn. A Doctor Bowes, initials unknown, was Frank's passenger. It has been established that the body of the pilot was in the plane which crashed but did not burn. No traces of the doctor have been found. It may be that he was wounded or, unharmed, had wandered off to find help. Because the nearest settlement, if indeed any Eskimos are in the neighborhood, would be about sixty miles away, he must have perished. No personal effects found.

July 22

A report says Farrel came back today after being away a week. No one knows where he went. I have again requested close surveillance.

August 9

Some Padlei Eskimos came in today and said that Farrel's wife and baby have been seen near Angikuni Lake, traveling alone. That leaves only the daughter's death unexplained. How the woman and baby traveled that far is a complete riddle. She must have had assistance of some kind for she had no dogs.

I have radioed this information and asked that Farrel be kept under observation until we receive a final report on the autopsy of the little girl. Meanwhile we must find his wife and bring her in for questioning. I have already asked that patrols be sent out to get her and her baby.

August 11

Telegram in from Hudson's Bay Company Back River post. *Both disappearances there remain a mystery.*

◆ 33 ◆

MEDICAL PATROL REPORT

Chesterfield—Baker Lake—Churchill—Eskimo Point—
Chesterfield and intermediate points

On February 5, at an early hour after extensive preparation, the M.H.O., Eskimo guide Sheeniktook and a team of eight huskies pulling a thousand pound komatik[1] load, set out northwest for Baker Lake. To make a journey of such magnitude in February requires considerable preparation and attention to the most minute details. The dogs have a substantial load as it is necessary to carry enough equipment to erect dwellings, maintain nutrition and do medical, dental and minor surgical work.

The first day was clear and cold with temperatures ranging to forty-five below with little wind. A few camps of Chesterfield Inlet Eskimos were visited and one family d.d.t. ed[2]. Dental work was also done and advice given by interpreter on the changing of igloo when the one became dirty. After a lunch of tea and biscuits, which is difficult to eat while wearing heavy caribou gauntlets, we were on our way. Before us stretched one hundred seventy-five miles of uninhabited waste. But since the dogs were breaking in fast and the traveling was good, our spirits were high.

By the end of the first day, we were about thirty-five miles from Chesterfield. The Eskimo had been so exuberant about our

190

good progress that he miscalculated the time and had to build most of the igloo by starlight and candlelight. This being my first experience with a snow house, it was with more than a little trepidation that I awaited its completion and door cutting so that I might enter and view our temporary home. Later, after our double sleeping bags were laid out on and surrounded by caribou skins and our caribou stew consumed, our snow house seemed fine. As this igloo was well constructed, the central zone reached forty degrees above zero—a marked contrast to forty below zero outside and therefore, comparatively warm. The worst part of the day was undressing and crawling into the sleeping bag, which certainly causes shivers lasting for minutes.

At 5:30 A.M. we arose and lit the candles. The stoves had been lit about fifteen minutes prior to our climbing out of the sleeping bags in order to warm the igloo a little. By 7:00 we had iced the runners[3], loaded our equipment, hitched the dogs and were on our way. The sun had not risen, but in the Arctic at sunrise and sunset, the reflected light is as powerful, and at these times it is easy to see objects.

Again the day was fine, but at 2:00 P.M. the inevitable northwest wind began in earnest. By 4:00 P.M. we were facing directly into it and forced to stop and build our house. By bedtime, the wind had built up to forty or fifty miles per hour, but we were comfortable in our home. The guide had to go out and put up a snow barrier around the dogs, which cuts down on their heat loss leaving more energy for pulling instead of heating. The husky is an exceptional animal and, without question, irreplaceable on the trail. Small kindnesses to these supposedly vicious animals are repaid by them a thousandfold before a trip is finished.

February 7, the third morning, found the sun bright but the wind still blowing furiously. Consequently, at 10:00 A.M., we were still seated in our igloo. Sheeniktook, the typical Eskimo in philosophy, was content to sit and wait. But the M.O., a fairly typical Kabloona, was showing more and more impatience when it became apparent that miles were being wasted for every hour we sat. Finally at noon, the wind velocity dropped a little, and I, impatiently but unwisely, ordered our departure. It was impossible to ride as the dogs could scarcely pull the load into the wind and had to be continually coaxed along. After four hours, we halted and built the third snow house. Our faces were slightly frozen and our bodies chilled but the double caribou clothing was doing the job that only *it* can do.

Weather now became the main topic—will the wind blow or will it stop—always the wind. Forty below and properly clothed with no wind is only nippy; forty below and a twenty-five mile per hour wind is vicious. The fourth day, the wind was still blowing strongly. Since we had only covered an estimated sixty miles of our two hundred twenty-five mile trip with no signs of the wind abating, we decided that we would wrestle with the gales if the dogs could maintain their pulling power against them.

The seventh morning found us fifty-five miles from Baker Lake after working through extensive ice fields and open water areas. The wind and snow was still in great evidence, having only decreased for a few hours in five and a half days. At this point, we were to encounter a camp where a boy had pneumonia. However, after hunting for two hours, we couldn't find any trace of his people and we had to continue on. Soon after we discovered that the feet of one of our best dogs had become frozen during the night[4]. The animal tried to continue, but when he began to bleed from the bowel with extreme reluctance, I gave the order to shoot him.

The day that followed was the bitterest yet—the temperature was fifty-two below zero officially with winds of twenty-five miles per hour. It was absolutely impossible to face this and we had our backs to it all day. We were determined to reach the post that day, and at 8:00 P.M., we saw a point of light in the distance which was the army light on a bulldozer. At 9:30 P.M., thoroughly fatigued, we arrived at the community of Baker Lake covering fifty-five miles on Wednesday, February 11.

Next morning after a good night's sleep at the Hudson Bay Company, I started work. Thirty-one Eskimos were examined and treated. Eleven teeth were pulled and two filled, one delivery attended and one heart condition treated. Medical work was done for practically everyone in the community including the whites. Two cases requiring major surgery were advised to come to Chesterfield. One case of tuberculosis was found. Medical supplies were checked, a number of complaints attended to and ironed out on the spot. The Army signals were visited and their new quarters found to be clean and bright—a marked improvement over last year. After contacting the R.C.A.F., H.Q. Winnipeg, they kindly agreed to allow me to take my guide and dog team to Churchill in order to make a patrol up the west coast of the Hudson Bay.

---

1. Komatik—a strong travel sled pulled by a team of dogs.
2. D.D.T. ed—d.d.t. powder shaker. Dusted on body and sleeping bags to kill lice.
3. Icing runners—the bottom of the wood runners of the sled were coated with mud. This mud in turn was coated with layers of water which froze immediately on the mud. The runners were iced and the sled slipped easily along.
4. On intensely cold nights, sick, old and pregnant dogs were usually protected in the igloo tunnel entrance. Unfortunately, due to my inexperience, our old dog was not so protected.

✦34✦

OUTPOST PATROL

That entry in my diary about the Eskimo killed in a frenzied drum dance recalled other bizarre things I had heard about in the remote Wager Bay region—and particularly about the almost legendary area north of Wager Bay to the Gulf of Boothia.

Here, in a few widely scattered camps, dwelt the Central Eskimos, a band reportedly quite different from others. They had been influenced very little by our civilization. I was told that the entire area never contained more than about twenty white men at any one time. For all that—perhaps because of it—they were said to be in better shape than their brethren of the Kazan River district farther south. In fact, they were still largely self-sufficient.

Because few caribou migrate so far north, these Central Eskimos lived mainly on sea food, clothing themselves in seal skins rather than caribou fur. The amount of seal products they exchanged with the southern Eskimos for caribou hides was insignificant.

Although white infiltration was spearheaded by the missionaries—the clergy still forming a majority of the few white settlers—I understood that the Central Eskimos either adhered to their own religious beliefs or lived according to their own distorted interpretations of white teachings. They were said to have many superstitions, and often to show hostility to visitors. On our first unforgettable train trip north to Churchill on the

Muskeg Express, Viola and I had caught the overtones of this in frequent references to "when Mr. Brown was almost attacked by those Eskimos."

In the nearly three years that had passed since that train trip, details of one white man's near death and the Brown incident had accumulated to enlarge and color the picture. As an official of the Hudson's Bay Company, Mr. Brown, it seemed, was making an inspection trip through part of this little known area. One night he and his guide were camping very close to a band of these Lord Mayor Bay Eskimos when, shortly after their arrival, one of the children of the band died.

A few hours later both men were awakened to hear angry and guttural voices close by their camp. It was not too long before Brown and his guide realized that they were being chosen as the center of attraction for the so called knife or spear dance. Recalling the situation of another white man who had recently passed through the area and had almost lost his life in the spear dance, Brown and his companion harnessed their dogs and left at once as fast as the dogs would go. Their retreat was none too soon, as frenzied cries and beating drums began to increase in tempo and echo over the moonlit frozen wastes.

The explorer who had passed through at another time was not as fortunate. His guide was away seal hunting when a child in the camp died. The white man, hearing a furor, stepped out to see for himself what it was all about. Instantly he was encircled by Eskimos armed with harpoons. They began to dance around the man, meanwhile jabbing toward him threateningly with their weapons. Not understanding the dialect of the district the man had not the slightest idea what the trouble was.

Soon the jumping and dancing developed into a sort of ceremonial ritual. The sharp harpoon points, thrusting ever closer, began to touch, then actually pierce the white man's clothes. Just when death seemed inevitable, his Eskimo guide returned from hunting seals. The guide stopped an instant in amazement, and gesticulated, and managed to catch the attention of the maddened crowd. The Eskimos halted and stared about them as if awakened from a trance. There was a long discussion, following which they slowly dispersed.

After getting hold of himself a little, the explorer managed
to ask the guide what if anything, he had done to make the
Eskimos want to kill him.

"No want to kill—not *quite,*" was the enigmatic reply.
Further explanation came by degrees. When a child died, the
Eskimos assigned its death to bad spirits. And who but the new
arrival could have brought evil spirits into the camp? In accor-
dance with age old tradition, they had hoped to drive the
demons away from those possessed by them through the ancient
method of the spear dance. There was always a chance, the
guide admitted, that the Eskimos might become overexcited and
really kill the white man. It was a risk one took when venturing
among Central Eskimos.

That was the story of Brown, Burwash and other white
travelers of the region, parts of which Viola and I had picked
up, largely garbled, on the Muskeg Express three years before.

Although my own records since then had included several unsolved disappearances in that wilderness north of Wager Bay,
there were three reasons why I wanted to make a patrol into
those parts. First, Dr. Rawson, my predecessor, had not had the
opportunity to do medical work there, so that it presented almost
a new field for medical examinations and immunizations.
Second, the few patients that I had treated by radio were due for
a much needed checkup. Third, a message had come through
from remote Igloolik Island indicating that a missionary was
seriously ill there and should be flown out.

Viola knew as much about these mysterious tribesmen as I,
but had the fortunate gift of placing my calling above the
personal feeling of either of us.

"Anyhow, I'm thankful you have Fogbound piloting the
plane," she announced, when that detail had been arranged.

I outlined our course on the chart. "Here's our headquarters,"
I said, pointing to Repulse Bay, at the foot of Melville Peninsula, some 250 miles northeast of Chesterfield "as the plane
flies."

Two hundred miles northwest of Repulse Bay was a mission
known as Pelly Bay. "This," I explained, with my best lecturing
pose, "is only about 200 miles southeast of the north magnetic
pole."

"Oh," said Viola, more concerned with people than poles. "How about this sick missionary?"

"He's at Igloolik Island. Right here, at the top of Melville Peninsula, 250 miles northeast of our Repulse Bay headquarters, Repulse, Pelly and Igloolik. There's work to be done at all three. I wouldn't feel right not visiting them once before quitting this medical job."

But I wondered privately just how these people would react to a Kabloona doctor and his urges to vaccinate them against evil spirits of a more tangible kind. The patrol should at least be interesting.

Fogbound and I took off one very cold day in late March. Our flight across Wager Bay was rugged, although we succeeded in avoiding several small storms. But the waste areas beneath us failed to put me at ease, even flying with Fogbound. The ice was rough, with many pressure ridges, streaks and humps of snow showing where the wind had whipped a pattern into the white mass. The coast was steep and rocky, bare stone visible in many places and snow filled crevasses ominously showing their raw, unfriendly edges.

Once a bear, disturbed by the noise of our engine, galloped off across the snowscape with weighty scorn. Peaks of the Prince Albert Mountains were faintly visible in the distance.

Landing on the ice in a small inlet near Repulse Bay, we were welcomed by Sergeant Hamilton, who had been at the post a few days to register the Eskimos for family allowances and old age pensions. We were doubly welcome because our plane brought all the supplies for distribution among the needy.

The Repulse Bay post was a pinpoint huddle of desolation compared with the size and "magnificence" of my own Chesterfield. A mission! A Hudson's Bay Company store! Little else could be seen save some Eskimo igloos. Here was a real outpost of civilization, planted hesitantly by people ready to fall back should the opposing forces prove too strong. I had the odd thought that a cautious child had pushed its toys toward a playmate, then remained alert and fearful, ready to reach out a grabbing hand if they seemed in danger of being snatched up.

It was the Eskimos, of whom there were quite a few about, who made the place seem a little more cheerful. I started examining the patients and checking the healthy ones as well. These

Eskimos were a bit darker than the ones I was accustomed to. The men in particular had more pronounced Mongoloid features. They showed the little tuft of hair on the chin, the tendencies toward a mustache. Most had a dark blue pigmented zone near the base of the spine, characteristic of the Mongolian races.

One man interested me especially. Years before, it seemed, the explorer Rasmussen had picked him out as one of the few pure-blooded Eskimos he had ever come across. I found him rather tall but a trifle slighter than the others, his skin very dark and his features beautifully carved. He was built more harmoniously, too, than his fellows.

I discovered quickly that walking around the little settlement was a hazardous business. Contrary to police regulations, all Eskimos let their dogs run around freely. As a result I was frequently surrounded by a growling pack of wild looking dogs that made me mighty uncomfortable. No R.C.M.P. post existed at Repulse Bay and no one paid much attention to the minor regulations, even though a police sergeant happened to be there on registration business.

I boarded with the Hudson's Bay Company manager and set up a clinic in their store. It made a good place for collecting blood samples to be sent to Ottawa for general research. No one could have been more cooperative than the subjects themselves, who submitted patiently to vaccinations. Detecting one serious T.B. case, I isolated the man and decided to fly him out on our way back.

Fogbound had never landed at Pelly Bay, our next "port of call" and had misgivings about the terrain. The plan was for him to fly several trips from Repulse Bay carrying the Pelly Bay people's quota of supplies.

"I can get in somehow," he had assured me beforehand, "but I want to get out too."

"What's the answer?"

The answer was to send an Eskimo on ahead to Pelly Bay to explain how they must lay out an airstrip pending our arrival there. As Sergeant Hamilton wanted to register the Pelly people, Fogbound agreed to fly him in first. Later, he would take some of the Repulse Bay mission fathers who were anxious to inspect the place. On the last of these ferry trips I would go in myself.

It all seemed quite simple when at last Fogbound and the sergeant took off and soon became a black speck in the northwest sky. On their safe return, hours later, the sergeant looked grimly amused, but Fogbound was furious.

It wasn't the oil seal that had broken while they flew over the Prince Albert Mountains, necessitating a precarious landing and temporary repairs made with a piece of cardboard Fogbound found in his pocket. That was more or less routine with him. But when he took off again, looking forward to an easier landing on a well prepared airstrip at Pelly Bay, he was badly disappointed. The Pelly Bay Eskimos were so little interested in white men and their flying machines that not only had they carelessly laid out the new airstrip in a *cross wind position* but had done such a slipshod leveling job that the little plane, bouncing fiercely over the rough ground, ran into considerable damage and all but cracked up.

The fuming Fogbound was a sight to remember as he stormed through the Repulse community yelling at the amazed populace to help him collect all the shovels in the place.

"I'll make the goddamn airstrip myself," he roared, "if I have to shovel every goddamn native under in the process!"

Ordinarily, Fogbound was not what you'd call a profane man.

◆35◆

FATHER HENRY'S FLOCK

When on his last trip he flew me to the Pelly Bay mission, it was difficult to imagine what the airstrip was like before Fogbound gave it his personal attention. The ice surface was still bad enough to bounce us dangerously so that the tips of our wings knocked off some bags placed on heaps of snow along the runway. We came to rest at last.

I sat still a moment for fear we might zoom up into the air once more. Then, crawling out, I looked around me and said to the pilot, "Where's the post?"

He motioned vaguely. "Quite a way from here, Doc. They've been transporting our supplies by komatik. Be here with their dogs in a few minutes and drive us over. They're a funny bunch."

The Eskimos who finally arrived with their komatiks struck me as rather haughty and reserved. I have seen the same reservation in whites who, stiffly polite, fancy themselves a cut above the average. Nevertheless, they treated me with considerable respect as being their first white doctor of this era. I was reminded, however, of Dr. John Rae who was graduated from Edinburgh University as a surgeon over 100 years before. He is said to have walked more than 23,000 miles in the course of arctic and subarctic expeditions while a member of the illustrious Hudson's Bay Company. In 1854, Rae met a group of Eskimos at Pelly Bay and found that they had some items of Franklin's unfortunate expedition, and could reluctantly advise of the death of Franklin and his men.

In my wildest fancies I never had expected to see Eskimos dressed like these in front of me—wide, bell bottomed trousers standing out two feet from the leg and open at the bottom. They were just the thing for "Pinafore," but hard to understand in a land where wind and cold must be kept out, not let in. Their owners wore them with pride, maintaining that they enabled them to run faster. This seemed hardly possible, with the big flaps of loose material getting in the way at every step. As our guides said, their claim was probably a joke meant for the Repulse Eskimos, because the Pelly Bay people felt that they could get around farther and faster than their friends on the coast. My own opinion is that fashion alone was responsible for the grotesque mode.

Our route from Fogbound's so-called airstrip to the settlement was curiously marked by beacons built of rocks and topped by caribou antlers. In a region where caribou are scarce, the Eskimos apparently attached special significance to the display of trophies from farther south. They looked incongruous—those huge antlers perched high above the landscape, silhouetted against the cold gray sky.

One outstanding physical feature peculiar to the Pelly Bay settlement was that, unexpectedly planted among the igloos, were three stone buildings neatly put together from local rocks. They dated back fifteen years to the time Father Henry, the Roman Catholic missionary, arrived and singlehandedly built the mission house and two storage places out of this material.

I can testify to one thing. The buildings, cold and damp, were none too practical. But the complete absence of wood had presented the father with a choice between an igloo and a stone structure. He chose the latter—and it almost cost him his life. A stone house of this type was so unusual in the arctic that when he started building these, the Eskimos thought one of their age old mercy killings quite suitable for anyone crazy enough to build with stone. It required considerable time and lung power for the father to convince them of his sanity, his good intentions and the value of his religious message.

Those gray, rectangular structures will long remain symbols of his courage and perseverance.

I found Father Henry himself a lean, youngish man with a reddish growth of beard and the absent look that comes to people who live long in isolation. Looking at him, I wondered if perhaps he hadn't stayed a little too long. He was terribly shy, and he felt so much one with his people that he was painfully uncomfortable among us who had burst in on him so suddenly. Not even the family allowance supplies we brought overcame his reticence.

"These provisions and supplies should help, Father," I said, cheerfully, in an effort to thaw him out.

The attempt fell flat.

He eyed the supplies indifferently. I found out later that he had had them stored on top of his buildings, as if to put their evil influence as far away as possible.

"He doesn't act as if his people needed the stuff," I observed to Fogbound, when we found what he had done.

"Nor needed any other interference from white outsiders," Fogbound added, and shrugged.

Yet in many respects Father Henry proved helpful and hospitable. His main building, where he insisted I must stay, was largely used as an assembly hall for religious meetings. He had reserved for himself only a tiny kitchen—living room/bedroom cubicle somewhat crowded and cluttered. Pieces of equipment mingled with bedding, furs and many undefined items.

We had been in there only a few minutes when we were actually shaking with the cold. Noticing this at last, the father hastily threw some seal oil and coal into his old cast iron stove. I suspected that he rarely used it for himself as he was accustomed to sharing the hardships of his flock.

With the seal oil-coal mixture going full blast, the stove soon got white hot and we had to peel off our parkas, then layers of underlying clothing in rapid succession. The trouble was that the father paid no attention to unimportant creature comforts such as warmth, so that, after another twenty minutes the fire had stopped roaring and the little room started to get cold again. As the temperature fell, we gradually reclothed ourselves, ending by wriggling back into our parkas. That was what we were doing when our host again noticed our predicament, raised his eyebrows and started the whole heating operation all over again. There was no halfway point about that stove. Its motto might have been "All or nothing." So it was more seal oil—peeling— cooling—dressing—seal oil—peeling—cooling and so on. That was the heating cycle all during the days we were there.

The church part of the building had its walls decorated with pictures, though only a few were of a religious nature. Most of the space was taken up with photographs of members of the community. Loving snapshots, these Eskimos took pride in viewing themselves pinned up on the wall. The father knew his congregation well; knew that such a gallery furnished harmless, good natured fun since the Eskimos liked to tease one another over physical peculiarities. Big ears, crooked noses, pot bellies, lack of chin—these were typical. And the people excelled in the art of creating nicknames derived from anything unusual, whether a somewhat lumpy posterior, a hammer toe or a broken nose.

As I had long since discovered, all whites in the arctic are nicknamed as soon as they arrive, and are known to the Eskimos by that given name as long as they stay in the region. Since many of these names are embarrassing to their involuntary owners, they become a source of amusement among the whites.

But the Eskimos don't spare themselves either. The photo gallery on the church walls in Pelly Bay served their love of this kind of humor to perfection. Seldom did I hear spontaneous bursts of laughter without tracing them to some group of Pelly Eskimos standing around the mission house merrily chatting about the candid camera shots of themselves pinned on the church walls.

Gathering his flock around him, Father Henry explained my purpose in coming, and, after he had added his own endorsement of the project, turned to me with the suggestion that I start my work at once.

After immunizing them against smallpox, diphtheria and whooping cough, I finally got around to individual cases. Some of these had eye trouble, some frostbite. Serious illness was rare, yet I found some.

"These two boys," I told the father, "are pretty sick. They ought to be in a hospital."

"I know," he nodded. "If you can take them back when you leave, I'll arrange it with their families."

Besides being sick, one of the boys had a club foot which, of course, had never been attended to. Considering the custom of mercy killing, the father probably had been responsible for keeping this cripple alive. Perhaps his own narrow escape from being killed as a crazy person when building the stone structures left him sensitive on that point.

We had our meals at the mission and I shall never forget the first one. The father had cooked fish for us and while I was eating mine with all the enthusiasm I could muster for so haphazardly a prepared dish, I noticed that he refrained from eating any himself. But every few minutes he would slip away from the table and disappear into an adjoining room. My curiosity grew until at last I bent over far enough to see what he was doing. In his hideaway back there he too was eating fish—but eating them raw.

He had taken over this Eskimo habit but at the same time found that he couldn't bring himself to demonstrate it in front of us. The more I saw of Father Henry the more I understood how thoroughly he had integrated himself with his Eskimos. All he really wanted now was to live their simple life. The entire time we were at the post it was clear that he was only waiting for a chance to join a group of his hunters going to Lord Mayor Bay. He must have been badly frustrated by the dictations of hospitality which caused him to postpone the trip, rugged as it would have been this time of year.

The night of our arrival, at his polite insistence, I slept in the father's bed and found later that he had lodged in an igloo with some of his Eskimo friends. I slept until about six in the morning. Suddenly, an unearthly "mooing" sound seemed for a moment to form a prolongation of the disquieting dream which the strange atmosphere of the place had given me. Half-awake, I leaped out of bed and stood in the midst of the paraphernalia which cluttered the cubicle, my muscles taut, prepared to face the worst.

Had the Eskimos, for all their polite aloofness, decided to dispose of the Kabloona doctor who had come to stick them with needles and take their cripples away?

Fuller awareness in me of a newly awakened world showed that the weird "mooing" noises emanated from Father Henry himself. He was calling his flock to an early mass!

Soon the sounds of bells and prayer reached me from the other side of the building where the missionary-turned-Eskimo was telling about the white man's God. A queer feeling came over me at hearing the proceedings taking place so far from the land in which this belief had originated—and only a short distance from the north magnetic pole.

Walking around the settlement after finishing my medical work that day, I came across the largest igloo I have ever seen. At first it looked like a rather high hill, only more symmetrical. I went over to investigate and saw the top of a ladder sticking out near the summit of the hump. Up the incline I crawled for a closer look. The ladder was about twenty feet long and led down through a hole in the roof of a huge snowhouse.

The space within seemed really tremendous. This giant igloo with its twenty-five-foot inside diameter, had been built some time before for a special religious celebration and had stood empty ever since. From a little distance the snowdrifts which partly covered it caused it to look more like a hill than an igloo. The construction of such a dome must have been a staggering job. I turned away with even greater respect for the father and his charges than I had felt before.

On our return flight to Repulse Bay we had to take along a great amount of furs. More than half the cabin was packed solid from roof to floor. Little space remained back of the furs for Father Pierre, a mild little priest from Repulse who had accompanied us to Pelly Bay. I sat up front with Fogbound.

We were high in the air and flying across the treacherous Prince Albert Mountains when suddenly the plane took on a strange jerky motion that had us off our course in no time. Before Fogbound could gain control we had lost considerable altitude. The rocks below loomed up in all their ugliness. It was one of the few times I'd seen Fogbound frankly worried. He had good reason. There would be no place to land should an emergency landing be forced on us!

Gradually the uneven motion of the plane resolved itself into a distinct back-and-forth rocking, as if caused by a regularly shifting load. We couldn't see behind the solidly stacked furs where Father Pierre had been left to make himself as comfortable as possible for the trip.

"You know, Doc," exclaimed Fogbound, "I think the father back there must be dancing up and down."

"*Dancing?* What on earth for?"

"To keep from freezing, probably. D'y' see the skimpy duds he had on?"

The jumping stopped awhile, then started once more, harder than ever. Fogbound was getting very annoyed because the little priest's antics were endangering our safety. On account of the way the cabin was loaded it was impossible for us to yell back and order him to stop. We limped jerkily ahead, Fogbound sweating in his efforts to keep us in the air. I had flashes of worrying over what might happen to the priest if we ever got back alive and Fogbound really let go at the little man.

The dancing finally stopped for good. The instant we landed at Repulse, Fogbound leaped out and ran around back to the cabin entrance to give Father Pierre a piece of his mind. I braced myself. I will say that Fogbound's remarks were surprisingly mild—for Fogbound.

"What did you keep jumping around for?" he demanded. "Didn't you know I was losing altitude and having a *hell* of a—er, a hard time keeping us off the rocks? If you had to be warm why didn't you wear—?"

"It wasn't that," the priest answered, humbly, adding, with a touch of unsuspected humor, "it—it was just the opposite."

"What d'y'mean, Father Pierre?" I put in.

"I'm very sorry," he explained, "but there was a fire in the cabin and I had to try and get it out."

"A fire?" gasped Fogbound. He turned a few shades whiter at thought of our belly tanks full of high octane gas that was separated from the main cabin by two thin metal walls only.

It turned out that while over the Prince Albert Mountains my sleeping bag had started smoldering, and almost continuously from that time on poor Father Pierre was trying desperately to trample out the fire.

Searching my mind, I reconstructed something like this as the probable cause. While going to the airstrip at Pelly Bay, an Eskimo, seated on top of our gear on the komatik, had been smoking his pipe and once had appeared to drop some glowing embers on my sleeping bag. After we were well up in the air, the eiderdown with which the bag was lined, began to catch fire. The smoldering process was a slow one and extremely difficult for the father to stop, dance hard as he would.

Fogbound's ire was swallowed up in his profuse thanks. He explained that we would have been lost had the father failed to keep the fire from the furs. All the frantic manipulations he had been forced to perform were preferable to being blown up in midair and scattered in little pieces across the arctic landscape.

◆36◆

IGLOOLIK—
"PLACE OF THE LITTLE HOUSES"

Fogbound was ready to leave for Igloolik Island at once. "And take the sergeant with me so he can start his registering," he suggested, "then come back for the bulk of the supplies. I'll get you for the last flight, Doc, eh?"

That sounded logical enough to the sergeant and me. Unfortunately, the weather stepped in at this point and prevented any flying at all. Fogbound took off twice, but was turned back by woolly fogs a few miles north of Repulse Bay. Finally he decided, rather grumpily, to wait for better weather.

Our forced stay of several days gave me a chance to gather information—legendary or otherwise—about the Tunit men, members of an ancient Eskimo civilization who lived in the Repulse area two or three thousand years ago, and whose last remnants were said to have died five hundred years ago. Their unusual height may be legendary. But I found proof of their exceptional strength in my examination of their graves, several of which were in the vicinity. Rather than leave their dead on top of the frozen group wrapped in skins and covered with small rocks, as was the custom later, they buried them in "tumuli." These were mounds built of huge stones weighing as much as 1,500 pounds. No pygmies could have handled such stones.

A feature of this old Tunit civilization, with its stone-and-whalebone homes, was that very often in the sleeping section the chief item of furniture was a large slab of stone placed at a seventy-five degree angle with the floor. Our Eskimo hosts declared that their Tunit forefathers slept with legs propped up against these stone slabs, thereby obtaining complete rest. If true, the modern practice of assuming a similar position for resting the legs had its origin in the mists of arctic antiquity.

How much of what I listened to while weatherbound at Repulse Bay was imagination, I don't know. One thing was certain. The Tunits were a colorful people, living long before the white man had placed his stamp of doom on the region.

At the end of our third day of waiting I was brought back from my dip into the long ago in the time it took to scan a radio-telegram just in from Igloolik. I called Fogbound.

"This says the sick father seems pretty bad and for me to come in a hurry. What do you think?"

Poor as weather prospects were for the next day, Fogbound's instant decision was to take a chance on the 250-mile northward hop along the length of Melville Peninsula. He was just as quick ruling out our original plan of flying several trips back and forth.

"We'll all have to go together, Doc, taking as many supplies as we can and letting the rest go. Weather will probably get worse the next few days. If we don't pull out of this country mighty soon well be stranded here for weeks."

Luck was with us next day when the heavily loaded plane staggered into the air and swung north. The weather was good. We had a beautiful flight.

The rocky landscape of Melville Peninsula, partly bare of vegetation, was on our left the entire way. To the right of us lay the waters of Foxe Basin. They were almost completely frozen and "freckled" with small islands. The sun colored the ice which, much like the water itself, took on hues which varied according to depth. At times I had a feeling that Fogbound was more interested in our speed and altitude than in the grandeur lying below.

At last, horseshoe shaped Igloolik, one of the larger islands in the Fury and Hecla Strait, loomed up and stood out clearly among the others. A few low swoops to reconnoiter the terrain, and Fogbound put our craft down smoothly near the small post.

Igloolik, Eskimo for "the place of the little houses," was an important island in earlier days. The natives of the place, calling themselves the Aivilingmiuts, derive their name from the fact that they are great walrus hunters. Walrus meat they use for food, and the tusks for their artistic carvings.

Directly north of Igloolik Island one can still find a few narwhals, the peculiar animals of the dolphin family which sport a single spiraled tusk. These tusks can be as long as eight feet, are found only on the males, and formerly were traded in Europe where people believed them to be the horn of the fabled unicorn. Pharmacists of the middle ages ground the tusks up for use in their medicinal concoctions—and doubtless made customers pay plenty for the stuff.

Specifically, the tusk is an outgrown tooth on the left side of the jaw; the component tooth on the right side never grows longer than about nine inches. The narwhal uses his long left one to dig into the muddy bottom of the sea and kill the fish thus disturbed. It has another—and more domestic—use, too. You'll find few Hudson's Bay Company officials in the arctic who have failed to transform a narwhal tusk into the standard for a floor lamp.

Originally, there had been a Hudson's Bay Company store on Igloolik Island, but this had been abandoned, leaving only a small mission post and a deserted house. Since that time the post has been reopened by the Hudson's Bay Company.

At the time of our patrol, in 1948, the Eskimos who welcomed us were a cheery, happy lot, and not afraid to show their pleasure in our arrival. We looked about us for some white men. There were none to greet us. Only two fathers lived on the island, it seemed, and the ill one was too badly off to be left alone.

We hurried over to the mission. There I examined the sick priest and reached the conclusion that, although suffering mostly from the strain of prolonged isolation, we'd have to fly him out.

Sergeant Hamilton and I then set up what, at that moment, may have been the world's most northerly "production line." As soon as Paddy finished registering a family for food allowance, he'd hustle them over to my improvised examination table for a checkup. Many had bad teeth, due to the change in diet brought about by white man's foods—especially starches. Otherwise the people seemed in good condition. Very few had major ailments of any sort.

It was only natural, perhaps, for a smile to lose something of its spontaneity when I started in on the owner with so fearsome a thing, as a stethoscope, or prepared to extract a badly infected molar.

Thoroughly familiar with Eskimo psychology, the grinning sergeant called me aside for a helpful suggestion. Then, lying flat on his back on the table, he pantomimed for me to take one of his teeth out, his groans and facial contortions drawing much sympathy from the Eskimos crowding about. With a flourish, I accommodated. Only, instead of extracting one tooth, I removed Paddy's entire upper plate. An instant of horrified amazement was followed by shrieks of laughter as our deception caught on. Like most Eskimos, these walrus hunters and ivory carvers could appreciate a joke. During the rest of my examinations the atmosphere was very cheerful indeed.

On the second day of our stay a stocky Eskimo I hadn't noticed before came to me and said his wife was ill. Would I have a look at her? I asked him to bring her in at once. When neither had shown up two hours later, I came to the conclusion that he'd probably got cold feet, and presently forgot the case.

Toward evening, however, in he trudged, bringing his wife with him. She was not in very bad shape and with a little medicine I managed to get her going again. What had taken him so long? He'd simply neglected to tell me that he lived twenty miles from the post, so he would have to travel forty miles merely to have his wife examined by the Kabloona medicine man. Thoughtful of his wife, like most Eskimos, he was pathetically grateful for what little I did and the pair turned and started off happily on their long arduous trek home.

In examining and treating various bands of Eskimos throughout my district, I had found them generally uncommunicative as to what they really thought of my strange antics. But not the people of Igloolik Island! Those lonely ivory carvers were among the most rewarding patients that it was my fortune to treat in the north. I said as much to Fogbound.

"What tickled them most," he answered, with a disarming smile, "was probably the diversion they got out of our coming to this Godforsaken island at all."

From tales told by the father, life could be very rough for these Eskimos. Several, he said, were lost every year hunting walrus. Often they drifted around hundreds of miles while marooned on an ice pan, hoping that the tides and currents would somehow set them ashore again. If not, their chances of reaching home were slim.

Land travel also had its perils, as raging blizzards collected numerous victims. The father pointed out one woman known as the Queen, and regarded by all the Eskimos with awe and respect. Her looks belied the title given her. If I stared hard it was only because I never had laid eyes on a less attractive Eskimo lady. But she must have been quite a girl in her day.

A good many years back she had been traveling with her husband and two children when they were caught by one of those storms. It was very bad and lasted for days. When they began to run out of food, the father, as was the custom, turned his share over to his wife and children, and soon died from hunger and exposure. One of the children followed him shortly afterward.

To keep herself and the other child alive, the Queen finally ate parts of the two dead bodies. Only in this way was she able to survive and drag herself and child back to camp to relate her gruesome experience.

A certain amount of cannibalism undoubtedly was practiced in earlier times. But the fact that her act had won for this woman a title of honor, besides spreading her story throughout the arctic, seemed good proof that cannibalism has become rare, if not nonexistent, in recent years.

Our days at Igloolik Island had to be few. Fogbound paced around, restless and anxious to get away while this was possible. With the sick priest on board, we took off and headed for our half-way station at Repulse Bay. The shouting and farewells of the Eskimos died away in the distance. With our mind's eye we saw them turn back soberly to their walrus hunting and ivory carving, hoping that maybe a year later another group of visitors might drop out of the sky to brighten their existence.

The result of our side trips to Pelly Bay and Igloolik Island was to accumulate at Repulse quite a number of patients and furs. It took elaborate planning to determine how best to transport everything safely back to Chesterfield. We decided on three separate flights, Fogbound taking the most serious cases first. I was almost sorry when he finally came back to get me—and a final planeload of furs.

A few months later, when I was given leave after completing more than three years of arctic medical service, I knew that my tour of duty would not have been complete without these last outpost patrols.

I shall always remember the grateful cooperation given me at Repulse Bay and Igloolik Island; and at Pelly Bay the embarrassing shyness of a stouthearted bearded missionary who had "gone Eskimo"—and perhaps stayed a little too long.

◆37◆

CALCULATED RISK

Besides the two kinds of arctic fever—the claustrophobic, in which the victim craves to leave the arctic in a hurry, and the opposite urge which draws him back, often to "go native"—is what is facetiously termed the "arctic bug." When *that* bites, you do what I did—if you too happen to be a prospector at heart.

Viola had appreciated my deep interest in geology even during medical school days. She watched it grow into an absorbing hobby while I was practicing my profession among the Eskimos. But the question of my ever turning to prospecting in earnest didn't come up until my transfer, for a brief, restless period, to a warmer medical post in Saskatchewan.

"Well," said Viola, after I'd thrown out a cautious feeling in family council, "why *don't* you?"

"You mean—take a leave?" I gasped.

She nodded. "I'm backing you, Joe."

There was no more argument than that. I promptly got extended leave from the medical service and made plans to go back to my old eastern arctic district—only this time free to do all the exploring and prospecting I liked.

During my years with the service I had studied the area intensively, traveling close to 50,000 miles by aircraft, dog team and canoe. But I had never been able to visit places that I wished particularly to see, not stay as long as I wished in spots

214

of more than average interest. Having fallen completely and irrevocably in love with the arctic, I now wanted above all else to go back and uncover some of the hidden resources of that tremendous stretch of little known land. I had in mind, too, taking motion pictures for a full length feature film. But my chief objective in going back was to *prospect.*

Of course, the lure of a challenge may have had something to do with it. Certainly, popular belief offered no lure. For years the Canadian East Arctic had been known as the "Barren Lands." Devoid of trees, its great stretches of bare rock, its forbidding climate and its history of death and desolation—all this contained little to inspire the homesteading type. But for another kind of people, inspiration can spring from a different source.

Before I left the region I had seen promising rock formations and mysterious veins. The Eskimos had told me of rich deposits that meant little to them but would make any prospector grab his sledgehammer. I wanted to go back and find out for myself.

People thought me out of my mind. Even the prospectors, eternal optimists, were far from happy about the "Barren Lands." Too many of them had tried and failed. Several big companies had sent their expeditions, only to be disillusioned. "Nothing there worth the hardship" had been the general verdict. The western arctic, yes. That had shown promise. The *eastern* arctic—hopeless!

I knew all the theories. I understood the hardships better than many. But I had always felt that the future of the region, especially the rehabilitation of the Eskimos, depended on the development of its natural resources. Familiar with the failure of those who had gone before, nevertheless I had an overpowering desire to prove that they had been wrong.

After all, the facts were on my side. The Laurentian and Precambrian Shields, which yield uranium bearing minerals, together with several important ores where they cover the northern regions of Saskatchewan and Manitoba, stretch out over the greater part of the Canadian East Arctic. Why, I kept asking myself, should not one find similar ores farther north? Perhaps still *other* ores?

I bought modern equipment, including film and cameras, chartered two Eskimo guides and outfitted my little expedition.

I planned to go in May and, for several months, travel alone with my guides. Later in the summer Viola would join me for an exploratory trip to Wager Bay. I read every mineralogy book I could find. Then I added to my equipment its most valuable asset, a Geiger counter, and so became the first prospector to take a Geiger into the Eastern Arctic.

My first discovery was the prompt realization that I hadn't known all the hardships, after all. Wishing to prospect along the coast, I had unwisely chosen to make the entire trip by canoe. Now, in those parts canoe travel in May makes as much sense as hunting a polar bear with a popgun. For one thing, it is difficult to get in close to shore because of land locked ice.

Whenever I wanted to examine an interesting rock formation on the distant mainland, we had to, first, run the canoe in to the edge of the ice; second, unpack the canoe and haul it up on the ice; *third,* fasten it on top of the komatik (which had formed part of the load); fourth, repack the canoe with the rest of the supplies.

After a trip of three or four miles across the ice, we would finally get to my rocks. Here it took perhaps twenty minutes to look around and check the formation. Then we had to struggle back to the outer edge of the ice floe, unload, reload—and travel on to the next point of interest.

Ice navigation proved extremely difficult. We had to do a lot of turning and twisting, and sometimes make detours to avoid big, dangerously shifting ice fields. I lost our position several times. Once we landed on a bare island and it took three days to figure out where we were. Sudden gales surprised us in the middle of open water. Just why the canoe wasn't swamped is a mystery. The bitter cold forced us to shorten our trips and camp often. We seldom found enough snow for an igloo and had to use our tents.

These were double, the sort of tent used in the arctic, but they lacked an igloo's warmth. Some nights none of us got warmed up at all. One incident made our misery more bearable. I shall long remember that night. We were camped on a tiny island still surrounded by winter ice. As can happen in spring, a terrific rainstorm suddenly swept over us, freezing the instant it came into contact with the tent canvas. With this thin layer of ice neutralizing the canvas's water repellent qualities, we were soon sitting in a steady drip, equipment getting wet, even the primus stove refusing to work.

When it came over me that I'd seldom felt more downright wretched, Tuga, one of the guides, started to *sing*. Tuga had often listened to the white man's radio and picked up some songs without in the slightest understanding of their meaning. His selection for this cold, rain drenched occasion was, "Any Place On Earth Will Do, As Long As I'm With You."

While I refused to be unduly flattered by the title chosen, my roar of laughter seemed to inject a ray of warmth into all of us. At least the cold tea tasted better.

The expedition had other unexpected aspects. For example, some of our maps, while good, were rather superficial. It was confusing to discover that between the Lorrilard River and the Connery there was really a third stream not shown on the map. But I could find no fault with that particular omission. The unmapped river led to the discovery of high-grade deposits, and I have the satisfaction of being the only one who knows where they are.

When we started to weave in and out of the small bays and inlets which indent the west coast of Roes Welcome Sound, we suddenly found ourselves deep in granite formations, with little likelihood that any prospector had preceded us. The large motor vessels and "peterheads" which navigate the Roes Welcome waters have no occasion to enter these little inlets which, for that reason, have remained unvisited.

Beneath the shelter of towering hills, we inspected Eskimo camps of the Thule culture. There were igloo-like houses built of rocks, with only the tops of the domes open where hides must have been thrown across. We uncovered stone arrowheads, graves, implements—all untouched through the centuries.

Elsewhere we came upon remnants of whaling camps of a more recent vintage; camps containing knives and pans—even the keel of a small boat. There was a simple grave whose inscription long since had been obliterated by sun and blizzard, but whose lone occupant no doubt died of pneumonia or scurvy. For a while, I spent more time on these discoveries than on prospecting.

However, the minerals disclosed by our search were most rewarding, ranging all the way from garnets to kyanite, a rare mineral of considerable value found in sizeable quantity in only one other place in Canada, and whose particular crystal is not found any place else on North America.

While a great deal of the ground we covered was certainly barren, some of the prospectors of old must have done their job badly. We identified quartz veins, with good copper values, of thousands of feet length. One morning we found that we'd been camping on top of a very large deposit of high grade asbestos ore stretching over many square yards, with unusually long fiber. We encountered gold in innumerable small pockets, and lead-silver ores in the form of very high grade galena in massive outcrops. Magnetite and hematite ores popped up in long ridges. My nickel and cobalt finds were of greater than average importance. There was more chromium in the area than anyone would have suspected. In particular, *radioactive material seemed to be all around us.*

Not long after this became evident, I slowly climbed a hill of solid rock carrying the Geiger counter in my left hand. That the instrument was clicking lustily brought no great excitement. Wherever I went I had found mild radioactivity. Any form of granite usually gives a certain amount that can be recorded on the instrument. Now I was out for bigger stuff; something really sensational; something that would justify a mining enterprise here in the middle of unexplored land.

As I climbed, the clicking grew more insistent and I switched the Geiger to the number two scale. The needle indicated a steadily rising count. When it registers on the number two scale at all, things begin to get interesting.

I hauled myself up over the ledge and walked across a level surface, the Geiger held loosely in my hand. Suddenly, its staccato clicking changed into something like a burst of machine-gun fire. I switched the counter to scale twenty—and held my breath. After subsiding a trifle, the "machine-gun fire" became so noisy that I had to take my earphones off. The needle danced madly back and forth. I stood still and turned slowly around, whereupon the needle jumped and the counter gave such a "whirr" that I shut the machine off for fear it would wreck itself.

There I stood, everything around me apparently as calm as if nothing had happened—the sun still shining, the little clouds moving along their windswept path. But beneath me lay a greenish rock giving out more radioactivity than a self-respecting Geiger could swallow. I had found what I had hoped to find!

Kneeling down to chip off hunks of the greenish stone, I muttered to them, amid hammer blows, "There, I guess these samples will show a good many people what sort of resources are stacked up in the arctic!"

This was one of three discoveries which I reported to the government, in keeping with the laws of uranium prospecting. Along with my finds of gold, kyanite, galena, chromium, magnetite and nickel, it amply justified my recent decision to take a chance and do a little prospecting on my own.

Considering the small amount of prospecting done in the East Arctic, and the tremendous finds that have been made, there is no question that the East Arctic will some day be one of the largest mineral storehouses in the world. Few Canadians are familiar in any way with this zone, and fewer still realize that this area will some day make them the wealthiest citizens in the world.

About a week after I had located and mapped the sensational deposit of radioactive material, Viola flew up from our new home in Saskatchewan to join me.

Together we set out for Wager Bay.

◆38◆

ESCAPE

Skirting endless land locked ice floes, we guided the motor driven canoe up the west coast of Roes Welcome Sound, rounded Cape Dobbs and pointed our craft through the rocky gorge that runs inland for twenty miles until it opens into Wager Bay proper.

Several days later, in the midst of our foot-by-foot exploration of the bay's shore line, we met the first human beings, save ourselves, that I had seen in many weeks. We were pulling into a wide cove when we sighted several tents in the distance. As we drove the canoe closer, a group of Eskimo children, yelling with excitement, came tearing out to meet us.

"Look at their clothes!" Viola exclaimed.

She had seen poverty during our stay at Chesterfield, but nothing like this.

We landed and approached a group of older Eskimos who had begun to emerge from the tents. Their clothing was tattered, their tent skins full of holes, their equipment worn and dilapidated. Their dogs seemed completely starved. The people themselves looked pinched from hunger.

They had come from the Pelly Bay area, a good 150 miles to the north. "Certainly," I told Viola, "these people are nothing like the prosperous crowd I found at Father Henry's mission."

It turned out that this was a roving band of hunters who had wandered south to catch the caribou. Having missed the herds completely, they were in desperate need of food. The men had been fishing, but the few fish they managed to spear would hardly keep them alive.

We pitched our tents close by and it did us good to be able to give them food from our ample supplies. The dogs didn't wait to be fed. They ran all over the place, gulping down every scrap, however microscopic, that was left unprotected. They tore labels off cans and chewed them with relish. Their drooping tails took on the barest hint of a curl.

These Eskimos had one admirable trait. Despite the hardships they had been through, and still were suffering, they were friendly folk; even good humored about it all. They told of their trek of many weeks across the mountains in the north, through stretches of rugged rocks where no white man had put foot. It must have been a ghastly trip, made more heartbreaking by the fact that not one animal was sighted. Storms and weakened dogs had so slowed their progress that there seemed no possible chance now of their coming within pursuing distance of any caribou.

After I had succeeded in making them understand that I was interested in rocks, I saw by the way their faces brightened that they had information for me. More talk drew mention of copper deposits somewhere back in the interior. Finally, following a heated discussion among themselves, they offered to take me there. I was greatly tempted, Viola somewhat less. In the end I decided that lack of time precluded any long overland excursion such as they proposed. These copper deposits would have to wait for a later trip. I took notes, though, of everything they said.

The only thing that worried us about these Eskimos was the way they kept eying our stores and equipment. We were afraid they might be driven to stealing—or worse. It meant keeping close watch day and night, and because of the strain of this we decided to make our stay with them a short one.

Before we left, however, I took some of the men out seal hunting. They had no skill in that direction and only killed one. Even that brought such exclamations of joy that I felt more than paid for my efforts. One seal would help them get by for a while, anyhow.

When, on leaving, we steered the canoe away from shore and looked back at their miserable excuse for a camp, we couldn't help wondering if they would ever reach their hunting grounds again. Their silhouettes stood out forlornly against the sky like black phantoms who, seeing no possible escape, were quite ready to vanish.

Viola and Joe Moody, on ice pan at mouth of Wager Bay, August 1950.

The most westerly point of Wager Bay was marked by an eerie, deserted Hudson's Bay Company post; also by a reversible waterfall. One was caused by the phenomenon of supply and demand, the other by a phenomenon of nature.

This last was brought about by the odd antics of a small river which flowed into Wager Bay through a deep fissure in the rocks. Tides in the arctic are unpredictable. I have been in places where three tides occurred in twenty-four hours. The peculiarity of the tides in Wager Bay is that they rise and fall very rapidly. This is due to the funneling effect of the narrow, twenty-mile entrance through which we ourselves had come from Roes Welcome Sound.

The first time I saw this reversible waterfall was when the tide had just started to go out and we were attempting to go up the channel which leads to the waterfall. The engine was wide open but the canoe was standing still as though held by a giant hand. Gradually, as the tide dropped faster the canoe was buffeted backward and the falls became more and more evident. As the tide in the bay reached its most rapidly dropping rate, the falls became a raging torrent and it looked as though the bay was threatening to drain the river and basin into which Brown Lake fed. Gradually the tide in the bay leveled off and began to return into Wager; and as it rose it forced the river in its western end to reverse its flow, thereby causing a new set of rapids as the water, pouring upstream over the channel rocks, created what amounted to a waterfall in *reverse*.

For some reason this fantastic oscillation of nature gave me the same sensation of smallness that came over me when first I gazed up into a night sky illuminated with northern lights.

Vague Eskimo reports of a "mountain that held gold" came to mind on seeing an unmapped inlet which ran almost parallel to Wager Bay and was separated from the main bay by a high, narrow tongue of rock. The alleged mountain, as I recalled, lay somewhere back of an inlet shaped like this. A huge cliff, visible beyond the inlet, might conceivably be the "mountain that held gold." My decision to investigate it nearly proved fatal.

We were rounding the rocky tongue and starting to cross the inlet, when a sudden squall hit us with a force that all but threw us out of the boat. The wind continued to tear through the inlet, churning the water into foaming waves that seemed to tower over the canoe.

Knowing that we'd certainly capsize if hit broadside, I tried to head back into the wind, a maneuver which lifted our bow clear out of water and spun us sidewise. Seas came splashing in, threatening to topple us over any instant. We bailed desperately. It wasn't enough.

One thing alone was left to try: Turn around and, with the wind at our back, scud directly away from our shore and head boldly for the opposite shore line, barely visible through the driving snow. We managed to turn around. Then we swept along with the fast traveling seas until a new danger arose of being overtaken and sunk.

I took to cutting the engine each time we rose on the crest of a wave, allowing the water to carry us forward like a surfboard. We bobbed around for more than an hour, the opposite shore coming into view at intervals through the horizontal sheets of snow. Even when we drew closer, we were being carried along too fast to try for a landing. Big boulders loomed ahead. I swung around them or scraped past. Only a miracle enabled us at last to nose our bow onto a beach of fine pebbles. The impact threw us over but the canoe was not badly damaged.

We lay motionless on the pebbles a few minutes, feeling like bedraggled rats. Gradually our breath came back and with it enough strength to haul the canoe up properly and make camp.

Next morning I started climbing after breakfast, taking my Geiger along as usual. Although the rocks weren't very steep, the weight of my equipment made for slow progress. Gradually a strange uncomfortable feeling came over me, as of being watched. Finally, I stopped and looked all around. Above me, two "hawk like" birds, probably falcons, were wheeling in the air, circling closer with every whirl. Soon they swooped so near my head that I felt currents of air stirred by their wings. It would have been easy to touch them had I a hand free.

To be blocked by a pair of angry birds seemed silly. But obviously I could move no nearer their nest without risking a full attack—and I needed my eyes for future prospecting. I lowered myself and rather ignominiously made my way back down, under their watchful glare. That part of the "mountain" remained unexplored, but I reached the summit by another approach. There was gold there, but only small, unimportant stringers of it such as I often had encountered in more interesting deposits.

I mounted a pinnacle for a good survey of the surrounding landscape. Undulating formations of rock rolled away into the far distance. To the right ten small rounded mountains, strikingly identical, formed a neat semicircle. Straight ahead, but many miles away, I made out a green, snow topped hump of tremendous proportions. It intrigued me, that hump of green. Since no plant masses of that dimension could grow for miles around, why was that great mass such a decided green? *Had it been colored by titanium oxide?*

I should like to have traveled there to see for myself. But the distance was too great. Solution of the mystery would have to wait for another expedition.

When entering Wager Bay from Roes Welcome Sound some days before, a rising tide had helped us through the twenty-mile cut that leads into the east end of Wager Bay. Now we were preparing to return to the waters of the sound. Again the tide was high because of a full moon, but that didn't bother us much. Our ten-horse-power motor would drive us against the current.

What I'd forgotten was the accumulation of drift ice which the high tide had locked between the rocks at the entrance. If this ice were to block the entrance completely, we would be prisoners.

When the situation dawned on me, we abandoned any further projects and headed full speed down Wager Bay to reach its narrow mouth before an unfortunate ice jam formed.

The currents in that area are very treacherous. The south side of the mouth contains powerful whirlpools which one must keep away from at all costs. Even large ice pans are churned to pieces in the swirling waters. The Eskimos told of small boats sucked under. Once a polar bear had been caught and drowned, roaring with fear.

Before getting very close to this dangerous area, dense clouds of vapor hanging above the pools told us which side of the entrance was to be avoided in our rush toward freedom. The trouble was, the other side, through which we had hoped to pass into the open water of Roes Welcome Sound, seemed pretty well blocked with ice.

"We'll try it, anyhow!" I yelled, and throttled the motor down in order to thread our way more slowly between the bobbing ice pans which kept closing in behind.

There came a time when we reached a point beyond which further progress looked impossible. I stopped the engine—and could feel us immediately start to drift sidewise toward the whirlpools. Half rising in the canoe and glancing around desperately, I made out a narrow lead—perhaps 300 yards long—momentarily opening up ahead. It seemed so providential that I stared a long moment for fear it was an hallucination. But there it was—a nearly straight lane of open water not over ten feet wide.

Even had I hesitated to take the chance of crushing the canoe, there was no choice left but to race into the near end of the lead and hope we'd reach the other end before the ice clamped together again.

We spurted forward. The V wave thrown up by our bow appeared to disturb the equilibrium of the loose ice floats around us. Those behind began to move with almost human restlessness, and nudge others close by. An ominous wave of motion was set up which raced on ahead of us and threw both edges of the lead into motion. In the distance I could see ice pans floating closer and closer together, as if forming a conspiracy to block us. But they were big and clumsy and their movement slow. Our craft, small and fast, squeezed through a last opening five feet wide —and roared out exultantly into the open sea.

Isolated grave at Cape Fullerton, near Wager Bay, of a Royal North-West Mounted Police Physician, 1904.

After the nerve strain of escaping from Wager Bay, I felt that we could do with some rest before resuming prospecting. In previous months I had shot a few thousand feet of film, but had had little chance to include wild animals in their natural surroundings. Roes Welcome Sound seemed an ideal place, and right now an ideal time.

"May not be too exciting," I thought, "but we'll have a good rest doing it."

I didn't know then that filming wild animals in Roes Welcome Sound would be anything but restful.

◆39◆

CAMERA HUNT

I was fortunate in having Ayranni with me.

Ayranni was known to be quite a hunter and would be invaluable in rounding up wild animals for me to film.

I carried a gun, but so far had refrained from firing a shot. That is the law. In a commendable effort to preserve animal life in the East Arctic, the government has limited all hunting for Eskimos and whites alike. But whereas Eskimos are allowed to shoot a specified number of animals a year, since this provides their staple food, the Kabloona is prohibited from hunting at all, except in isolated cases when he has been a long time resident or because of serious shortage of food.

It is next to impossible to control the hunting habits of Eskimos, and most of them sneak in a few extra bears, walrus and caribou. But, in general, the whites stick to the rules and shoot only if attacked. In the past they were free to accompany the natives on their hunts and even help stalk the animal. But it is the Eskimo who, legally, must pull the trigger.

There aren't too many polar bears in Roes Welcome Sound. Capturing one on land is difficult. He smells you miles off and disappears before you can get near. If you manage to locate one in the ice fields, the chase is easier. The bear will keep in sight, and with a fast boat and a good guide you can catch up with him and get him in your sights.

It must have been quite a task in former days to hunt the polar bear. The Eskimos had only bows, arrows and spears or harpoons with points of ivory and bone. Dogs formed the important weapon.

The Eskimo himself, with his strange lack of interest in the past, knows little about ancient hunting methods. One can only imagine what must have gone on.

Accompanied by a pack of dogs, several men probably attacked together, first waiting until the dogs had the animal at bay. This gave the hunters a chance to throw their spears at the bears neck in an effort to sever the spinal cord. When one considers that with one slap of his paw a polar bear can throw a 100-pound husky forty feet through the air, it isn't hard to understand the dangers of a close range battle with this animal.

Squatting forward with movie camera ready, I tried to visualize one of these ancient struggles while Ayranni guided our canoe among huge ice pans far out from shore.

We had started our hunt that morning. I had taken great pains beforehand to explain that what I was most interested in getting was some good action shots. If we found anything worthwhile his job would be to make the animal angry before he even thought of shooting it. I wanted my film to show the drawn out excitement of the chase. Ayranni thought I'd lost my senses.

An hour later, when we had the exceptional good luck to sight a polar bear on a distant floe, I suspected from his sudden tenseness that some of my instructions might be wasted. The canoe shot forward. After long contemplation of the strange sounding "ice berg" approaching his floe, the bear retreated to the farther edge and finally slid into the sea.

We followed his bobbing head for several minutes, then lost sight of it. We were cruising idly about in the vicinity when suddenly I dropped my equipment and groped around for my gun, yelling,

"Watch out, Ayranni. Watch out!"

The head of the bear was about five feet away from the canoe. He was making ready to lash out at us with a claw.

Ayranni, his eyes gleaming, swung the canoe around at the last moment, leaving a surprised animal in our foaming wash. We speeded away, then turned again for another approach.

"For God's sake be careful," I told Ayranni, "and don't get excited. You can't swim," I reminded him.

I doubt if he heard me. He wasn't interested in movies now. To him a bear was a bear and something to be slain. Ever since sighting this fellow he had thought only of killing. Fifteen hundred pounds of meat for men and dogs! That was the important thing.

"Ayranni!"

Something in my tone recalled to him my previous instructions. Reluctantly he fired several shots close to the swimming animal, deliberately refraining from hitting it. But after watching the anger mount in the animal's vicious little eyes, he decided that this was fun and started to take unbelievable risks in maneuvering the canoe around the maddened bear.

With danger so close it was I who thought about shooting. It was I who threw the camera down and wanted to save our lives with a well-placed bullet.

"Steady now," I muttered, when the tide of the chase had turned in our favor. I picked up the camera again.

We were now pursuing the fast swimming beast. When near enough I started grinding away. The boat veered. I looked again. With amazing nimbleness, the bear had climbed up on an ice pan where he stood a moment, the thick fur sleeked against his great muscular body, his small head swaying from side to side like a pendulum. He didn't growl. He uttered a throaty hiss.

Planning to follow him up onto the ice, Ayranni steered against one edge of the pan, only to have the animal turn and, with a seesaw motion of his shoulders and buttocks, gallop off to the opposite edge.

I checked my film. Luckily there were twenty-five feet left. I looked around us. What a picture this would make! The sky was clear blue and the water reflected the blue in deeper hues. Ice pans of various sizes floated around in the choppy sea. The coast, barely visible, was at least ten miles behind us.

A splash brought my eyes front again. The bear had disappeared, plunged overboard from the far side of the float. Swinging the canoe around the ice pan brought the animal into view again, only now all that was visible was the streamlined head with its shiny black nose, pushing through the water.

Ayranni throttled the engine down to enable us to follow at a distance of about fifteen feet.

Suddenly the bear reared up in the water and turned as if to attack us, but changed his mind when Ayranni opened the throttle wide. Heading for the nearest chunk of floating ice, the animal lost no time climbing onto it. This was a much larger ice pan than the one he had just left and its spacious area put the idea of a closeup into my head. I spoke to Ayranni. He hesitated a moment, then nodded and ran the canoe into a little cleft on our side of the float, about thirty feet from where the bear stood watching. We dug our mooring pin into the ice and cautiously climbed out.

We stood still a few moments, then walked slowly toward the bear, who retreated to the top of a little hump three feet high. I remember how the sun's rays pierced the ice at his feet so that it burst into a spectrum of brilliant colors. When we got closer, the bear growled and showed his sharp teeth. Suddenly he rose up on his hind legs. His front paws, raised high above his head, made him seven or eight feet tall.

This inviting posture proved too much for Ayranni's Eskimo blood. He fired fast. Two shots. The bear came down groggily. He swayed on his feet, blood crimsoning his fur. Gathering the last of his strength for a final effort, he gave one leap and landed almost at our feet. Then he turned over and lay very still. It was the first polar bear I had ever seen close up.

Just as I was bending down, rather nervously perhaps, for a better inspection, a yell from Ayranni made me jump. The bear had nothing to do with it. Another ice pan, swinging around, was about to close the opening in which our canoe was moored. We rushed over and pulled the boat up on to the ice. There was a thump and earsplitting crunch as the two huge blocks of ice crashed together. Another second's delay would have pulverized the canoe, leaving us stranded miles from shore on ice that was slowly drifting out to sea.

While I stood there marveling at our good luck, practical Ayranni was skinning the bear.

◆ 40 ◆

PRIVATE LIFE OF A SEAL

Besides using the skin of the seal for boots and summer clothing, Eskimos relish its tasty meat and fat. The main use of the fat, however, is as a fuel for their combined lamp and stove, known as a kudlik.

This device is a fair example of the way Eskimos can adapt available materials to their needs. The kudlik is a shallow, semi-oval dish of soapstone, the rim of which is slightly higher on one side of the dish, which also holds muskeg, caribou hair or rope to act as a wick. As the chunk of fat melts away, it provides a steady flow of oil for the lamp. Trim the wick well and you have a pleasant, yellow-blue light; besides which, the kudlik gives off quite a bit of heat.

All Eskimo cooking used to be done over a kudlik. Today, with the introduction of kerosene, only a few coastal Eskimos use the old method. But back in the interior you'll find many igloos in which the kudlik is still the sole source of light and warmth.

In northern areas, where the Eskimos find no caribou to hunt, they live mostly on the meat of sea animals, including whales. Killing whales and walrus, therefore, is their principal object in life, and here again the *seal* is important. Not only is his meat a staple food but, until recently at least, his skin was a necessary adjunct in capturing whales. This is how the skin was used.

An ingenious technique enabled the Eskimos to remove the seal meat, bones and intestines through the opening left by cutting off the head. The skin, intact, was carefully scraped on the inside and any small holes sewed up. The airtight balloon, or float, formed in this way was blown up and attached to one of the harpoon lines used in hunting white whales, narwhals and the dangerous walrus.

Now, one common characteristic of whales is that they submerge when hit, many sinking immediately if fatally wounded. The Eskimos learned how to prevent this loss with their sealskin floats. Advantage was taken of the fact that the whale hunters traveled in groups, since no whale could be killed by a single harpoon. A number of harpoons with lines attached would be hurled at the same time. The whale would submerge as usual, but if there were enough sealskin floats attached to the lines, he couldn't go far without tiring. Nor could he sink. This gave the hunters time to close in for a leisurely kill.

In the old days it must have been a much riskier job to hunt a big carnivorous killer whale or temperamental walrus from a kayak than from the small sloops of later whaling history. Many Eskimos perished. But their occasional reward made the danger worthwhile. The group would camp near a killed whale for months, feeding off the cadaver until nothing was left. Some Eskimo tribes must have lived on whales alone. The coast of Melville Peninsula contains the remnants of whalebone houses, the very existence of which may well have depended on little floats fashioned from the skin of the seal.

So important is the seal even today that Eskimos are allowed to kill him in unlimited numbers. Fortunately, there are plenty still around, and in great variety. The two best known, perhaps, are the bearded, or square flipper seal, sporting tremendous whiskers on his snout, and the ring seal, which has beautiful silvery hair on the underside, while its back and sides range in coloring from a black mottling to a solid black zone.

To hunt these animals takes more patience than skill. They are not hard to get in open water, especially when weary. But endurance is the main requirement for hunting them in the ice fields. They cannot stay under water more than about ten minutes, then they have to come up for air. In winter, when they seek their food beneath the ice, they keep several holes open through any of which they can emerge for a breather.

They possess great resourcefulness, these seals. For example, they plan ahead for winter, getting their holes started as soon as the sea begins to freeze over. They move from one spot to another, piercing holes in the ice, smashing the first thin layer with their snouts. And they have to keep these holes open during the long winter months. I often imagine them hurrying from one hole to another all day and all night, making certain that no icy film cuts off their vital air supply.

Nanook, the polar bear, the king of the Arctic jungle of sea ice.

When they sleep on the ice, as often happens, they keep close to their holes. Only if a hunter has the wind in his favor and approaches carefully can he hope to catch one of them before the alert animal plops through the nearest hole down out of sight. Eskimos sometimes crawl along on their stomachs or push themselves forward on small sleds, imitating the movements of a seal. The animals never sleep long, but doze and wake up every so often to look for danger. When a seal raises his head the Eskimo hunter looks up too and moves his head seal fashion. Such tricks sometimes work. More often, though, the seal gives one look, then slithers into his hole in ample time to escape capture. Sometimes two scared seals, making for the same hole, get stuck. If you're not hungry and depending on them for food, it can be very amusing to watch them wriggle, each trying feverishly to reach safety under the ice. On other occasions a seal will crawl onto the ice through a crack and quietly fall asleep. Suddenly the ice pans will come together closing off the crack and the seal's escape. It was always amusing to watch the surprised and frightened seal wrestling himself across the pan to the next crack or hole.

Oojuk—a friendly sea mammal. It is the biggest seal weighing up to 700 pounds.

If not fortunate enough to trap a seal on the ice, you must wait patiently at his hole for him to come up. As soon as his snout appears you throw your harpoon and pay out the line attached. Even then much time may pass before you have him under control. Assuming that both harpoon and line are good, you are bound to win in the end because the seal will weaken through loss of blood, besides needing to come up for air.

A little trick in seal hunting is to ascertain how many holes the animal has. If he knows you are waiting at one, he will select another for his breathing spell and you will wait indefinitely without sighting so much as the tip of his whiskers. If, however, you post a dog at every hole within 300 feet, you can be sure to catch him somewhere.

Atlantic walrus—an aggressive and dangerous animal in Arctic water.

This sort of hunting didn't appeal to me. Because I was more interested in filming seals in open water, Ayranni steered our canoe one day to an area where they hadn't been hunted much, and therefore knew no fear.

A good distance away from the coast, we found ourselves caught in a group of square Flipper seals. Dozens of them playfully chased one another around the boat. With expert precision, Ayranni sent his harpoon into the neck of a 600-pound beast, which submerged at once. The Eskimo paid out his line. We waited. Suddenly, the seal surfaced only a few feet away from us. He seemed to have plenty of strength left and, seeing him swimming directly toward us, I grew anxious. So did Ayranni.

"Keep him off!" he cried, sharply. "Him trying come aboard."

It was quite true. The poor animal, gasping for breath and not realizing that we were his hunters instead of another ice pan, was about to climb on top of us. I shoved my camera aside and leaped up. I was genuinely sorry for the seal, but it was more important to save the boat. Already he had rested his head on the gunwale and was trying to get one flipper over the edge. We tipped dangerously. When all our equipment started to shift, Ayranni fired three shots and the seal grew limp. We had quite a time hauling him in, the canoe heeling so far that we hung out over the opposite gunwale to keep it from going under completely.

Walrus herd—although some sun and sleep, there is always at least one on alert for enemies.

As we turned homeward that day, a beautiful ring seal broke water a few yards away. He turned his head and scrutinized us most intelligently through bright, round eyes. Completely unafraid, he seemed to wink at us drolly with one heavy eyelid.

"Don't shoot," I begged Ayranni, as the Eskimo, less amused than I by the animal's comical expression, seized his gun. It must have been a strain on his attachment for me not to pull the trigger.

I have been glad ever since that he didn't fire. The footage on which I succeeded in recording the pranks of this curious seal is among the best I have shot.

◆ 41 ◆

QUIET INTERLUDE

I had photographed seals and a polar bear at close enough range to make my little camera excursion less restful than planned. When I suggested that the ice fields would form a fitting background for a quiet filming of sleeping walrus, Ayranni first discouraged the idea, then, failing in that, lectured me with a seriousness I hadn't known the Eskimo possessed.

"Walrus *dangerous,*" he warned. "He'll attack when mad. He'll kill when wounded."

"But isn't that true of nearly every animal?"

"Maybe," he admitted. "But walrus very bad. With tusks he will smash boat, pull under water. You stand on ice pan close to water, he will come and hook with tusks. When shot he will come at you even if nearly dead. Him stretch neck out two feet and get you when you think safe."

"Then," I said, smiling, "don't get as careless as you did with that bear the other day. Remember, Ayranni, I want to take motion pictures and *that's all.*"

"Oh, yes, me careful," he promised. As if he hadn't stressed the danger quite enough, he added: "Walrus swim faster than boat with ten-horse motor. You watch."

With that warning in my ears, we took off for the distant ice fields where, from a distance, we had spotted many of the huge sausage like animals the day before. All during the night I had

238

listened to their screeching and grunting, for in the still of an arctic night you can hear them miles away.

Soon it became apparent that I had more respect for my guide's warning than he did himself. With gun across knees, he was running our engine and steering the canoe full speed into the ice fields. I sat near the bow, as usual, camera in lap, my 303 rifle within easy reach. Presently we saw them, a whole colony of walrus. More than a hundred of the monsters were spread around in groups on various ice pans. They were formless. Except for the identifying tusks, it would have been impossible to single them out. On one small ice floe two youngsters were fighting, striking their tusks together with tremendous force. The bony crackle resounded across the water.

Ayranni throttled down and guided the boat carefully through the narrow leads between the ice pans.

"They no move," he whispered. "You shoot pictures—quick!"

I hadn't waited but already was aiming my camera around, taking groups on the surrounding floats. But Ayranni had made a slight miscalculation. Slowly the ponderous beasts, alarmed by the sound of the boat moving among them, slipped off the ice, one by one, until several dozen were in the water. They seemed only curious as their bobbing heads began converging toward us. I could hear them breathe.

Soon they had the canoe surrounded and Ayranni was finding it more and more difficult to steer between the animals. He headed for a nearby ice pan but had to make a quick turn when a big bull surfaced directly in front of us. The water splashed and the engine growled, and these noises appeared to excite the swimming monsters all the more. They made hostile moves, coming at us in groups, then diving just when I thought sure they'd capsize us. I caught glimpses of gray bodies as, with the flick of a flipper, they slid under the canoe.

"Ayranni, they'll upset us!" I yelled.

"Never do that," he yelled back, actually seeming to turn a shade lighter. "Walrus always attack from side. Swim along canoe and hit tusks on boat like drum—rat—tat—tat. Must get off on ice now. Too many walrus."

He gave the canoe another sharp turn. The propeller came out of the water and with a "splut—splut" our engine quit. The unexpected lurch had nearly knocked me out of the boat and my camera dropped from my hands. As I bent down to put it in a safe place, I saw six walrus heads staring at me.

"Shoot, shoot!" called Ayranni, working feverishly to get the engine started.

I fumbled around for my gun, finally reached it. By this time we had drifted close to the ice pan, but now strong currents began to drag us away.

"SHOOT!"

I shot blindly and reloaded. I shot again and again, too excited to aim.

One of the walrus was hit and went down immediately, a red film spreading over the water above him. I hit another on the skull, but my bullet ricocheted off and merely left a red gash. Our attackers, keyed to a frenzy, came at us from all sides. And that was the instant when, whether due to Ayranni's sweating efforts or simply because that was the nature of the thing, our engine started again. We jerked forward, barely missing two ugly heads.

All the animals seemed as much surprised as we were, and for a few moments we left the herd behind. That didn't last long. They started in pursuit, and, although they gained on us without apparent effort, the slight delay gave us time to draw close to the ice pan again. As we approached this sanctuary, one big fellow who had never bothered to leave the ice, came slithering toward us. Ayranni shot twice. The wounded beast tumbled toward the water but came to rest on a ledge that stuck out underneath. An instant later the canoe bit the edge of the ice with alarming force, but we didn't worry. There was no time for that.

"Pull up!" Ayranni cried.

Between us we dragged the loaded craft, dripping, out of the sea. Within seconds, long, yellow-white tusks were digging into the ice where the boat had been.

Ayranni shot into their midst. "Don't let walrus come on ice," he cautioned, calmer now. "If they get up we dead."

We had beaten them off for the time being. Some were hurt badly; others had grown more careful. But this was no time to discount their loyalty toward their wounded comrade on the ledge—which probably was what had inspired the attack.

Again I heard my guide's voice: "Other side—get other side!"

One of the walrus was pulling himself up on the far side of the ice pan. I ran over close and shot. Even as his head dropped, he lashed out at me, missing by a few inches. Another came up behind me, but at the Eskimo's yell I jumped sidewise and the impact of his swinging head threw him back into the water.

After these direct attacks stopped, the beasts took to swimming around our ice pan, lashing the water, as if to remind us that we hadn't seen the last of them yet. But if they tried to climb up, we found it possible to scare them away simply by rushing over toward them. The block of ice on which we stood was red with the blood of the two we had shot. I turned to Ayranni,

"What do we do now? Try the canoe again?"

"No—no. We wait until walrus calm down." Suddenly he looked at me hard and added, worriedly, "But we no wait long. We drifting to sea."

He was right. With the walrus holding us at bay on this little chunk of crimson ice, we were being carried slowly away from land by tide and current. The beauty of our surroundings was in sharp contrast to the drabness of our predicament. The fast sinking sun threw purple hues across the water. Clouds formed in the northern sky, producing a palette of colors that would have made any artist catch his breath. But all this held no fascination for us since it looked as if a storm might be brewing.

Ayranni, resigned to whatever fate lay in store, had started to skin one of the animals, cutting wide rings of hide and pulling them off carefully. Later, assuming that all went well, these rings would yield tough ropes of thong thirty or forty feet long. Next, he chopped the tusks out of the two-inch-thick skull and cut up the meat. This walrus must have weighed some 2,000 pounds. The other was smaller.

"Well, we can't stay here, fifteen miles from land," I observed, after watching him work awhile. "We're still being carried out. If we don't quit this ice pan soon we'll not have fuel enough to get us back."

Ayranni shook his head. "We wait," he said, firmly.

"But, Ayranni, if we drift any farther out—"

"They watching. See."

Most of the walrus had climbed onto other ice pans surrounding us. They were restless and seemed to be eying us closely.

"Sometimes they go back in water when canoe is lowered," the Eskimo volunteered, after a look around. "They know we stuck. They try keep us here."

He didn't sound very hopeful. But when I saw a lead opening up in the direction of the coast, I decided we'd have to take a chance and told him so.

He thought it over. "We try," he announced and immediately began loading the canoe. He piled enormous chunks of meat and rolls of skin into the boat.

"Good God, Ayranni," I interrupted, "all that weight will nearly swamp us. We can't make any kind of speed."

If it cost his life, the Eskimo in him would never allow such waste. "I not leave this," he said. That settled the matter.

Carefully, stealthily, almost inch by inch, we slid the canoe into the water, all the while glancing furtively about. Nothing stirred. We stepped in noiselessly and took our positions. Still no movement from the floes around us. It wasn't necessary to start the engine in order to draw away from our enemies because they were slowly drawing away from us. The ice pans were drifting out to sea and our heavily loaded boat, although swept in the same direction, offered more resistance to the current and so tended to lag behind.

When Ayranni considered it safe, he started the motor. Instantly the shapeless gray forms on the ice pans roused into life and splashed overboard, by ones, twos and threes. But he gave the engine full gas, we sliced through the water and an occasional carefully aimed shot kept the vanguard of the pursuing herd at a distance.

We had cause to feel fairly safe until about two miles from shore when the engine gave an expiring gulp and stopped dead. No more gas! Except for a faint glow of northern lights, darkness had closed down on us. I broke the sudden silence:

"What can we do now?"

"Nothing. We wait." He glanced over the side and his voice had a new tone when he added, "But have tide now."

A look overboard had told him that the tide had turned in our favor, and ultimately should carry us in.

At that, it took nearly three more hours—which seemed a week—while we sat shivering in silence. Finally, pebbles crunched under our bow and, with a yell of relief, we leaped out to pull the canoe up on shore and get the blood circulating in our cramped legs. Another hour of walking brought us back to our camp, where the dogs we had left behind welcomed us with the greatest show of excitement—inspired mainly, I believe, by the smell of raw walrus meat.

Later, I caught myself smiling. Ayranni grinned back, a little uncertainly. He evidently thought that he was the object of the Kabloona's strange mirth.

He didn't know I was smiling at the whimsical notion that filming wild animals in Roes Welcome Sound would provide an interlude of rest and quiet.

◆ 42 ◆

INTO THE ICE FIELDS

One morning very early my old friend, Sheeniktook, awoke me by poking his head into the tent and announcing:

"Tuga him say no dog food. Him say dogs hungry."

"What do you say?" I queried, with a yawn, knowing that he was likely to be more concerned over our dogs than was Tuga.

"I say we not go prospect today. We hunt seal. Rocks wait long time, dogs no wait. They weak like this." He dropped his head and let his arms hang limp to show how the dogs felt.

Besides dog food, another reason to knock off for a day's hunting was that Sheeniktook, Tuga and I had just put in five exhausting days prospecting, going by canoe from cove to cove, landing often to investigate likely formations inland. When we traveled on land the dogs had a hard pull over the soft snow. Although these little excursions inland had furnished exciting rock samples, they had left us no time to hunt food for the dogs.

"All right," I agreed, rather reluctantly. "Tell Tuga we'll take a day off and shoot some seals."

I ate breakfast and walked to the top of the bluff beneath which we had camped and looked out over the sea. The sun hadn't climbed above the horizon yet, but the reflected light showed landlocked ice extending about two miles from shore. Beyond was closely packed drift ice which moved in and out with the tide.

The water glimmered grayish blue in the distance, the leads between the big ice pans taking on the same cold line. The ice itself looked gray at this early hour. Later, the sun splashed every ice float lavishly with color. There had been a great deal of movement in the ice field, as evidenced by the huge peaked formations built up by countless hummocks and pressure ridges. As a result, each ice pan resembled the stalagmite studded bottom of a grotto.

Breaking up time for the ice had arrived. We had been lucky so far, maneuvering our canoe along the edge of landlocked ice while the drifting field moved out to sea with the tide. Each time the tide came back, we'd haul the boat from the water and continue by sled. At night we had always been particular to camp far in on the solid ice, sometimes even on the shore itself.

While it would be impossible to get a boat through the outer ice fields today, they were still safe enough for walking. If we wanted to hunt out there we'd have to do it on foot.

I turned to Tuga, our best hunter: "You sure we'll find seals?"

"Seal out there sure."

As Tuga was seldom wrong about such matters, we started out, taking the dogs and sled as far as the outer edge of the land locked ice. There I freed myself of all heavy equipment, including a caribou parka which hampered my movements. I took along only my camera, gun, cigarettes and some chocolate. All three of us studied the movement of the ice awhile. It was still coming in and would be safe enough until it changed a few hours later.

We decided to split up. Tuga went one way, Sheeniktook and I the other. Walking on the ice fields was tricky, especially with breaking up time at hand. While most of the ice was solid, occasional spots were mushy and full of holes. Because the white field was moving in toward shore, the leads were narrow and easily crossed. What bothered us most were the many cracks and small channels filled with slush from snow and groundup ice. These were hard to see. We had to test every foot with a stick before advancing. Sometimes the stick found no support. That meant we had to walk around a few hundred yards to reach solid ice again.

As for seals, Tuga's usually sound "hunches" seemed to have failed him for once. All Sheeniktook and I found were a few seal holes and, to make it more aggravating, we nearly fell into some of these. We wandered around for hours, finally landing on the last of the big floats beyond which were only small pans and scraps and pieces of ice. I stopped in disgust, sat down on a hummock and lit a cigarette.

"Well, Sheeniktook, I guess this is as far as we go, eh?"

Rather than showing discouragement, the Eskimo swept his arm around and spoke: "More open water make this good place to spot animals. Come, we look around."

He was right. On climbing the next ridge we saw, about five feet below where we stood, a big square flipper sunning himself luxuriously on the ice. Sheeniktook shot the animal and we lumbered down hastily for a close look. Its size delighted us; around 500 to 600 pounds. We then debated the best way to transport such a huge load of meat. We could have cut it up and carried a few of the best pieces back with us. But the dogs needed food badly, so it would be better to move the entire animal if possible. Besides, I didn't know when we'd have time for another hunt.

Finally I took Sheeniktook's advice, which was to bring the dogs out here on the ice and let them drag the seal to shore. He cut off a few pieces to take to the hungry animals at once. Then, because it was so hot on a day like this, and to protect the skin of the seal, he wriggled out of his parka and flung the garment over the dead seal.

"Me back soon with dogs," he said, and took off across the ice field. He looked back once and called, "You stay here so I find seal easy."

When he was out of view, I sat down on the parka covered carcass and, comfortably relaxed, let my eyes wander over the scene. The early morning grayness had gone. The sun shone brightly and the sky tinted the water the deepest of blues. I noticed how the ice pans differed in color depending on just how the light hit them. Some were soft pink with high spots of light purple, others a sea green. Many hues of blue were to be seen. The little chunks of ice remained pure white as they danced and swirled around in between the heavy pans. I played a game with these little white chunks. When I closed my eyes part way and looked at them through my lashes only, colored stars twinkled in all directions, giving the effect of a dazzling fireworks display. On opening my eyes again, sea pigeons were winging overhead and eider ducks were moving along high up in the sky.

Something about the magnitude of that moment called for pleasant introspection. Here was I, Joe Moody, sitting on an ice pan in the middle of the sea. Under me was a freshly killed seal. All around me nature displayed a mystifying beauty. I was more than 1,000 miles from any city, more than 3,000 from the place where, just a few years back, I had worked my way through college.

"Doctor Moody," I told myself, "you have come a long way—and not in miles only. For over three years you've been the doctor for 2,000 people in a country of 600,000 square miles. You have amputated, operated, delivered, injected; you have pulled teeth and stopped epidemics. Good! And now you're leading your own expedition into this fantastic, forbidding land. You haven't done so badly, Moody."

This grandiose mental picture of myself was to be considerably deflated by nightfall.

The deflation, which took place gradually, began after I had been daydreaming there on the ice for some time. Where, I wondered, with a start, was Sheeniktook? Well, he might have had trouble finding the dogs. Surely he'd come back just as soon as . . .

I felt a sudden jar, and sat up very straight. There it came again, a movement in the ice. Not just a little movement, either. Something big was going on all around me. I glanced about. What I saw had a dreamlike quality, but the stark fact was there. I was drifting out to sea. Slowly but unmistakably my ice pan, along with hundreds of slabs of loosened ice, was moving away from the solid, landlocked ice which still fringed a shore line visible perhaps ten miles behind me.

I leaped up and hurried back, following the tracks left by Sheeniktook on the mushy surface. Speed meant everything. If I didn't get back to that solid ice I'd be carried out twenty, maybe thirty miles. And if my ice pan drifted *too* far out it might even get caught in other currents that would prevent it moving in again with the next tide. It would drift around in open water and melt away slowly, or else be ground up by other floating ice.

I followed Sheeniktook's tracks until suddenly a water gap lay at my feet. The Eskimo's next footstep was ten feet away on the other side. Desperate now, I searched in every direction. A few hundred yards off, my float seemed almost to touch another. I ran over, jumped across the small gap and, greatly relieved, walked back to pick up Sheeniktook's footprints from which I had been separated a few moments before by a ten-foot lead.

But the footprints weren't where I thought surely they'd be. They weren't *anywhere*. The next ice pan maybe, I thought. Again I jumped blindly—*and there they were!*

◆43◆

NIGHT WITH NO END

I no longer took precautions but hurried along as fast as I could travel, picking my way from hummock to hummock, around peaks and pressure ridges, across yawning cracks. The ice field was still staying together in a fashion, permitting me to jump across leads, even to step from one pan to another where they happened momentarily to be pushed together.

I lost and recovered Sheeniktook's tracks many times. When I lost them I guessed at the right direction and roamed around until I crossed them once more. I finally climbed a little ridge and looked in every direction. The two Eskimos must have noticed that the ice was moving out. They should be on their way to help me.

But no black specks were visible moving across the ice. Where could they be? Had I lost direction completely? Could Sheeniktook's footprints have been leading me *away?* Had the whole field turned with the tide so that actually I was moving toward more open water?

Curbing an urge to panic, I took out my compass and checked directions. No, I seemed to be all right, although it might not be for long. An offshore wind was coming up; not a strong wind but one strong enough to help the ice pans along on their way out to sea.

I jumped down off the hummock and knew right away that I shouldn't have. In landing, my right leg went through to my knee. Instinctively, I threw myself forward on the ice and crawled away from the dangerous seal hole that had filled with slush and snow. My leg was soaked but there was nothing I could do except stumble ahead, checking my compass every few minutes.

After climbing onto a particularly high float, I saw my two guides perhaps two miles away. They stood on a ridge. I waved. They waved back. They had the dogs with them and appeared to be walking back and forth. I sat down to rest, expecting them to come for me now. But they didn't. They kept walking up and down on that ridge without even trying to start my way. A bit put out by their thoughtlessness, I shrugged my shoulders, got up and started walking again. But I could go more slowly and carefully now, knowing that I was on the right track and fully expecting to join my team in a short time.

But on coming closer I saw what had been keeping them on their ridge. The last ice pan on which I was standing was separated from them by thirty feet of open water. However, they could have crossed this lead and rushed to me to warn me of my imminent danger.

Dare I try to swim it? Would a sudden change in the currents bring the ice blocks together and crush me when halfway across? I was weighing the chances when a shouted, "Wait!" came from Sheeniktook. He climbed down to a narrow ledge where a small float was hugging it. He had a tent pole in his hand. Carefully stepping onto the small hunk of floating ice, about ten feet in diameter, he pushed off with his pole. Luckily, he pushed hard enough to start the little block sailing my way, because when he jabbed the pole into the water for a second push it didn't touch bottom. I wondered a little at the time how such a depth could be consistent with landlocked ice.

Slowly Sheeniktook drifted toward me on his precarious little ferry. He moved as close to the edge as he could and reached out with the pole. I grabbed it and pulled him close to my piece. When I stepped across, the little block nearly capsized. Only by jumping to the other side did Sheeniktook keep us in balance. We pushed off again and wobbled across the widening gap to where Tuga squatted down with one arm outstretched to receive us.

If it looked like a posture of friendship on his part, I was in no mood to reciprocate. My temper had been rising ever since I realized how simple it would have been to get back if only they had warned me of the breakup in time.

"Why didn't you fellows fire a gun or something when you saw the ice breaking away? You knew I was out there with the carcass of that damned seal!" They nodded gravely. "If a lead had already formed, you could have crossed it on an ice float, like we did just now."

Again they nodded.

"What the devil's the matter with you:" I exploded. "I could have been lost for good."

"You see," Sheeniktook explained, mildly, "Tuga say I not go, I say Tuga not go. Too dangerous. We stay."

"You mean you *deserted* me. If I hadn't noticed the movement myself, I'd still be ten miles out there with that—that seal."

The pair looked at each other a little sheepishly. Now Tuga put in his explanation:

"Tuga say Sheeniktook him not go. Sheeniktook him say Tuga stay here. So we stay."

I waited for more but that was all.

Now that we were safe, as I supposed, the ridiculous side of their behavior struck me full force and I sat down and grinned at myself,

"That nearly finished you, Moody," I soliloquized. "They thought it was dangerous. Dangerous. So they stayed." Aloud, I tried hard to give my voice a scathing quality.

"You two are brave like the women who chew the skins to make your boots. You're really the most abominable guides—" They must have noticed my grin a moment before because the chastisement had no effect. "Well," I finished, lamely, "let's get back to the komatik and make camp. I'm starved."

A mysterious look passed between the two, but they said nothing.

The sun was slowly disappearing in a haze as we struck out across the ice in the direction of land. We knew the dark would be on us soon. Our progress was slow, however, due to the dogs pulling on their short leashes and constantly dragging us away from our carefully chosen path of solid ice. After walking about ten minutes Tuga, who was ahead, stopped with a grunt and an eloquent gesture, as much as to say, "You see?"

Before us stretched an open space of calmly lapping water at least 100 feet wide.

I glanced at Sheeniktook to make sure he saw the open water too. Then in a flash I remembered a while back, when his tent pole failed to find bottom, my mild surprise that it could be so deep at the edge of landlocked ice. It was all clear now, horribly clear. They had not come to me from landlocked ice. All the time they stood on the ridge deliberating, they and the dogs were moving out to sea as inexorably as I was myself. The irony of it made me smile—two faithful friends seemingly so concerned over each other's safety, when actually they had been in deadly peril themselves—and had not known it.

My ironic smile faded when I realized how desperate our position had become. Plenty of ice still lay to seaward, but landward the channel of black water was widening a little more each minute. There was no possible way to get across.

I looked at the two Eskimos in the growing dusk. Their dark faces no longer reflected the false hope with which they had bolstered me up so long. In its place was the fatalistic calm which I knew characterized the Eskimo, but which had never appeared more strikingly. I couldn't make out from their look whether they expected to live or die.

"We go get seal," said Tuga, casually.

"What for?" I asked. "It's probably miles away by now."

"Food," Sheeniktook explained.

I saw clearly then what we were in for. We might be stranded in the ice fields for days. The pan we were on was a big one and moved slowly, but there was no guarantee that it would ever move back to shore again. We seemed to be drifting out diagonally and might easily get caught in another current. If the wind got stronger or a storm came up tomorrow, it might blow us out for miles and miles, our float slowly crumbling and finally disappearing. But we needn't be concerned over that final act because we should long since have perished from exposure. The nights would be bitterly cold with temperatures of twenty-

five or thirty degrees below, and we didn't have covering
against that.

As these dismal thoughts raced through my head, the
Eskimos walked away to see whether they might perhaps reach
the dead seal. They returned in an ominously short time. We
were completely surrounded by water, they reported.

Huskies in canoe. Faithful friends ready to serve by aircraft or canoe, in harness
or as pack animals.

I struck a match and looked at my compass. We still drifted
in the same direction, on a ninety-degree angle with the coast.
The sun long since had sunk below the horizon and the darkness
was bringing on severe cold. The wind—perhaps five miles an
hour—appeared to be growing stronger. If it increased as I had
seen it do sometimes, we'd be dead by morning—at least
Sheeniktook and I.

Tuga was the only one thickly clothed. I had left my heavy
outer wear way back at the komatik when we started to walk in
the ice fields that morning. Sheeniktook's parka was out there
somewhere, draped over a dead seal. While Sheeniktook
stamped around trying to keep warm, it occurred to me that my
leg was getting very cold. The wet boot and caribou skin
legging were frozen. I stripped them off and wrapped a piece

torn from my shirt around the icy foot. There was no choice then but to put the frozen boot on again.

I watched Sheeniktook testing the surface of our ice pan to locate any hollow spots. Having marked out a safe area, he turned to me.

"You run around inside circle, get warm. Keep running around. But no step over line."

I ran back and forth over the tested area until I was breathless, if not overly warm.

Tuga proved himself more of a lone wolf. He seemed little concerned about us. Having silently built himself a shelter from ice blocks, he had folded himself up within it and was comparatively warm. We had built a shelter too, but could stay motionless only a few minutes at a time. Then we'd get up and run ourselves warm again. I divided part of my chocolate with Sheeniktook, a tantalizing gesture since it only reminded us how hungry we really were.

Darkness had grown so complete that we were prevented from seeing more than a few feet ahead. The sky was overcast, and neither moon nor northern lights brightened the ice scape. Only the faintest band of light hung close to where the horizon should have been. The band flashed to and fro, a little stronger one second, a little weaker the next. Once in a while narrow beams of color would shoot out, then crumble into nothingness. Sometimes the whole band of light, hanging low, would dance in the air as if mocking us with a cold, steel like grin.

All around us were the eerie noises of the ice; noises seldom heard in daylight but strongly suggesting the supernatural at night. We heard crushing sounds in the distance where similar floats were being pulverized. At times a loud thud or explosion would wake up the sea gulls perched somewhere near us, and send them squealing up into the air.

Finally, a tremendous squeaking and grinding noise began and continued until, after a final rending crash followed by a series of splashing noises, all was silent again. No doubt a large pan had overridden ours and either broken itself up or smashed large parts of ours from the main mass. This left our pan momentarily on a sharp slope, with us clinging fearfully to it. A few more of these occurrences and we would have no pan left. Then, after a spell of rocking around, we found our ice once more horizontal so that we could get up and run around again.

A fresh crackling near by sent me back headlong to our shelter. I wondered if the ice we were on was slowly breaking into pieces. Another sound that held me breathless was a walrus squealing loudly in the distance, each squeal seeming to bounce around in the ice a long time before dying away.

I was utterly miserable and close to freezing in spite of all efforts to keep warm. I fell to wondering, quite calmly, whether I'd have to amputate my leg in the morning. How would I accomplish it? I went through all the routine motions in my mind-leg amputation, well, let's see . . .

But other thoughts fought for preference. What were Viola and my family doing at that moment? What would they do if I were lost? Would we ever see land again; get the feel of it under our feet? How would we finally die? Would it be from cold and hunger? Or would we drown far out at sea when the ice broke up? If worse came to worst I still had my gun . . .

Fighting any such idea back I took out my compass again and succeeded in lighting a match. But I'd lost my sense of direction. The compass told me only that north was north. And even that wasn't too certain so close to the magnetic pole.

Sheeniktook must have suffered tremendously as he was wearing even less than I. I had offered him my sweater to cover himself with, but he wouldn't take it. Tuga might have given his friend something to cover himself with, but Tuga was snoring. Occasionally he hiccoughed in his sleep. I could keep my thoughts to myself no longer.

"Sheeniktook," I said, more for conversation than information, "what can we do?"

"Don't know," he chattered.

But he did a curious thing for him. He crawled over and looked at my compass. He never paid any attention to that before, having no confidence in such Kabloona inventions.

"Maybe tide bring us back," he continued, in a matter-of-fact tone, "maybe not." After a pause he added brightly, "Can eat dogs."

◆ 44 ◆

MIRACLE?

True, we had the dogs. I looked over at them curled up on the ice asleep and tried to imagine the degree of famishment needed to relish their stringy, slippery meat—as I had heard dog meat described by some who knew.

Sheeniktook knelt down, bent over and held his ear close to the ice. "Can hear when tide changes," he said. "You listen."

I listened, too. I heard nothing but the slosh of water and a peculiar soft creaking in the ice. It meant nothing to me.

"No change," he said, and got up and started running and beating his chest to keep the blood in motion.

We went through another hour of torture. My leg was numb. But I checked it and found it wasn't frozen yet. It ached, when rubbed, and that was encouraging. Between spells of muttering to himself, Sheeniktook urged me to keep running.

More hours dragged by. It must have been about four o'clock, still completely dark, when Sheeniktook once more got down on his knees and stayed in that position for a long time. At last he got up.

"Tide changes," he said.

I dropped down and held my ear close to the ice again in an effort to catch the language of the sea. To me the noises sounded the same as before but the Eskimo insisted that if there was any movement in our float it was now definitely in the other direction. I was willing to take his word for that. But who could tell whether we were moving back or north or south? No doubt we'd know at daybreak.

The movement became more noticeable. A quarter hour later a thump told us that we'd hit another ice pan. Sheeniktook awakened Tuga immediately. They held a long talk in their own language. After that Tuga got up and went away.

"Tuga go see other ice," Sheeniktook explained.

The first reflection of sunlight, its source still far below the horizon, began to tint the sky. I saw faint wind streaks high above us. If they brought a storm and it came down, we should be pushed out to sea again.

Tuga came running back from his investigation.

"Much ice around," he said. "We try get off."

As Sheeniktook agreed that the time for action had come, we gladly broke up our miserable camp. I looked at the circle of trampled snow and ice where Sheeniktook and I had danced around half the night to keep from freezing and thought how silly it looked in the gaining light.

We walked along the rim of our ice pan, first in one direction then another. Numberless ice floats surrounded us; mostly big ones on which a man could walk for quite a distance. A collision shook our block and, catching Tuga off balance, threw him down. We all laughed a little and it helped our morale. Presently another pan hit on the shore side, or what I took to be the shore side. Tuga hurried across. Sheeniktook looked at my compass again, then we too crossed onto the new slab of ice. We were on our way!

Cautiously we picked our course from one pan to the next. It was necessary occasionally to wait patiently for leads to close. There were a few times when our progress was blocked by a wide channel. This meant a retreat until we could find a way around. Our biggest scare was when the ice on which we stood was suddenly pushed under by a bigger pan that slid up over it. With the air full of creaking, crashing sounds, we all had to jump for our lives.

Two hours of this and we hit solid ice and thought for certain that we had reached the shore. Still we kept walking ahead blindly, as if life consisted only in walking over ice—on —on—to the end of time.

Tuga broke the spell by climbing a ridge and scanning the horizon with the telescope he carried. He pointed to the left.

"Komatik," he said.

Another hour passed before we reached the sled. There Sheeniktook and I wrapped ourselves in warm clothing and we all ate a little before pushing on. The sun rose in a purple sky and lent its color to the ice. But now the ice we were on was no longer safe either. Big cracks made their appearance everywhere. Once we stopped and looked back and saw that the tracks of our komatik had moved apart some six feet.

From then in, our final flight to the shore line became a desperate race, with the cracking ice seeming ready to break afloat any moment . . . We made it to the good, solid rocky shore and breathed freely for the first time in twenty-four hours.

I took the telescope and looked out over the sea. The ice was breaking up everywhere. Much of the field where we had camped a few hours before had not moved in at all. Out beyond that, big pans drifted aimlessly in open water—one of them, no doubt bearing the dead seal covered with Sheeniktook's parka. Even the ice we had raced across a few moments before—ice we had thought solidly landlocked—was now shifting and cracking open.

This bird's eye view of the chaos we had left behind gave special emphasis to the hairbreadth nature of our escape.

"How often can a man face death?" I mused, handing the telescope to Sheeniktook.

He scanned the ice in silence, finally muttering a disconsolate, "Two."

For a moment I thought this his belated answer to my question. But it was only that he had spotted a pair of seals sunning themselves on a distant ice pan, and was regretting our inability to get them for the dogs.

Part II
The Eskimo of Yesterday and Today

♦ 45 ♦

A LIVING HISTORY PANORAMA

To get a better perspective about this land and the historic pressures that have dominated it for centuries we have to look to Asian, European and American history.

Originally it was thought that the ancestors of the Inuit came from Siberia, across the Bering Bridge about one thousand years ago. Archeological sites near Igloolik Island now indicate the Denbigh culture arrived in this area about 2000 B.C., having crossed the Bering Bridge much earlier than originally was thought. The Denbigh were the first human settlers in this region.

As the centuries went by, they would be followed by the better known Dorset–Thule cultures. These are the precursors of our present day Inuit. This indicates nearly 4000 years of unbroken Eskimo habitation of the land.

Most of the animals that sustain these people also came across the Bering Bridge. The musk ox is perhaps one of the most amazing of these creatures. Estimated to have lived in the Arctic for 90,000 years, it is one of the few animals in the world that is of the mammoth and saber-tooth tiger era. These animals have also survived a number of ice ages living precariously on the few ice-free islands in a vast sea of ice.

The first white men to visit the North American Arctic were Norse, led by Leif Erikson, who landed in the Ungava and touched the southeast shores of the Baffin Island. The Vikings also had a colony in North Newfoundland at L'Anse aux Meadow. It is not difficult to comprehend this, as the Norsemen settled on the east coast of Greenland in 982 A.D. These colonies existed from two to three centuries. All these Arctic settlements were to die out, however, and it would be hundreds of years before another group of explorers would reach these polar regions.

The first is believed to have been Martin Frobisher in 1576. His main objective was to find a short route to the riches of the east via a northwest route in the north polar region.

Over the next hundred years many maritime voyages were to follow, including those of Davis, Baffin, Hudson, Foxe and Bylot. All failed to find the fabled Northwest Passage. One of the main problems, of course, was ice. The early ship's crews failed to realize that the sea ice did not clear the bays and islands until late July, that travel was best in August and September, when ice problems were minimal.

Nevertheless, a good deal of knowledge was gathered and mapping done during these early voyages. This was to prove of inestimable value to later explorers. Contact with the Inuit had been made, but the extent and value of their knowledge was not generally recognized to any degree.

In the meantime, a few voyagers had traveled overland to Hudson Bay and had observed the huge resources in furs that existed in that region. One voyager was M. de Grosseillers, who tried to interest the King of France on his return to Europe. Grosseillier was unsuccessful, but he was undeterred and took his cause to Prince Rupert of England—who indeed was very interested. The formation of the far reaching and powerful Hudson's Bay Company in 1670 was a result of this historic meeting. Now the ships that sailed into the Arctic were mainly interested in fur, and later in whaling, rather than a route to the far east.

Other powerful English merchants, angered by what they perceived as a monopoly by the Hudson's Bay Company, sent sailing vessels into the Arctic in 1742 to find another trade route. Again the push was on to find the Northwest Passage to the west, and a route to the riches of the Indies.

The English government, needled by these trade feuds and the lobbying that followed, offered a reward of twenty thousand English pounds to the discoverer of the polar route to the Indies. This reward would go unclaimed for over one hundred years.

It would be 1815, after the Napoleonic wars, before serious maritime voyages were again attempted to find the elusive Northwest Passage. Many bays and inlets carry the names of the better equipped ships and crews. Ross, Parry, Beechly, Back, and the well remembered Franklin are among those whose explorations are so remembered. Even today, the Northwest Passage is still considered international water by some nations.

The Northwest Territories—as all the east, west, arctics, and sub-arctic zones came to be known—emerged only as a political entity on July 15, 1870, when this area was transferred to the recently confederated Dominion of Canada. The imperial order in council that permitted this transfer was passed July 23, 1870.

The next historic step for Canada occurred on July 31, 1880, when all the Islands north of this mainland area were also transferred to Canada. These almost unknown land transfers to Canada have become of immense political and economic significance to this nation.

During the period from 1870 to 1920, Canada's attention to the East Arctic was minimal. Most of the exploration and attention was focused on the territories north of the Prairie provinces and the Yukon—which was called, along with east and high arctic—the Northwest Territories. In fact, the Northwest Territory and Yukon government branch was only created on July 27, 1922. The finding of gold and oil in the west and northwest naturally focused the governments attention in this direction.

Canada is fortunate that few sovereignty challenges were made to the east arctic zones; there were certainly other nations that could have legitimately launched just such a challenge. In fact, Norwegian explorers Sverdrup and Nansen had explored the Ellesmere Island complex, and in 1902 the Norwegian flag was raised over this area. It was not until 1930 that Norway accepted Canada's sovereignty over the area.

Each wave of explorers would accumulate some knowledge, which would benefit subsequent ones, who would inevitably follow. It would be Captain Robert McClure of the Franklin search party who would find the Northwest Passage. McClure did only part of the passage by ship; much of it was done by dogs and on foot over the ice. The full traverse was not accomplished by one ship until Raold Amundsen in the forty-seven ton *Gjoa* made the passage from the east to the west in the period from 1903 to 1906.

The search for the last Franklin Expedition stirred tremendous exploration of this area. That was soon to translate into the great whaling expeditions of the Scots and Americans. To reach the North Pole also became an obsession of some nations.

American whalers were busy in the Central and Eastern Arctic, as were American explorers Kane, Hayes and Hall. They pushed deep into the Greenland, Baffin, Frobisher, and Repulse Bay areas. Peary the American, eventually reached the North Pole in 1909.

Under international law it was necessary for Canada to explore, map, inhabit, and administer the area to maintain legitimate sovereignty. Until the turn of the century it is obvious few if any of these requirements were met.

The Hudson's Bay Company had been trading into the area since 1670, but it was not until 1909 that they began setting up permanent posts. The first was at Cape Wolstenholme. The Royal Northwest Mounted Police continued patrols into the Eastern Arctic, and eventually set up posts in Cape Fullerton from 1904 to 1908. Men such as Low, Bernier, Bell, Stefansson, the Tyrell brothers, and many others did valuable field exploration and mapping for Canada during the 1897-1914 era.

The Roman Catholic church set up their first mission in 1912 at Chesterfield Inlet. The first Anglican mission had already been established by Reverend Peck in 1894 on Blacklead Island, Cumberland Sound Baffin Island.

In the first half of the century, the Inuit inhabitants of this territory were ignored in all these original transitions. Gradually, however, the Canadian Government cemented their hold on the land by establishing a Department of Transport, radio transmitters, R.C.M.P. posts, and the East Arctic government patrol—which carried various government services on the Hudson's Bay ship, *Nascopie,* to the hospitals of Chesterfield and Pangnirtung. They set up mapping and scientific surveys, and extended these further. The first census was not done until 1948. And even in the 1950s the Inuit had no vote and little say in their land management.

Unlike the Indians, there were no treaties. These people were relatively unknown and of little concern to most Canadians. These were the barren lands.

The Inuit themselves called the land Nunaga, or "The Land," and to most of them, that was the world. This had been all they had known for thousands of years. They had considerable difficulties understanding where the white man had come from, let alone what motivated him to do such seemingly foolish things.

The Hudson's Bay Company's ice breaker, *Nascopie,* first sailed these waters in 1912 to supply company posts. In 1933 this vessel was chartered to carry the Canadian government East Arctic Patrol. This patrol—which carried R.C.M.P., administrative, medical, and scientific personnel—continued to render valuable service to the Arctic communities until 1947, when the *Nascopie* grounded on a reef and sank near Cape Dorset Baffin Island.

A substantial amount of scientific work was accomplished in this period. Prospecting in the 1920s was vigorously carried out by such companies as North American Mineral Explorations, Dominion Explorers, and Cyril Knight and Associates.

Airplanes were first used at this time for exploration, but with no maps or navigation gear, as much time was spent rescuing lost pilots as prospectors spent in prospecting. Epic rescues were made and some pilots became renowned for this type of flying. Dickens, May, Spence, and Reed were a few of these well known pilots. Most died in tragic flying accidents.

A few mineral discoveries were made—nickel at Rankin Inlet, and a few gold occurrences. It was 25 to 50 years, however, before even these developed into mines such as the North Rankin Nickel mine and Nunansivik Pond Inlet. The Great Depression of the '30s dampened an interest in this area and curtailed exploration.

In 1939, Canada became involved in World War II. This terminated the depression; most arctic endeavors now had a military focus. The Second World War was at a crisis. This signaled a change in the East Arctic. The Americans decided to build air bases at Frobisher Bay, Baker Lake, Southampton

Island, and Greenland, as an alternative staging route over the Canadian Arctic. This was called the Crimson Route. Built at great cost and waste, it was never used for its original purpose.

In 1944, the R.C.M.P. vessel *St. Roch* completed the Northwest Passage east to west in one season. This epic voyage was the first such traverse and created great interest.

However, this era was to herald changes that later would overwhelm this polar area.

We end the '40s with some changes, but they were minimal, isolated, and reversible. The Inuit generally lived as they had for centuries.

Following World War II, the cold war era set in with the threat of Soviet bombers coming over the North Pole to attack America. The United States decided in the early '50s to build the Distant Early Warning line (DEW line) in the Arctic. This was an extremely costly megaproject. A multitude of airstrips were constructed for the movement of massive amounts of material.

Sophisticated communication networks were established. Some Inuit labor was used, but a great deal of community disruption occurred.

Another occurrence, not of the magnitude of the DEW line, but as important in its effect on change of Inuit life, was the opening of North Rankin Nickel Mines at Rankin Inlet, Northwest Territories in 1955.

There had been no communities here before 1955, when Inuit were recruited for the mine from nearby villages. Suddenly families were drawn from centuries old communities. Soon Rankin Inlet became the largest town in the East Arctic. In 1962, the mine closed. The social and economic situation in the town deteriorated seriously for some years. The Canadian government did attempt to improve conditions with various programs. Gradually and painfully the town evolved into a fairly stable community. Today it is the site of the territorial government of Keewatin.

◆ 46 ◆

A '90S OVERVIEW

Nunavut, the Eastern and High Arctic Inuit homeland, was officially established as a national political entity in 1990. I call my '90s overview of this land "Nunavut" because it is the one word that seems to embody the geographic, cultural, human, and political changes that—like a giant Tsunami—have literally rolled over this huge territory in the past few decades. Cataclysmic changes from the stone age to the nuclear-computer era had now begun in earnest in the East Arctic. This overview will not attempt to cover these enormous changes in detail. Volumes would be required.

On approaching a typical East Arctic Community before the 1950s, you would first hear the howling of at least a hundred Husky dogs. As you came closer, you would see komatiks by the dozens near the entrances to igloos both above, and below the drifted snow. Innumerable items would be scattered about: whips, wooden snow shovels, harpoon handles, snow knives, skins and other paraphernalia. From the igloo domes' air holes, wisps of vertical steam would be rising. You would be greeted by Inuit dressed in double caribou, and speaking Inuktitut.

The situation was similar in summer, except the dwellings would be tents and people would be dressed in a mixture of seal skin and white mans' clothing. The smell of rotten walrus meat and rancid seal fat would be overwhelming.

266

There were no roads, no overhead wires, no satellite dishes, and no snow machines. The few widely dispersed framed buildings were those of the Department of Transport, Hudson's Bay Company, Royal Canadian Mounted Police, the Medical Health Officer, and missions.

Now the sights you would see at the same community would be startlingly different. On approaching the same community the first object you might see is an aircraft getting ready to land on a gravel, lighted airstrip and guided by excellent navigation equipment.

As you entered the community in a truck or van, you will have noted the poles carrying telephone and electrical cables. There will be few if any dogs to greet you, as they are replaced by three- or four-wheelers and snow machines. You are now in the community of a hundred or more one- to two-story frame buildings—no tents, no igloos. The homes have electricity, plumbing, satellite TV, telephone, and the other usual amenities. The Eskimo will greet you in fluent English or Inuktitut—as you wish.

If you had been a Government official with a house here decades ago, you may have trouble finding it in the maze of buildings. I had this strange, unsettling experience at Chesterfield Inlet.

The communities now are known by their Inuit names, and are called hamlets. They have municipal buildings replete with mayor, council, and the usual municipal administration. You may even meet legislators in one of these communities. All hamlets have schools and nursing units. The main center, Rankin Inlet, has a hospital with full medical staff, and medical attention can reach almost anyone at anytime.

Even in 1949, medical service was spotty, almost nonexistent in many areas, and completely subject to the vagaries of weather. Frequently in the winter, dogs could get the doctor to a community quicker than a ski-equipped airplane. In a true life-and-death situation, the patient either survived the crisis with minimal medical aid, or died. Not so anymore.

When you traveled out on the land, you were on your own with your dogs for days to weeks. Now with a medium frequency portable radio transmitter, when you canoe or go out on snow machines you can be in immediate contact with your base at home. The communication web now covers the entire land.

The animal population has increased dramatically with the improved regulations governing conservation and hunting. This is especially true of the musk ox, caribou, and bear. But the great whale species are still endangered. The polar bear was always a hazard during travel, but with dog teams there was ample warning to take protective steps. Now travel on the barrens without dogs and with an increased aggressive polar bear population can be very dangerous.

North Rankin Nickel Mines—a major force in the destiny of many Inuit families.

As is often the case, all changes were not for the better. Alcohol became legal and substance abuse became widespread with its usual effects: illness, family problems, crime and death. Most hamlets still have problems, but the people, their elders, and the council, have taken measures to help themselves.

Many communities by Plebiscite have banned or controlled the sale of alcoholic beverages. Support groups for substance, family abuse, and suicide prevention are active. These and other problems are addressed at the Inuit Circumpolar Conventions.

On a visit to Rankin Inlet, Hakoluk—one of my old guides —took me to the graveyard and pointed out the graves of some young people who have committed suicide due to substance abuse. Such deaths were unheard of in past decades. In fact, during my medical tour in the Arctic from '46 to '50, I don't remember one Inuit suicide.

Another casualty of the rapid change is the family unit. Over prior centuries—as in many cultures—the grandparents, parents, and children comprised a vital unit of care and love. So it was with the Inuit. In the past it was extremely important. It was their way of imparting knowledge and experience for their survival of the family, and indeed the whole band. This unit began to have difficulties in the 1960s to the 1980s, when children were taught only English in schools. Thus a serious communications and cultural problem arose. The grandparents spoke only Inuktitut—the parents Inukitut and some English —and in most cases the children spoke English and little Inukitut. Communication within the unit was difficult. Of course, this created a dangerous cultural abyss. Today this has been corrected, but in many cases it was too late.

However, the Inuit are out of necessity adaptable; this has allowed them to meet these challenges. Many are returning to using dogs for transport, to hunt, and to trap. They are survivors, blending their necessary cultural ties with the sea and the land with those of the modern communities in which they live.

It is remarkable that these people with limited materials to make weapons and tools, could tenaciously survive down through the millennia in one of the worlds coldest and most inhospitable region. This race has quietly survived in the Polar regions during the latter era of the Pyramids, the Dynasties of the Caesars, the birth of Christianity, the Vikings, and European centuries of upheaval and death.

We have seen immense changes so far, but the most remarkable change of all was to take place in Ottawa in 1990.

There were no treaties between Canada, and the Aboriginals of the East Arctic, but after the relative short period of two decades of negotiation an agreement in principal was signed between the Tungavit Federation representing the Inuit of the Nunavut settlement area, and Canada.

The biggest land settlement in Canadian history was now completed. A vast area of Canada had now officially become the homeland and hunting ground of the East Arctic Inuit. Nunavut (Our Land) was officially born.

The trip from Stone Age to the Nuclear-Computer Age had been traversed in just three decades.

♦ 47 ♦

THE DOCTOR'S PRESCRIPTION

The story of our Eskimos, in many respects a sad one, is quite similar to that of other races exposed to white man's colonization.

Through the ages white men, who considered themselves more civilized than their brothers of different color or nationality, have tried to impose their habits, morals and religion on many peoples who should have been left alone. Not only did the races to be "enlightened" often have a noble civilization of their own, like the Aztecs and Incas, but usually their inherent culture was better suited to the areas in which they dwelt.

With the Eskimos, this is still the case. Their old way of life was singularly well adjusted to the peculiarities of weather, terrain and food supply. The whites who came to the arctic could well have learned from the Eskimos, and copied the habits and philosophies which had enabled these people to survive happily in one of the most forbidding areas of the world. But we felt, instead, that we were bringing the Eskimos a more desirable existence. The inroads thus made on the established Eskimo culture have, in many instances, proved quite detrimental in preserving the Eskimo race and what it stood for.

How many Eskimos once roamed the Canadian arctic? Estimates of over 50,000 have been suggested, but if we take a minimum of 35,000 we shall not be too far wrong. The most recent census taken in 1950, gave 9,000, a figure showing an increase over previous counts. This increase, however, is because each year more Eskimos are counted for the first time through more expert statistical research. A recent estimate for the same territory quotes a figure of 16,000 Inuit people in 1994.

Ever since the first whaling expeditions into the Arctic there has been considerable formal (and informal) intermarriage, and the mixing of races will undoubtedly continue as more and more whites settle the area. Intermarriage and a gradual leveling off of racial characteristics need not be bewailed. But the fact that thinning Eskimo blood coincides with the degeneration of native culture is cause for deep regret.

The Eskimo used to be self-sufficient, all his necessities supplied by the land in which he lived. Food, clothing, and summer housing were provided by the animals he hunted. Bones, ivory and native copper were the raw materials from which he shaped his implements. Snow supplied the igloo. With natives from the interior bringing caribou skins and meat—and receiving the coastal Eskimo's sealskins, blubber and oil in return—the Eskimo economy ran its full cycle of hunting, foraging and exchange. Neither need nor desire called for piling up earthly goods. The Eskimo's health apparently thrived on a well balanced diet.

White men changed much of this. Whalers started undermining the Eskimo's health by bringing in unknown diseases against which the natives had no immunity. Pneumonia, measles, influenza, the ordinary cold, and more complex illnesses like dysentery, diphtheria, typhoid and other contagious infections raced through the Eskimo population like a forest fire after a dry summer. They killed thousands within a few years. The whalers brought tuberculosis, which nested on fertile ground and has been taking a staggering toll ever since. The 1948–49 epidemic proved that the infiltration of disease had by no means reached an end.

Another factor that had a dramatic impact on Eskimo life was the useless slaughter of arctic animals. The white man's whaling methods of those early days were certainly more devastating than the Eskimo whale hunts, and depleted the herds faster than native hunting might have done. It has been estimated that each whaling trip brought the white man profits of at least $30,000, and that between the years 1863 and 1885 a total value of more than $2,500,000 in oil and bone was taken from the waters of Hudson Bay. Considering that an Eskimo family could live off the carcass of one whale for months, you can imagine how disastrous was the attack made on their food supply by the white whalers.

To me it seems the height of irony that the cost of women corseting themselves into an unhealthy hourglass figure should have been so high. It cost hundreds of human lives, the near extinction of the Bowhead whale in the arctic, and a considerable portion of the blame for the near extinction of musk ox and the serious depletion of caribou. Records show that in 1884 as many as 200 porpoises were caught by the whites during one single tide at Churchill. The end results of untold costs, past and present, to the Canadian government will never be known.

Reliable stories are told of hunting parties of white traders and whalers only a few short decades ago killing thousands of musk oxen and caribou on one island during a single hunt. Some past expeditions, both government sponsored and private, have also killed arctic animals needlessly.

Authorities once considered the musk ox to have been 1,000,000 strong in the Arctic and Subarctic. In the 1940s there were about 500 left on the mainland and a few hundred more on the islands. Happily today this animal population numbers around 100,000. The musk ox is not a migratory animal and could be domesticated and herded. It could provide excellent skins, milk and meat for the Eskimo.

Where depletion of herds was breaking down Eskimo economy on one side, the introduction of the white man's economy began tearing at it from the other with the employment of Eskimos by the whalers to help them with the catch. They paid their new employees with trinkets and with food strange to the natives. Soon the Eskimos took to hanging around whalers' camps waiting for boats to come in, anxious to perform work that would yield fascinating products which the Kabloona brought with him. The result was they paid less attention to their own hunting, now that they could get food from the whites.

But the white man's food introduced starches to the age-old Eskimo diet of meat and fat. The change disrupted their metabolism which had been adapted to the climatic circum-

stances of the zone. The new foods ruined their teeth and made
the Eskimos more susceptible to disease. The long period of
transition that weakened the strain has not yet come to an end.

The natives learned to use the white man's firearms. But
because at first they did not handle these properly, or know how
to adapt their hunting methods to the use of firearms, they killed
many animals needlessly. Countless walrus and seal were slain
—and lost for want of sealskin floats on harpoon lines to
prevent their sinking. Significant numbers of caribou, shot and
wounded but not killed, staggered off into the tundra to die and
decompose.

The complete turnover in the Eskimo economy came when,
in later years, the whites began to pay high prices for white fox
fur. The Eskimos found it lucrative to provide the traders with furs,
and so became even more dependent on the Kabloona. The cycle
of native self-sufficiency was broken.

Introduction of the fur trade contributed a further disaster in
Eskimo life. It kept the people from following their own habits.
The simple method of trapping tended to lower their hunting
skills more and more. They were too busy trapping foxes to
exchange for white man's foods to take time for their seasonal
hunts.

They began to feel not only a curious desire, but a definite
need, for the staples they received at the trading posts. Although
technically they could be paid in money, few Eskimos ever were
given cash. Instead, they received in trade those products the
whites could readily dispose of. Trading was new to the
Eskimos and the early barters were rarely fair.

However, one should not misunderstand the position of the
trading companies which soon dominated the economy of the
district. The traders did not come to the Arctic as do-gooders.
They were businessmen; trade was their business. They made a
small profit on goods they gave the Eskimos and a large profit on
the furs brought in to them. Their winnings thus came from two
sides, a type of commerce appealing to most keen businessmen.

While the first decades of trading resulted in considerable
exploitation, it must be admitted that the companies changed
their policy in later years. Bilateral profits are still being made,
but generally the trade is now fairer. The fact is that bitter
realities soon confronted the budding economy that had been

brought to the Eskimos. Over a number of years the price of fox fur dropped from around $40 a skin to $4 or $5. Those, of course, were the prices paid the Eskimos. The European and American markets slumped accordingly, but on a higher scale. When the bottom thus dropped out, drastically reducing the Eskimo's income, the trading companies had to abandon the artificial economy which had kept things in temporary balance.

They turned, instead, to aiding the demoralized natives, who didn't know what had hit them. The companies started to extend credits, knowing well that in most cases they would never be able to collect. They also gave outright relief. But the great damage had already been done. Although fox furs have sold for somewhat better prices in recent years, there is no doubt that the white man's economy, upon which the Eskimo so trustfully placed his own way of life, brought deep distress.

With a dwindling supply of foxes and lower prices for furs, they can make hardly enough income to keep themselves alive. With fewer caribou, walrus and whales, not to mention poorer hunting skill, they cannot get as much meat and clothing as their habitat once provided. In fact, it was found that not even the help extended by the trading companies was enough. The government has had to issue relief year after year to a high percentage of Eskimo families.

The trading companies have suffered, too. The main reason they haven't closed more of their posts is that Eskimo relief and family allowances are issued through the posts, and in the products they carry. They still deal in furs, but this trade will never again become so important as it was once.

This, then, is one instance in which white infiltration has backfired. The change in the Eskimo economy that came about after our influence had spread across the Arctic was obviously not a change for the better. If the breakdown of a native economy and the attack on the health of the Eskimos are the most regrettable effects of white colonization, other subtler influences have also contributed to the crumbling of Eskimo culture.

Christians, Moslems, Hindus and other believers have, through the centuries, striven to bring others what they considered the true religion. Some conquests of the soul have been peaceful, others not. Some brought more tangible results than conversion alone, others did not. But in most cases a delicate,

indefinable something that was an inherent part of native life
was destroyed. Or, if not destroyed, it was overpowered by the
new code of morals and religious dogma introduced. In considering the effects of conversion, the real merits of missionary
work need not be questioned.

While true that the Christian religion can help other people
do away with unnatural fears and abolish destructive taboos, one
must also consider the physical change that it brings to the
natives. We like to believe ourselves helpful to converts in
matters of the soul. Yet only too often are we confronted by the
knowledge of having destroyed other values which might be
equally important.

Although the Moravians are said to have entered the Arctic
as early as 1740, the Christian invasion of the arctic began
formally in 1770 when the Moravian missionaries set up their
headquarters at Nain on the Labrador coast. One writer, after
visiting Nain, described the mission there as a place, "Where the
sermon in Eskimo is made for the good of his soul and the sake
of his trade."

There is little doubt, however, that these early preachers had
the Eskimo's welfare at heart. They were the first to teach
reading and writing, and they utilized a system of syllabics
whereby the Eskimo language could be consigned to paper. This
script is still in use and has proved of great importance in
furthering Eskimo education.

The Anglican and Roman Catholic missions came to the
Arctic in later years and settled in different regions. The fact
that more than one mission took on the task of converting the
Eskimos had one unfortunate result. Different groups of natives
—having gained different beliefs—became distrustful, even
hostile, toward one another. Where for centuries they had lived
in peace, they divided into camps, each under the sponsorship
of a different Bible. In some zones they were a divided people.

The Eskimos responded slowly to Christianity. This is quite
understandable, considering their age-old philosophy, their many
superstitions and their inherent code of morals. It is hard for
them to understand teachings based on ideals rather than on the
practical facts of everyday life—Arctic life, in particular. There
are, of course, many Bible references quite beyond their
comprehension such as corn and wheat, trees and deserts,

swords, chariots, lions, tribes and emperors! Such words had no meaning for them because these things were utterly unknown and without a place in their culture.

Eskimos can only try to take religion at face value, to accept the teachings and follow the rules where they affect their own everyday life. That they can grasp the spiritual values contained in our religious dogmas would be extremely difficult to prove.

Religion and education often go together. But attempts to teach Eskimos what we would like them to know have not always been satisfactory. For example, confusion followed the era of Moravian teaching when Eskimo grammar systems were issued by two different missions, by one of the trading companies and by the government. In each case the compilation of a native grammar system was inspired by a desire to teach the Eskimos a common language and abolish their many dialects. The result of this well-meant effort was, in some instances, ineffective because the different native tongues had been replaced by different interpretations of what was considered the basic Eskimo language.

Today the territorial government carries most of the burden of educating the Eskimos, making educational facilities available to the people as well as to promote a general teaching policy. The government has taken important steps toward helping the Eskimos adapt themselves to the makeshift way of life that has supplanted their old existence. We are late in doing this, but not too late. There is hope that, under intelligent and purposeful guidance, some of the damage done previously may be repaired. Now that white infiltration has torn them away from their once happy lot, about all we can do is make their status quo more acceptable, and assist them in overcoming the lethargy which settled over them during the long decades of transition.

The government's rehabilitation program follows very definite lines. We know now that nothing must be allowed to disrupt what is left of the old Eskimo economy. They are being taught to depend once more on what their own land can provide, rather than to rely totally on other economic factors.

Closed seasons on several Arctic animals have been introduced and each Eskimo family officially limited to the amount of game it can kill, all in the hope of avoiding further depletion of the herds. Emphasis on trapping has been lessened.

An attempt is being made to revamp the Eskimo economy where it concerns the individual's contact with the outside world. Should it prove to be the Eskimo's lot that his traditional habits no longer suffice to provide a decent existence, he must be able to find employment in his own region, regain his personal pride and once more become the family breadwinner. This will help solidify his economic position.

Much time is given to the teaching of handicrafts and artistic expression for commercial purposes. Eskimo art has always found its expression in carvings and needlework. The natives are being strongly encouraged to use their basic skill and artistry in creating products that can be sold in the white man's markets. In certain parts of the Arctic this occupational therapy has already met with great success. It is hoped the movement will continue to spread to include all those individuals who are capable of artistic expression.

But the most important development that could put the Eskimo back on his feet has yet to come. The vast mineral resources of the Arctic will not go unexploited much longer. Once the mining industry has settled in the area, there is bound to be another boom that will far surpass the economic upsurge of fur trading days.

Although many people find difficulty in accepting the fact that Eskimos will have to find prosaic employment in order to live, it is better to have them do any honest job than watch them dwindle while trying to return to their old mode of life. That old mode is destroyed. Too much of what once constituted his basis for existence has vanished. We cannot just tell the Eskimo to "go back to your former habits and shift for yourself," any more than we can revive the thousands of his brothers killed by our diseases, or the hundreds of thousands of animals slaughtered by our hunters.

With proper encouragement from the administration, such as subsidies or tax deductions, private mining companies could start Arctic operations in which the Eskimos would find their place. With government-sponsored training programs they could be taught to make proper use of their mechanical skills, and could be employed in many decent, honest, uncompromising jobs. Tourism, and land claim settlements now have opened a new life for the modern Inuit.

I have tried to diagnose and prescribe for a "patient" whose condition is still far from satisfactory. I have neither concealed nor excused, but have tried to point out new hope for a proud race which—through the blundering ignorance and conceit of the white invaders—has been brought dangerously close to its doom.

Only in recent times have we forced ourselves to recognize our mistakes. And while we concentrate on a new, progressive policy for the Eskimos, we might remember how in the past we fell far short of our own ideals, far short of demonstrating that culture of which we are so proud. No one man, organization, institution, mission, trading company or whaling firm can be blamed for what happened. It goes deeper than that. The damage was caused by the white man who, in his surging quest for new frontiers, often forgot to pay due attention to the welfare of the frontier people with whom he dealt.

It is time we learned from our past mistakes. Otherwise we may yet have to hang our heads in shame because our "shining progress" destroyed a colorful group of human beings who once dwelt in peace and asked only to be allowed to live a life that had suited them perfectly for a thousand years.

Joseph P. Moody, 1995

BIBLIOGRAPHY

Adamson, Moody, et al, *Poliomyelitis in the Arctic,* Canadian Medical Association Journal, Ottawa, 1949.

Baird & Robinson, *Brief History of Exploration and Research in Canadian East Arctic,* Canadian Geographical Journal, Ottawa, September, 1955.

Blancet, Guy, *Search in the North,* MacMillan Co., Toronto, 1960.

Canadian Geographical Journal, Ottawa, 1950.

Dunbar and Greenaway, *Arctic Canada From the Air,* Queen's Printer, 1956.

Finnie and McKeand, N.W.T. and Yukon Branch, Department of the Interior, Volume 1, Government of Canada, 1930.

Hudson's Bay Company, *A Brief History,* Hudson Bay Co., Winnipeg.

Noss, John, *Man's Religions,* MacMillan Co., New York, 1949.

Nunavut, Settlement Area Agreement in Principle, Northern Development, Ottawa, 1990.

Oblate Fathers, *Eskimo,* Volume 37, Churchill, Manitoba, 1955.

Sargent Epes, *The Arctic World and Its Explorers,* John E. Potter Press, Philadelphia, 1873.

Scoresby, Capt., Life of *The Norwegian Colonies in Greenland,* 1860.

Shipley, Nan, *Churchill,* Burns and McEachern, 1974.

Tuttle, Charles R., *Our Northland,* Blackett, Robinson, 1885.

Order this Exciting and Adventure-filled Book for Your Friends, Colleagues, and Loved Ones!

ORDER FORM

YES, I want ____ copies of *Medicine Man to the Inuit* at $22.95 each, plus $3 shipping per book. (Colorado residents please include $1.68 sales tax.) Canadian orders must be accompanied by a postal money order in U.S. funds. Allow 30 days for delivery.

My check or money order for $_____is enclosed.

Name _____ Phone _____

Organization _____

Address _____

City/State/Zip _____

Card # _____ Expires _____

Signature _____

**Check your leading bookstore
or call your Credit Card Order to:**

1-800-507-BOOK (2665)

Please make your check payable and return to:

Arctic Memories Press
200 Union Blvd., Suite 425
Denver, CO 80228